Making Modern Lives

SUNY Series Power, Social Identity, and Education

Lois Weis, editor

Making Modern Lives

Subjectivity, Schooling, and Social Change

Julie McLeod and Lyn Yates

STATE UNIVERSITY OF NEW YORK PRESS

Published by
State University of New York Press, Albany

Printed in the United States of America

For information, address State University of new York Press,
194 Washington Avenue, Suite 305, Albany, NY 12210-2384

Production by Kelli Williams
Marketing by Michael Campochiaro

Library of Congress Cataloging-in-Publication Data

McLeod, Julie, 1958-
Making modern lives : subjectivity, schooling, and social change /
Julie McLeod and Lyn Yates.
p. cm. — (SUNY series, power, social identity, and education)
Includes bibliographical references and index.
ISBN 0-7914-6767-8 (hardcover : alk. paper) — ISBN 0-7914-6768-6
(pbk. : alk. paper)
1. Education—Social aspects—Australia—Longitudinal studies.
2. Students—Australia—Longitudinal studies. 3. Subjectivity—Australia v
Longitudinal studies. I. Yates, Lyn, 1949- II. Title. III. Series.
LC191.8.A8M35 2006
306.43'2'0994—dc22 2005018998

10 9 8 7 6 5 4 3 2 1

For Clara and Eva,

and Katie and Clara,

and for our parents

Contents

Acknowledgments

This project has now been over ten years in gestation, and during that time we have drawn upon support and assistance from many sources. Over the course of the study, our own lives have changed and taken different turns—new jobs, interstate moves, the birth and growing up of our own children. Longitudinal projects require a lot of commitment and depend on generous contributions from many people; the experiences and encounters that have happened along the way have been immensely enjoyable.

We particularly want to thank the students who agreed to be part of this project, and who continued to give time to us for seven or eight years of their lives. Without their willingness, this study would not have happened. We also thank the teachers and schools who facilitated our research, who set aside time for our visits, usually in the midst of busy school days, and showed an interest in our work.

The 12 to 18 Project (on which this book is based) was made possible by grants from the Australian Research Council (1996–99; 1999–2000). We were given further support—through research grants and conference and research leave—by the universities in which we worked during the course of this project: La Trobe University, Deakin University, and the University of Technology Sydney. We are extremely grateful for this as well as for support provided by research administrative staff in our departments.

We were fortunate to work with many skilled research assistants and project officers. Those who worked on and provided support to the project at different stages include Karen Halasa, Geraldine Ditchburn, Sera Arnold, Chris Brew, Esther Faye, Kathleen Orr, Jasmina Radulovic, Malcolm Turnbull, Terri Yates, Jodie Arrow, Renata Atkins, Miranda Hughes, Katie Wright, Ann Findlay, Dar Weyenberg and Michelle Arrow. We appreciate both the practical assistance and the terrific company provided by these people, and particularly acknowledge the work of Michelle Arrow, who steered the administrative work of the final years of the project, and did invaluable groundwork in bringing together a report for schools and participants.

Many people, both in Australia and internationally, contributed to our work in a variety of important ways: providing feedback on writing; hosting seminars and conferences to which we were invited to present papers in progress; offering accommodation, conviviality and friendship on international visits; organising and hosting periods of research for us at other universities; and encouraging us in our work and helping us to see things from different perspectives. We would like to acknowledge in Melbourne Johanna Wyn, Jane Kenway, Barbara Kamler, Stephen Lamb, Cherry Collins, and colleagues in the Deakin Difference and Identity in Education Research Group; and in other countries Rachel Thomson, Janet Holland, Miriam David, Gaby Weiner, Madeleine Arnot, Diana Leonard, Valerie Walkerdine, Mary-Jane Kehily, Debbie Epstein, Helen Lucey, Kathleen Weiler, Sari Biklen, Jane Gaskell, Jo-Anne Dillabough, Hildur Ve, Harriet Bjerrum Nielsen, Monica Rudberg, Tom Popkewitz, Mimi Bloch, Bernadette Baker, Michael Apple, Sue Middleton. We also thank our Feminist Theory Reading Group that met for 10 years, and was a great source of social as well as intellectual support, and particularly in relation to this project Georgina Tsolidis, Sarah Paddle and Andrea Allard.

Our research work was also sustained by the good humour and generous support of our close friends and family. We especially appreciated the hospitality and practical help given by Lois and Ray in relation to our fieldwork and the willingness of Katie, Clara, Anna and Mikhaila and their friends to help out with pilot work. More generally, Lyn would especially like to thank Lois and Ray, Tom and Libby, Tony and Liz, Lorraine and Libby, Nicky, Clive and Mark and of course Katie and Clara for ongoing support and reminding her that there is more to life than work.

For friendship, holidays, and making life rich, Julie thanks Karen and Henry, Lizzy, Mick, Lena and Rachel, Miranda, Leonie, Stephanie, and Paul. David came on research trips when our children were young, gave much domestic and emotional support throughout, and was always an astute critic. Clara and Eva's lives span this project—both born in its early stages; they have learnt much about working mothers, and I have gained much more from them.

During the eight years of interviews we saw the participants change and grow, and we thought often about our own children and the world and situations they face. Our project was concerned with schooling and identity, and with retrospective and prospective visions of that. Doing this research evoked emotions and memories for us of our own growing up, our own schooling, and the support we had from our own teachers (in country high schools) our families, and especially our parents.

CHAPTER 1

Modern Lives, Subjectivity, Schooling, and Social Change

There is never a single set of constitutive criteria to appeal to in characterizing complex social practices. (Benhabib 1995)

Every act of research is simultaneously empirical (it confronts the world of observable phenomena) and theoretical (it necessarily engages hypotheses about the underlying structure of relations that observations are designed to capture). (Bourdieu and Wacquant 1992)

This book is about young women and men shaping their lives as they move through the years of secondary schooling and into the world beyond. It is also a discussion about how both the personal and the big picture are significant in researching and theorizing social change, as well as an ongoing reflection about how one researches subjectivity. The book is framed by concerns about education and inequalities, differences, and changes in education. The stories we tell and the arguments we make are an attempt to foreground things we think matter both in education and in understanding subjectivity, schooling, and changing times.

The book emerges out of a longitudinal project in which we set out to explore how dispositions, attitudes, and identities develop over a period of significant personal change—the adolescent years—and during a social era often characterized as "New Times." We designed this study to examine more specifically how such dispositions, attitudes, and identities develop in particular (and different) school settings, and against particular (and different) biographical experiences. We are interested in how individuals form themselves and in how social patterns and inequalities are created.

Over a seven-year period (1993–2000), we interviewed and videotaped 26 young Australians (14 girls and 12 boys) as they aged from 12 to 18 years, from diverse social backgrounds, attending four different types of school. (We called this the 12 to 18 Project.) Twice during each year of high school, and in the first year afterward, we listened to these students talk about their sense of self, their values, attitudes to the future, and their experiences of school. Their individual narratives illuminate the uneven and differentiated impact of contemporary social and gender change, and the profound influence of school community and culture on the shaping of subjectivity.

In following young people over the significant years from 12 to 18 we were engaging with broader questions about social forms today (of class and gender and race, as well as contemporary schooling) and with the problem of what this thing, subjectivity or identity, looks like, and how you might empirically research it. Take Keren's story for example.

Keren lived in a small country town with her mother and sisters; when we first met her, she was 11 years old and at the end of elementary school. She smiled a lot, told us that she would like to be a teacher, and that she was excited about going to high school. When we interviewed her again in the first years of high school, she was not so happy and enthusiastic about school, indicated that she was being bullied, said she liked "technical subjects" but was not any good at math, and was seeing a remedial teacher, She did not like the way she looked—her hair, her teeth, her body. She saw herself becoming a cook, or a preschool childcare worker. When she talked about the future, she said she would "just take it as it comes." She wanted enough money to have "a car that works" and she dreamt of having a nice house, but that was "imaginary, very very imaginary." Throughout high school "taking it as it comes" remained a prominent theme in her thoughts about herself and her future. She attended a school in which the majority of students left before graduation, but Keren stayed on and passed her final exams. When we last interviewed her, she was enrolled in a one-year training certificate to become a nursing assistant and was saving to move into an apartment of her own.

The questions we are interested in and which we explore in later chapters include: How is Keren's sense of self and subjectivity shaped? What does she bring from her family, her biography, and what does she encounter at school? What is our own role in the story we elicit from Keren and the stories we make from our conversations with her? How are changes in education and work patterns affecting Keren and her peers? In what sense is one person's story "evidence"? In what sense is Keren's story a familiar one of a working-class girl and her path through school and life, and in what respects are there signs of a new era, new experiences, a new "detraditional" world? How would we tell?

Questions such as these are about theory and substantive focus; they are also about methodological ways of proceeding and writing, about how to do research.

To begin with, consider our decision to examine issues of schooling, social change, and inequalities by a longitudinal focus on subjectivity. Subjectivity has become an object of fascination for contemporary theory, and the reasons for this, as well as the questions being posed, warrant attention from those who are concerned about young people, or schooling, or social power and inequalities. For some theorists, the new attention to subjectivity is responding to broad social and cultural changes. It involves questions about what is required of the person in this era—what fashioning of subjectivity or identity does the new work and cultural order require, and how do young people shape themselves, over time, in the context of their family and school life? For others, the interest in subjectivity is a continued development of a range of theoretical, practical, and political attempts to address "difference." It is part of an ongoing engagement with questions about how gender or class or race and ethnic formations work today, with how individual identities as well as social patterns are made and remade; and with how inequality, advantage, and disadvantage are produced and might be changing.

This book is one account of young people in current times, and of the theories that try to understand them. Our stories of what happens and what is said by the young men and women we follow are set against and in dialogue with some of the different claims and theories being made about these times, about gendered identity today, about schools and what they do. We set out to study, for example, changes in how girls today are seeing their lives and thinking about their future compared with girls of their mothers' generation. We look at the aspirations and dreams they develop in the school years, and the meaning of the choices they make as they take their first steps of their work or career path beyond school. These changes are evident in both middle-class and working-class girls, although their stories are not the same. It is also a study of changes affecting boys, of new forms of uncertainty about who they are and where they are going—though, here too, the story is differentiated by class and ethnicity. For both males and females, some of the assumptions and conscious expectations they have about men and women today, both at school and in future public and family life, have changed.

But this book also argues that the constant theoretical and political focus on "change," "New Times," and new forms of identity has been overdone and the extent of change somewhat exaggerated. The new types of work and opportunities, new modes of entry to work, the intensified push to govern and present the self in new ways foregrounded in the "new times" rhetoric, are taken up and experienced very unevenly by different groups of young people in our study. And many of the patterns and claims theorists have noted about previous periods, such as inequalities and class or gendered ways of being, or schooling's role in producing and consolidating difference and inequalities, are still apparent, even though they may have different substantive forms today.

When Keren's mother was in high school in Australia in the mid-1970s, the average age at which women had their first child was 23; far fewer women went to university than did men; employed women were concentrated in three types of occupations (sales, clerical, and service); and, on average, women earned only two-thirds of male wages. From the 1970s onward, new "equal opportunity" policies and initiatives for girls were introduced in schools. By the time Keren left school in 2000, the average age at which women were having their first child was 28. Over one-third of marriages now ended in divorce, single-person households were the second most common statistical norm, and the likelihood that a woman would have a single lifelong marriage was greatly reduced. Also by the mid-1990s, slightly more women than men were going to university; yet the great majority continued to work in a relatively narrow range of occupations, with many adult women concentrated in part-time or casual jobs and in the service and hospitality industries. For men, many traditional jobs in factories or farms have disappeared and divorces as well as decline in marriage rates mean that many fathers do not live with their children. While there has been some closing of the gap in the wage differential between women and men, women nevertheless earn significantly less than men. Notwithstanding well-established Australian policies for girls' and women's equal opportunity in education and in the workplace, in 2002, women's average earnings in Australia were

$555 per week while men earned $839, a larger gap than 10 years earlier (Summers 2003, 3).

Since the 1990s, new debates about gender and schooling have become prominent in most affluent countries, with a turn away from concerns about the education of girls to a focus on the educational experiences and outcomes of boys, evident in a huge growth in books about boys and men, conferences about boys' needs, and, in Australia, two parliamentary inquiries into the educational experiences of boys. In 1995, we asked our participants, then aged about 13, what they thought of the media debate about girls doing well at school, and boys needing more special programs. Most of them, girls and boys, agreed that girls did apply themselves better at school, but almost all rejected the idea that boys needed any special attention, since "boys are just normal." In relation to gender, education, work, and futures, the late twentieth century was a time of major change. Our longitudinal project set out to see how these changes are being lived by girls and boys from different backgrounds.

The stories of two young men in our study, Brett and Marcus, suggest how some of these changes are being differentially experienced.

Brett lives in a rural town, attends the same working-class secondary school as Keren, leaves school early, and, when we last interview him, is seeking work in a factory or a manufacturing trade. He was tired of school, and longed for the adult world of work where he could be with his "mates." Friendships were important; in many respects, they replaced the sociality and purposefulness once derived from paid work. But Brett's self-identity remains linked to getting work, being independent, and facing a traditional future as a "breadwinner." He has a taken-for-granted view about who he is that is not shared by Marcus.

Attending an "arty" state school in a middle-class suburb of a large city, Marcus has also not completed his schooling. After some time abroad on an exchange program, he cannot seem to find the motivation to return to school (though he thinks he will do some more study eventually) nor does he feel inclined to think too much about his future in a strategic sense. Rather, he is committed to "sorting himself out," to being true to his values, to exploring options, independently of the world of paid work. Marcus is consumed with introspective work on the self. His biographical project is his work.

In making sense of these different lives, we engage with a range of theories of subjectivity, gender, and contemporary times. Throughout the book, we explore the fit between the large-scale, macro analyses that these theories offer and the situated, embodied, and uneven effects of social change, read through the lives of our participants. Much contemporary social theory, as we noted earlier, analyzes the form of late modernity in relation to the production and characteristics of the "self." Giddens's (1991, 1992) arguments about "narratives of the self" and reflexive biographies and Beck and Beck-Gernsheim's (1995, 2002) related examination of "individualization" and the "detraditionalization" of identities and social relationships have been very influential. They analyze the emergence of new forms of identity in tandem with transformations in social relations and with associated imperatives to make oneself. Many scholars influenced by the work of Foucault provide a different and less optimistic vision of this process. They see it in terms of "government" of the self and "technologies of the self." They examine the emergence of a new "culture of the self" evident in the contemporary concern with therapeutic practices of the self and strategies for making the self an object of knowledge (Popkewitz and Brennan 1998; Rose 1996, 1999). Other theorists address the making of the self in terms of capacities they see called up for a new kind of worker, shaped in new capitalist times. James Gee, for example, describes the formation of a "shape-shifting portfolio person" (du Gay 1996; Gee 2000/01; Gee, Hull, and Lankshear 1996). The vocational literature (and policy-making) today is full of calls for the development of new lifelong learners, people who reshape themselves as needed (Chappell et al. 2003).

In a longitudinal study of a new generation of young people, what connections do we find between such theoretical accounts of the current era and the young people we study? How do they in their adolescent years now construct their lives and imagine their futures? Are new forms of self-making evident, and are they part of a general change or reasserted in forms of social differentiation?

We argue in this book that the forms of change and continuity in relation to gendered subjectivity are not adequately encapsulated in the types of theories that are now widely embraced. It is not simply a story of the pervading spread of "risk biographies" (Dwyer and Wyn 2001; Furlong and Cartmel 1997; MacDonald 1999), nor a unitary narrative of the "detraditionalization" of gender (Adkins, 2000, 2002a; Beck and Beck-Gernsheim 1995, 2002). The usual contrasting options of either "reproduction" or "transformation" do not capture the complexity, unevenness, and double-edged quality of "gender changes" today. For example, influential theories of women's gendered psychology have emphasized themes of connection and autonomy as problematic developmental agendas for women (Gilligan 1982; Gilligan, Lyons, and Hanmer 1990). In our repeated interviews with the young women of different backgrounds, we certainly saw how issues of connection and relationship continue to be highly important for them; we also observed how issues of autonomy and public achievement are equally important. Different things are now taken for granted by young people in terms of possibilities and future lives; for the young women, connection is neither irrelevant nor something to which all else must be sacrificed. It also seems to be the case that the achievements of feminism and girls' ways of being today have produced both new possibilities and dilemmas for them. And dilemmas arising from the desire for connection and community together with independence are taking on a distinctive salience for many young men today (discussed in chapter 8). Masculinity is being renegotiated in relation to changes in work, cultural imperatives to be "your own person," and social and political legacies of feminism—and again, the combination and salience of such factors are unevenly experienced.

Other feminist theorists have discussed women's self-perceptions and psychology in terms of their mediated sense of themselves through the "male gaze" and their culturally derived awareness of what is required to be judged as a "good" woman. We emphasize in our story of the young women in our project, particularly the young women from middle-class backgrounds, what we have called a highly honed reflexivity. This is a keen awareness of how they are being heard and interpreted by others—in the research interview, in their concerns about friends and families, in relation to schools and their teachers. But this reflexivity and the forms of femininity we explore are not quite the same in the specific temporal context of our study, contemporary times, and the high school years, as they have been in the past. This reflexivity is double-edged: it can take a self-punitive mode, a relentless self-scrutiny of seeing the self through the eyes of others, or a sense of never being good enough (Walkerdine, Lucey, and Melody 2001). Yet the reflexive personal style and ways of being are also an asset in the contemporary school and workplace, contexts in which self-regulating, flexible, adaptive, and reflexive identities are highly valued (Chappell et al. 2003; Gee, Hull, and Lankshear 1996). What is valued by school curricula and by work today has changed and this has different consequences for gendered ways of being. In other words, there is some rearticulation or realignment of the cultural significance and effects of gender difference.

At age 14, many girls in our study were dreaming about a future of almost unlimited possibility: travel, combining different glamorous jobs, fast cars, adventure (McLeod and Yates 1998). At 18, a summary of their postschool pathways (see Appendix 2a) looks like a pattern that would make the "girls can do anything" feminist reformers of the 1970s wring their hands in despair at the gender-stereotyped choices: three enter nursing, others go into arts and commerce, music therapy and law. The young men chose equally gender stereotypical occupations of mechanical engineering, medical technology, computer studies, and gardening. These are the kind of summary data that one expects to find in tracking studies of destinations. But neither the pathways to these occupations at 18, nor their meaning to the individuals or their significance in terms of social power, can be assumed from this simple summary. Our close-up and recursive study of subjectivity follows the antecedent influences on destinations and the shifting cultural and subjective meanings of those decisions. Following young people's strategies and narratives of identity-making over the six years of high school through a focus on what they say to us about their self, their school, their future—repeatedly, prospectively, retrospectively, contradictorily, recursively—provides a different way of seeing "pathways" than the tracking from outside that databases and large-scale survey-based research provide. It shows practices of meaning-making, and the ways in which identity is developed and reshaped over the course of the high school years.

We started our study with strong interests in understanding contemporary relations of difference and inequality and in the wealth of sociological theories on what schools produce and reproduce in relation to this. Many of these sociological studies focus on difference, and the ways in which the dispositions and embodied ways of being young that people bring to school and to their future-thinking are deeply differentiated by class, or gender, or race, or "habitus." Recently, there has been a renewed upsurge of interest in the writings of Bourdieu and Bernstein and their attention to class or habitus and differentiated processes of interaction between individual and school (Arnot 2002; Ball, Maguire, and Macrae 2000; McLeod 2005). There has also been a rash of new studies examining schools from the context of what the "new middle class" is doing in the changed environment of current times and current education and economic policies (Ball 2003; Brantlinger 2003; Power et al. 2003). Following people from different backgrounds at the four schools in our study reiterates the continuing relevance of what these well-known theories have shown, particularly the ways in which socially learned dispositions, knowledge agendas, and ways of being are taken up by schools and by individuals experiencing schooling as signs of their capacity or incapacity to be successful, to be certain kinds of people. But our study of particular individuals located in four different schools, and including close attention to two schools "in the middle" as well as to more elite and more disadvantaged locations, tells a more micro and differentiated story of identities and pathways being shaped in the course of schooling. Our story is consequently not just about schooling, but about particular schools.

While acknowledging and not detracting from the broader picture of how schools shape and produce inequalities, we show how, at the individual and family level, these processes do not produce uniform effects. Accepting that people from certain backgrounds will only, realistically, have access to certain schools, we can still see the effects on young people's formation of attending different schools and encountering different configurations of school agendas and cultures. For each of our four schools, some of our selected students were supported more than if they had gone to one of the other schools; at least one young person in each of the schools we studied would, hypothetically at least, have been better served by a different school. This, however, only intensifies one issue that clearly affects young people and their families today, one that we also discuss (chapter 3), and this is the pressure to make perfect choices, and the greater weight on schooling outcomes and associated focus and pressure on making (successful) futures.

Our study was designed to investigate patterns and experiences of difference and inequality and was framed in dialogue with the sociological literature on inequalities arising from class, gender, and race/ethnicity. Whatever words were used, this literature tended to portray what happens to young people in schools as a story of reproduction. The project was also set up with attention to the "school effectiveness" literature that had so dominated the decade before we commenced our longitudinal study. That literature often bracketed big differences out of the picture and compared like with like to show that some schools did better or worse. We tried to bring the different starting points of these two perspectives together in the initial design of our project. We aimed to encompass elite and disadvantaged and address the big patterns of social inequality that frame schooling experience, but also to select schools and individuals so that we might be more aware of schools "in the middle" (where outcomes are not so predictable), and could compare young people from different backgrounds in the same school and from similar backgrounds in different schools. Focusing on subjectivity and meaning-making longitudinally, and selecting schools and participants in the way that we did, offers a different type of perspective from both the "reproduction" and "school effectiveness" research. The question becomes not only "who gets what" in terms of retention, success rates, entry to higher education, and so forth, but "what kinds of people and agendas are formed by particular school environments?" This is an issue that tends to get discussed more in relation to elites and those who are most disadvantaged by the system. However, in countries like Australia, the great bulk of people are in neither of these situations (Pusey 2003). We had a sustained attention to these people in "the middle" and to "ordinary" high schools (Yates and McLeod 2000).

One of the most interesting aspects of the project for us has been seeing how, over time, two schools with roughly comparable student body demographics shaped different types of identities, aspirations, and values. This increased our sense that the individuals we had begun to study in that school did take on some cohort characteristics. This was very evident in our interviews with the young people at age 18, when most had left school, but also noticeable at points when political values are discussed, midway through the project (see chapters 3 and 7). Elaborating the effects of particular and contrasting school cultures on biographies is a significant focus of this book. As we discuss, the pattern seen at Regional High School was of people embarking on vocationally oriented courses, working hard, analyzing their next step, seeing their life outcomes as the result of how hard they worked, planning strategically, and expressing relatively unsympathetic views to the unemployed or to social discriminations. In other words, an "enterprise school," where life is a CV. At the other school with some comparable demographics, Suburban High School, at 18 the young people were mainly preoccupied with inner-directed self-discovery. They were finding the transition to university difficult, and a number were dropping out. They appreciated the care their school had given them, and spoke out about social injustices. But, in most cases, they were rather unsure about where they themselves were going in life, but nevertheless regarded self-understanding and introspection as worthwhile pursuits. Here we have a "therapeutic school," in which life is about examining and nurturing the self.

Here, and in stories from the other two schools in our study, we show how "pathways" and subjectivity are closely intertwined. It is not simply a story about what examination results a particular school achieves—though we do not discount that in the expensive private school in our study, the norm for students in the final year was to get marks that would put them in the top 20 percent of students in the whole state, and, for one student in our study, even going on to a university other than the most prestigious one feels like an aberrant path.

The effects of different school cultures are also evident in how students articulate their political values. In chapter 6 we show how different ways of talking about race and unemployment developed in different school environments. We also demonstrate how these orientations developed in relation to students' sense of personal and national identity, their sense of "who am I?" In other words, their views were shaped in the interaction between processes of schooling and processes of subjectivity. Our study is based in Australia, and this means that issues of race and national identifications are set up in nationally specific ways, ones likely to be different from how they are addressed elsewhere (by researchers, by participants in popular debate and historical imagination). But the reasoning of these young people about who they are, their sense of national belonging and identity, express dilemmas that are likely to be encountered in many different countries, where questions of "nation," "migration," "colonialization," and reconciliation with Indigenous peoples have become prominent. How do the young people in our study orient to a history in which the existing inhabitants of a country were displaced and now have rates of mortality, morbidity, and poverty that are significantly worse than non-Indigenous Australians (ABS 2004)? How do they think about who Australians are, given that, on the one hand, almost one-quarter of the population is born overseas (ABS 2004) and, on the other, there has been a long history of public fears about immigration? During the course of this project, one backdrop was a major political campaign about the unfair advantages of so-called Aboriginal welfare and multicultural groups, the dangers of further immigration, and the disadvantaging of older working-class and especially rural families. In the ways the young people in this study talked about these issues, we hear their own identity-making, their family experiences and projections to the future, and also the genres of particular school cultures.

Examining political attitudes, such as attitudes to race/ethnicity and racism, offers insight into processes of subjectivity and identification (who am I? who is "us"?). It also points to methodological and conceptual challenges in researching political views. This pertains to issues about who are the interviewees and what is happening in the interview relationship, and it also concerns issues of interpretation and the theories we draw on to construct our story about what their political values mean.

In this book, we reflect on our own activities as researchers, along with our own interpretive strategies and claims to truth. We work in departments of education, and we wanted our work to have something to show to that field. We began this project believing that a new longitudinal empirical study might help us and others address questions about inequalities, subjectivities, and young lives in the context of schools, particularly the contested terrains of "reproduction" versus "effectiveness" approaches to schools and inequalities, and sociological versus psychological versions of identity-forming. But when we began we were also immersed in the challenges posed by feminist and poststructural researchers about the constructing role of researchers and their claims to power and truth (McLeod 2003; McLeod and Yates 1997; Pillow 2003), a form of questioning that arose because of the stories that are inevitably trampled over, or rendered invisible, or marginalized as particular researcher claims are made. We don't subscribe to a view that research means nothing, is nothing other than power, is nothing but a construction. But we do consider that reflexive attention to the constructing or trampling over or making marginal is an important part of the research on inequalities and power. The issue of what we thought we were doing (and what effects we were having) when, as comfortable professional Anglo-Australian women, we asked working-class boys what they were thinking about in terms of their future or urged young people from different national and cultural backgrounds to tell us about their views on race and national identity needs to be part of what we look at.

Today we are writing in a climate in which there are powerful political moves to say that only "scientifically based research," only randomized controlled trials and quasi-experiments are good enough to count as real research in education (Yates 2004). We do not agree. We think that the type of research we discuss here, and the reflexive scrutiny of the stories we tell from it, do generate knowledge that matters for those working in education and youth and gender studies. We show schools as sources of biographical meanings, values, and trajectories over time. This contrasts with studies that view schools primarily in terms of statistically measured outcomes, such as retention and achievement at the end point of schooling. By attending to different types of theory and different types of interpretation in relation to our interviews, by keeping alive different perspectives that make sense of what is happening, we try to show that building "powerful models" is not the only form of research that matters. Situated and interpretive knowledges matter too. Again, to refer to chapter 6, attempts to "make sense of" how our Australian students talked about politics and race requires attention to place, history, situated specificity, yet also raises questions about how such values are formed and function in other countries and places.

The 12 to 18 Project: Design and Methodology

Our longitudinal and qualitative study is, from one perspective, a small-scale study, following 26 people. From another perspective, it was a major undertaking, with elements of four school ethnographies, and our intensive involvement in the project has now lasted a decade. Over seven years, we conducted over 400 lengthy interviews and generated multiple sources of evidence or "data" for each interview: notes at the time and subsequently, tapes and transcriptions, videotapes, our own recollections, as well as later comments by the people involved, including comments from a final interview after participants had watched a compilation video tape of extracts from the seven years of their earlier interviews. The project was structured to offer ongoing attention to interpretive comparison. We built it by selecting between six and eight main students from four different schools (initially we had interviewed all students in a class from each of those schools, and we continued through the first three years of the project to interview other friends together with the main students we were following). Unlike a more common form of qualitative research, school ethnographies, we did not want to focus only on the experiences of one "type" of student (e.g., working-class boys), or different groups of students within a single school. And we wanted to look at schools beyond the kinds that are usually chosen by researchers like ourselves whose interests are in difference and inequalities—that is, the most disadvantaged or most elite. We wanted to pay attention to "the middle," to explore what happens in ordinary high schools, where experiences are not so overdetermined. This, we felt, was a particularly important focus for "new world" countries such as Australia.

In the study design we wanted to set up some opportunity to consider what particular school experiences bring to the biographical characteristics of students differentiated by class or gender or ethnicity. So the four schools and the 26 students were selected to include students from different backgrounds in the same school, and students from similar backgrounds who attended different schools. There are, of course, important methodological questions about what we are assuming and doing here, what it means to do this kind of research with small numbers of subjects, and the implicit categories in how "different backgrounds" are selected; these issues are discussed in later chapters when we talk about "class" or "race" (see also Yates 2000, 2001, 2003).

In each interview, twice a year over seven years, we were asking our participants to talk about various aspects of three things: their views of self, their views of school, and their views of the future. In each interview we asked questions or embarked on the conversation in different ways. Sometimes we asked directly ("How would you describe yourself?" "What do you think this school views as important?" "Do you think much about the future?"), sometimes indirectly, asking them to bring along and talk about a favorite photograph, or what they thought of certain issues that were in the news. Our interview questions and style were more influenced by sociological and feminist perspectives than psychological ones. Our intent was to embark on topics in ways that were relatively nonleading, and nondirective, both in the sense of attempting to avoid setting up certain types of responses as the appropriate ones, and in the sense of not closely privileging a particular type of theory and theory-testing in the design of the questions themselves. We also had an ongoing interest in and concern about the meaning of the interview exchange and the effect of our own embodied personas on what those in the study would say or choose to say, and we will discuss that further throughout this book. These were not a "confessional" style of interview, and our approach, as all research approaches, set up some possibilities and foreclosed others (McLeod 2003; McLeod and Yates 1997).

One decision we made was to try to minimize the impact or significance of our study as an event in the lives of those we studied. Contrary to many feminist approaches, we did not seek an "intimate" relationship with those we studied, and we did not, as some other projects do, show previous videos or talk about what was said in previous interviews in subsequent interviews (until the end of the study when we prepared and discussed with each participant in our study an overall compilation tape from their individual interviews). This did not mean that no relationship developed between us and those whom we interviewed, or that the study had no meaning or impact for them. During the course of the study, we found that the mere event of appearing twice a year as nonjudgmental outsiders who gave people a chance to talk was specifically valued by some, whereas others were not particularly comfortable with this, but nevertheless tried to help us. Again, we will discuss this further throughout the book. But a longitudinal study, with repeated interviewing, does inevitably build a more significant research relationship than a one-off survey, and we attempted to minimize as far as we could having the research event itself shape the choices and thinking that we were setting out to study.

Our project was an interview-based study, not an ethnographic one. The methods are ones that elicit conscious and often self-conscious talk about what people are thinking, and what they want to say to researchers about this. We interviewed participants in a conventional interview setting (in an empty schoolroom, and later in a neutral outside location); in a space that was "time out" from their school day. We did not observe them in the classroom or in the school grounds with their friends; we did not follow them out of school, or interview their parents or teachers. Of course, in one sense, this is a limitation, and circumscribes what we can say. But it is not possible to be a fly on the wall; had we done any of those other kinds of research, that too would have shaped certain events and interpretations and foreclosed others. For example, to the people in our study, the fact that we were not having any direct involvement with teachers or parents was a feature of their interview space. The "buddy" ethnographer relationship by no means guarantees access to events as they would be if that ethnographer were not present. In any case, we too have families and lives, and other demands of our working life beyond this study. In terms of the specificity of our lives as researchers, we were also mindful of the effect of our presence as older women from the university on what the participants told us and the dynamic of the interview; we discuss this in the following chapter. The larger issue of what we, and all researchers, are able to do and not do as we try to study lives is an ongoing part of our account.

Although our study is not an ethnography, it draws on elements of ethnographic form in its design and interests. In particular, the study was designed not as a study of 26 individuals who might carry certain gendered, class, ethnic, and family features with them, but as a study of "biographies in interaction with schooling." The school is intended to be a presence in the study; it is part of what we are studying. The individuals were selected and interviewed in the context of their four different schools. One of the main interests of this study was to look more closely at the influence of schooling in the shaping of subjectivity. Many existing research projects and theories offer broad insights into how schools, or academic knowledge, or competitive curriculum work to confirm some advantages and confirm some students as disadvantaged or as "other." We wanted to deal with school culture and situation and context, as do ethnographies. By listening to what participants said about a particular school over many different interviews (including retrospective comments) and hearing how views and values changed or deepened over that time by school "cohort," we gathered a large amount of direct and indirect evidence about the school and the student's relationship to it. As well, we conducted all the interviews ourselves and twice a year, over seven years, visited the schools, and experienced their style of administration, bulletin boards, and publicity materials about the schools. This is part of the story we discuss in this book.

In terms of the selection of students for the study, we first chose the four schools. We wanted to include one that might be identified as disadvantaged and one that would be identified as elite and two "ordinary" high schools. Second, in terms of location, we selected two from the metropolitan capital city of the state and two schools from a regional or "country" city. This was to give comparative attention to the significance of a mid-sized city experience (as distinct from the "urban" or "rural" settings that have drawn much more research attention in Australia). Finally, we wanted opportunities to study people from similar backgrounds in different schools, so we chose schools (and individuals) in which at least some of those involved might potentially have gone to one of the other schools in our study.

This structuring of the study might seem to mimic, inappropriately for a small-scale and interpretive study, the quasi-experimental structuring that is more commonly found in large-number research designs, given that we have only six to eight students at each school, and similarly small numbers that might represent different kinds of class or ethnic backgrounds, especially in combination with gender. It might therefore be argued that for any type of comparison, the numbers involved are so small as to make the activity meaningless. But the comparison here is not a reading-off of "findings" guaranteed by adequate sample construction and computer-based technical methods. The object of comparison is itself constructed of interpreted texts, but comparison is also used in the process of interpreting the texts (the subjects, the schools): it is always a process of moving back and forth between whole and parts, between different extracted comparisons. And the process of interpretation includes reflexive attention to the context of production of our data, including the temporal context of our embodied interview. What we are setting up in the comparative design and method of the project is not a replication of "controlled comparison" in the ways done with large-scale studies, but the setting up of opportunities to think self-critically about the attributions we are making about the meaning of the texts in relation to the larger education issues that are the context of our study.

To select the students, we first interviewed and videotaped, in friendship groups of three, all students in a particular class. In the case of the regional schools we did this by taking one final year class of three elementary schools whose students would be proceeding to those two schools. In the case of the two capital city schools, we interviewed in similar groups of three, all of one Year 7 class—first year of high school—near the commencement of that year. We then watched the videotapes and tried to simply select about eight "different" students for each school, with equal numbers of girls and boys, and not just those who were particularly engaging or talkative. We wanted to include some "class" diversity and some "ethnic" diversity, but we chose not to do this by having the students fill in questionnaires about their family backgrounds. We did not want to predecide what "class" is, or in what way "ethnicity" should be categorized and then embark on a study to follow young person X because they "represent" this class or this ethnicity. In the ensuing interviews, we wanted their own accounts about the significance or nonsignificance and markers of these categories and relations (as well of those of gender) to emerge through what they said. This sets up a different type of interpretive work than if we had begun with each participant categorized.

After our first round of whole-class interviews, we approached the 12 year olds and parents of those we wanted to participate. Most were happy to do so, but a particularly inarticulate girl from poor circumstances and a boy whose parents were very wealthy did not agree to continue. Our participants did include some whose families were relatively poor, unemployed, single-parent, relatively recent immigrant, and some whose families were relatively wealthy, in high-status jobs, with holiday houses at the beach and in ski resorts and who took overseas vacations. Some parents were teachers, worked in small business, or did manual work. Our study did not include the students from the extremes, in terms of the most elite and powerful and the most powerless and disadvantaged. But the repeated interviews, with their glimpses of family over seven years, also indicate the inadequacy of these demographic one-word descriptors of people. Some mothers were returning to study; some fathers were having business problems and experiencing changes in work; some families were splitting up; some families were being dominated by a particular issue such as the health or behavior of one of the children. The brief biographical snapshot of each participant provided in Appendix 1 shows how imperfectly glib database categorizations of "SES" or "ethnicity" capture the complex mixture of experiences in family backgrounds that are the norm today.

The Schools and Participants

Pseudonyms have been used for all participants, the four schools and the regional center.[1] Appendix 1 provides a brief sketch of each of the participants, and Appendix 2 is a very summarized version of what happened to the people in each school—their outcomes—and the various ways they thought about their future over the seven-year period. However, given the small numbers, these summaries and destinations only become meaningful on the basis of the more interpretive account of how each school is producing certain kinds of people, values, and possibilities (McLeod 2000b, 2002; Yates 2001, 2003; Yates and McLeod 2000).

Our study was based in two Australian cities in one state. All four schools are coeducational, and none is academically selective in enrollment. Two schools were in Melbourne, the state capital city of over 3 million people. In Australia, schooling policies and administrative structures are state-based and directed from each state capital. Melbourne houses most of the universities in the state, including the most prestigious, and, until the 1970s, the only tertiary institutions that had university status were located here. Two schools were selected from Cubbin, a regional city of around

100,000 people, some two hours from the capital city. Cubbin is a substantial center of education, with a large number of state and private schools as well as technical colleges and a small university, of relatively recent status, and not prestigious. In comparison to larger cities in Australia, Cubbin is not very ethnically diverse, has had less post WWII immigration, and a greater proportion of families living in the area for three generations or more.

At the high school phase, for historical reasons, Australia has a relatively large proportion of students attending private (or "independent") schools, and this is particularly strong in the state where this study is based. Historically, the larger and elite private schools dominate the top ranks of results in the final school certificate and are very disproportionately represented in entrants to the prestigious universities (Teese 2000), and more generally in important and powerful positions in the society generally—as evidenced by inclusion in *Who's Who* (Peel and McCalman 1992). So private schools are a visible presence to parents and teachers in this state—and indeed a substantial number of teachers who teach in state schools themselves send their children to private schools. There is a widespread perception that private schools produce both academic advantages and social network advantages in relation to later social hierarchy, though when family background is controlled for, the academic advantages are not as evident as commonly perceived.

School 1 Regional High

This school of some 1100 students is one of the oldest high schools in the state. It is located in Cubbin, a city with many private boarding schools and a regional center of education for what was in the past a prosperous farming community. This high school, unlike all the other public schools in the same city, has long been an honorary member of the private school sporting association in Cubbin, and news of its students and events are frequently covered in the local newspaper. Within the state school system, this school is recognized as having particular distinction as a sporting center of excellence, as well as for its strong musical program. It allocates among its staffing a specialist rowing master, has its own rowing shed, and boasts a number of impressive buildings and playing fields. In Cubbin, among parents who want to send their children to a "good" school, but cannot afford the fees of a private school, there is competition to move into Regional High's selection zone (it is not academically selective, but geographically zoned, except for sporting prowess). In social demographics, the school has a mixed population, with students who might come from any of the categories represented in SES surveys. However, its composition overrepresents those from "lower middle-class" backgrounds (nonwealthy small business, some teachers, nurses, etc.) and underrepresents both the poorest groups (more likely to go to Regional Tech or other similar schools in the city) and the highest SES and more historically elite groups (more likely to go to a private school). At Regional High, the students wear uniforms that are similar in style and quality to the uniforms worn by the private schools—for example, high-quality wool blazer and pleated skirt or wool trousers.

School 2 Regional Tech

Historically, the education system in this state offered two kinds of secondary school: schools with traditional academic subjects, called high schools, and schools with overt vocational purposes and designed for those likely to leave school before Year 12: "technical" schools to train boys for manual occupations and "girls' [domestic] schools" to prepare girls from a similar class for lower occupations and then domesticity. In the 1970s, with gender equity reforms, schools were merged into coeducational technical schools, with both girls and boys formally offered similar access to "trade" subjects. By the 1980s, when there was a greater concern about "league tables" and relative Year 12 results, and when apprenticeships were no longer easily entered after Year 10 but began to require Year 12, a further reorganization of the system took place. In Cubbin, and throughout the state, technical schools were amalgamated and restructured to form junior campuses (Years 7–10; with students aged approximately 12–16) with students then moving to a common senior school for the final two years of secondary school.

The junior campus of Regional Tech, which was the site of our study for the first four years, was located on the edge of a public housing development, and also drew a number of students from some smaller, relatively poor, rural towns not far from this city. It had relatively new buildings, and was very well equipped with new computers and other technical equipment. The senior campus was an older, more run-down set of buildings in an adjoining suburb. At the junior school, the "uniform" consisted of the requirement to wear a sweatshirt in a dark color and leather shoes rather than trainers. There was no uniform at the senior campus, and students were encouraged to view the transition to this campus as an opportunity for greater independence and to be treated more as "adults."

School 3 City Academy

In Australia, in each capital city, a number of elite private schools associated with church foundations were established in the nineteenth century and have grown and maintained a status as "leading schools" throughout the twentieth and into the twenty-first centuries. Although they now receive high levels of funding from the Australian commonwealth government, they also charge high fees (and thus have much higher funding per student than state schools, as well as impressive buildings and extensive grounds and facilities). They are therefore socially selective. Although they may have some scholarships for academically gifted achievers or for particular occupational categories such as families of clergy or teachers in the school, compared with the broad population demographic, they overrepresent professional and managerial occupations and overrepresent those from wealthy backgrounds.

Within the group of elite private schools in each city, there is considerable advertising and "word of mouth" publicity about the different emphases and agendas of different schools. Today, the association with particular religions (Anglican, Presbyterian, Methodist, etc.) is a less strong part of the public profile of the elite private schools, although these tags may remain in both the name of the school and the composition of its governing board. City Academy was one of these elite schools, with extensive beautiful grounds and buildings in a desirable and visible part of the city. Unlike some other private schools, this school was not academically selective, and emphasized its breadth in curriculum choice, especially its support for the arts as well as sport and academic areas. In the senior years, it offered a choice of certification routes.

School 4 Suburban High

Public schooling in Australia is administered centrally as a state system compared with the U.S. system of local school boards, but there has been some variation in how different states have allowed schools to develop. Victoria, especially in the 1970s and 1980s, supported some diversity of style and approach by different schools. These schools were not specialist schools, and each was expected to offer the same broad curriculum as its core in the early high school years, and to enter students for a common final certificate. However, some variety in curriculum offerings and facilities was available between schools, along with differences in their organizational form and culture. Some schools were known for formality and discipline and others for pastoral care or informality; some emphasized science and language and music, others offered photography and drama. Suburban High was one of these "arty," more informal schools. We selected Suburban High because it was in a middle-class suburb very near the suburb where City Academy was located.

Suburban High was in a desirable and attractive suburb, with many large houses in beautiful gardens, but the area also includes some less wealthy sections, including those with public housing. Its school population included professional and middle-class parents who knew and liked its curriculum and values emphasis as well as those whose parents were in manual jobs or unemployed or recently arrived immigrants. This school had much more visible ethnic diversity than the other schools in our study. During the time of our study, the school underwent some changes in direction. It had been established in the 1960s, and through the 1970s and 1980s had shown its commitment to a more informal, "progressive" style of education by not having a uniform (uncommon in this state at the secondary level) and developing an impressive arts center and fostering related achievements, including photography exhibitions, and so on. Some middle-class parents in professional occupations chose this school because it appeared to value cultural diversity, to care for students, and to place less emphasis on the disciplining regime and competitive academic curriculum of many other schools. However, when we began our study, this school had been experiencing a declining popularity. In the media there was much attention to "school effectiveness" and university entrance scores, along with worries about drug culture. The state government too, in the wake of some unpopular cutting of school budgets and closing down of schools, had made a gesture to still criticism and show its commitment to "progressive" issues about gender equality by developing a new showpiece public girls' school and providing free public transport to take girls there. This school was located close by Suburban High, and had drawn potential students from that school. In the first year of our study, Suburban High had only a small Year 7 intake, and one in which boys outnumbered girls by around 3:1. As the study continued, this school took steps to reverse these problems: it introduced school uniforms, embarked on new publicity campaigns with local primary schools emphasizing its values and curriculum, and gave more attention to retaining students in the final years.

The Plan of the Book

In the following chapters, we do not set out to present the story of our project, in the sense of a chronological narrative, but to discuss themes and issues that we were exploring in dialogue with this project: questions about meanings, subjectivity, inequalities and social differentiation, questions about how particular schools and particular biographies come together. Some stories and incidents are referred to in more than one chapter. Readers can remind themselves of the characteristics of schools or individuals by returning to the quick sketches presented in this introduction, or by looking at the participant snapshots and summary tables of aspirations and outcomes presented in the appendixes.

Chapter 2 explores the value and theoretical rationale of embarking on a longitudinal study of subjectivities in the particular way that we did. A range of other recent work has been broadly concerned with the terrain that we explore in our project, and here we discuss some contributions of that work as well as our own particular framing. We consider some issues about what it means to do "theory" as well as discuss the particular value of a qualitative and longitudinal method that allows retrospective and prospective components.

Chapter 3 frames the stories of our seven-year project in terms of what we heard about what actually counts with schools today and with how this is differentially inflected in the sociocultural settings of the four schools. Some of the story we tell here is a familiar one, in terms of the practices that enhance the already advantaged and further disadvantage the already disadvantaged—a story already much explored by other theorists in terms of "codes" and "dispositions" and "reproduction" and effects of "school mix." But our project also shows some changes in the agendas of schools today (their emphasis on image-making, for example, on young people needing to be an advertisement for their school), and draws attention to the relational positioning of schools and the students in them—relative both to that school's population, history and community, but also to other schools in the same city. The chapter illustrates how individual engagements with being a good student are to some extent specific to their school culture and student makeup. In everyday words, we show that while (as databases attest) school outcomes are broadly in line with family background characteristics, for individual students a more specific or more differentiated sense of themselves and their potential is generated by the particular school. We can see how some students at every one of the four schools might have fared better or differently had they been to one of the other schools in our study. We show in this chapter that being a good student is not simply a result of enacting what each school formally endorses, but is shaped by peer interactions, by the history of both the school and the family, and that their history in the school over time constrains possibilities for an individual. The schools too are conveying agendas that engage with social differentiation and changing work possibilities in different ways. In one school (not the private school), being well noted in terms of social distinction is understood by the students as more important than final academic results. In two other schools, students see the school as heavily engaged in teaching them to be a certain type of person—a well-networked and distinctive individual in one case; someone attuned to and comfortable with difference in the other. We argue in this chapter that today students become part of the marketing of schools; the civic values they learn include the importance of marketing themselves.

Whereas chapter 2 discussed a longitudinal approach to subjectivity and our perspectives on doing theory, chapter 4 considers in more detail some specific sociological debates that have framed our own research and analysis. We outline here how our dual focus on processes of subjectivity and social differentiation led us to engage with different types of theory. A key aspect of our approach has been to explore subjectivity as both a project of self making—one that many theorists argue has intensified in the current era of late modernity—and as an ongoing process of "becoming" that is socially and discursively embedded but not reducible to either. We consider these debates in relation to associated arguments about transformations in gender identities and gender relations, and the manner and extent to which young people today are formed in and by processes of detraditionalization, including the de (or re) traditionalization of gender.

But we bring two additional perspectives to these debates. One is a cluster of discussions concerning the role of discourse in shaping subjectivity, and the attention to the psychosocial subject as in part a reaction against both social and discourse determinism. Here we argue that we need to keep in focus both sociological and psychological ways of seeing, not to compress one to the other, and to actively acknowledge the different kind of insights each does or does not make possible. The second perspective we bring to the larger debates about new forms of identity involves the practices of social distinction and differentiation and embodied dispositions that Bourdieu's concept of habitus emphasizes. Student subjectivities are formed in interaction with the ethos of the school, which cultivates dispositions and orientations that may contradict or correspond to the habitus formed in the family.

Researching subjectivity within a qualitative longitudinal study offers distinctive insights for seeing how the project and the process of becoming someone is embodied and happens incrementally and recursively over and in time; we illustrate this with discussions of two young women at different schools as they reflect on and describe themselves at different stages of the project. We consider the methodological dilemmas involved in asking young people to "tell us about yourself" and the challenges of making interpretive claims from interview material—text, encounter, visual record, and our own recollections—and develop a case study of one young woman's changing relation to her school that also illustrates the value of keeping in play different perspectives on subjectivity.

Chapter 5 considers "subjectivity and becoming" through a close-up study of one young woman and her dreams and planning about her future and her career choices. Central to this are her self-understandings about who she is and who she wants to become, and her positioning in relation to family, her school, peers, and broader social discourses. Our discussion of this is set against two divergent traditions of studying young people's orientation to the future in the high school years. Policy-makers tend to see "pathways," "transition," "career choice" in rational and instrumental steps. Cultural studies theorists are interested in the ways young people project, reflect on, and negotiate their own biography, revisiting their dreams, their values, and their sense of who they are and who they want to be. Even theorists who do attempt to meld the social and biographical with concepts like habitus do not usually examine the remaking of biography and the dreams that form individuals, but look to exterior readings of lives via gender, class, locality. Our focus in this chapter is both on the social (field, school, culture, discourse) working in individual lives—"how do discourses turn into subjectivity?"—and on how individual subjectivities turn into social patterns: "how do social patterns of unequal futures begin to get set up?" This chapter shows gender-differentiated patterns in the projections of the future; and it uses a comparative illustration of girls from different background to also demonstrate how class difference frames the dreams and pathways that we see.

In chapter 6 we consider who is "us"?—Australian students on politics, racism, ethnicity, and unemployment—and we also consider how they are talking about these matters to us and how we are complicit and awkward in the research and writing we do here. In Australia, discourses of racism are often voiced through judgments of belonging, of who is and is not "Australian." But the issue of who is Australian is also pervasively problematic, given the colonial dispossession of Aboriginal Australians. We show how, for these young people, their identifications of "us" and "them" are shifting ones and ones that relate to young people's own processes of identity-making and becoming. That is, they are about belonging and projected belonging as well as about demographic background, inherited values, and experiences. We also compare attitudes to racism and ethnicity with other political values in relation to unemployment. This chapter again indicates the significant effect of school ethos on the understandings and political values that individuals develop, as well as the different salience and consequences of being "different" in different schools.

Chapter 7 discusses class in the new world and the new economy. This is a period of change in work, social relations, and labor structures, and "class" is not a foregrounded identity in either Australia or the United States (or even, for many young people, in the United Kingdom). This chapter discusses the problems of working with a concept of "class" but also argues the importance of keeping alive a discussion of class in relation to the experiences of the individuals and the schools we studied and for discussing schools and society more generally. We take a new look at the large group who might be said to be "in the middle" in SES hierarchies—neither clearly advantaged in terms of school and work nor clearly disadvantaged. In terms of class consciousness and class identification, we show that class, in the sense of social distinctions, is salient in some subjectivities and not in others; that it operates differently in different schools, and for different individuals at a school. In terms of class reproduction or the story of how middle-class kids get middle-class jobs, we take up the issue of social change, and different formations of work today, and discuss how the schools and individuals in our project are engaging (or not engaging) with these changes. We point to patterns of both reproduction and change that are evident against this changing backdrop. And we discuss this story of reproduction and change with particular attention to class-gender subjectivities and situations, specifically what we see in this study happening to middle-class girls compared with working-class girls, and working-class girls compared with working-class boys.

Accounts of young people today often want to pin down a typology or come up with a key label. In chapter 8, we draw together a number of themes concerning gender, subjectivity, and change that emerge in earlier chapters of this book. In particular, these are debates about gender detraditionalization, reflexivity, and "enterprising subjectivity" as well as discussions about the changing social and work opportunities for girls and boys, and gender differences within class patterns, especially working-class patterns. We introduce two main new discussions in this chapter. The first is the large discursive picture of what "gender equity" or "equal opportunities" means for girls and boys today. On the one hand, the official language of equal opportunities has been well grasped, and men and women are said to be equal; there is clear evidence that some actual and imagined possibilities have changed for young women in particular. Most do not think of their futures solely in terms of domestic responsibilities; most imagine a future of emotional and economic independence. But, on the other hand, the young women and men tended to not hold a political view of gender, evidenced in the belief that "males are just normal," and an impatience with examining social issues and changes in relation to gender.

The second discussion we develop here concerns changing resonances of conventionally gendered dilemmas and cultural themes—namely, autonomy and connection. In discursive binaries, girls have typically been aligned with relationships—to self and others—and to seeking "connection" over "autonomy." Diverse theorists have outlined the dilemmas young women encounter as they negotiate these apparently conflicting desires. Here we look at these themes in relation to the experiences and thinking of young men and consider how those conventional markers of gender difference and gender identity are changing and being mediated in class and school differentiated ways. The binary of autonomy or connection does not seem to be holding for either young women or men. We suggest that characterizations of the current era as one marked by a "culture of the self" (Rose 1999), where autonomy is foregrounded, need to take into account gendered and situated mediations of the quest for autonomy, and the different cultural and subjective resonance that quest offers for men and women. Similarly, accounts of the transformation of gender must attend to the ways in which young women and young men are differently responding to changed economic, social, and discursive circumstances as part of their project of the self.

Our concluding chapter returns to some of the contextual and sociological issues with which we opened this first chapter. It considers the specificities of our study in relation to large-scale social changes, particularly in relation to gender and work and to current debates about the purposes of schooling. It shows, as Benhabib (1995) argues, that understanding complex social processes, such as schooling or subjectivity—and the interactions between the two—cannot be reduced to single explanatory frameworks, to single "constitutive criteria" (Benhabib 1995, 27), or to discussions that privilege either subjectivity or schooling. Throughout this book, we try to keep both processes simultaneously in view.

CHAPTER 2

Researching Subjectivity and Schooling—On Method and What It Means to Work with Theory

In any longitudinal study, it is not only participants' lives that are subject to change. During the time of our research, world politics changed dramatically, new wars were started, some political voices and struggles emerged, others declined or intensified. The political and intellectual context in which educational research is located also shifted, and new agendas became prominent, such as policy concerns about the education of boys, or calls for "evidence-based" research, and challenges to the value and utility of educational research itself (Yates 2004). Our lives too moved on, our work and family commitments changed, babies were born, new jobs started, one of us moved to another state. While the interviews for the study remained a constant reference point for both of us over the seven-year period, the theoretical debates that framed our enquiries shifted and this, in turn, influenced the way we developed our interpretations. We turn here to recapture the questions and theoretical agendas that motivated our decision in the early 1990s to embark on a qualitative longitudinal study and framed our design and methodological choices.

There were multiple starting points for this study—biographical, intellectual, and sociopolitical. We both had researched and written about policy changes concerning gender and schooling that had begun in Australia in the mid-1970s. By the 1990s, we wanted to see the effects of such reforms on a new generation of school students. The period from the 1970s to 1990s was an era of significant and well-documented social change for countries such as Australia, and gender reform in schools was one part of that. Such changes include the effects of the women's movement and globalization and associated shifts in work and family patterns, the expansion of the knowledge/service economy, overall increases in school retention, decline of manual and industrial work, and the demise of the concept of a lifelong job (Bauman 2001; Chappell et al. 2003; Dwyer, Tyler, and Wyn 2001), smaller average family size, and decline of lifelong marriage (Summers 2003). There had also been a considerable change in social discourse or the cultural backdrop of what is taken for granted or what is silent. In the 1970s, the women's movement demonstrated that inequalities for women existed in schools and in public institutions; that there was "a problem that had no name," and that "sexism" was a real social phenomenon. By the 1990s, gender issues and gender reform were beginning to seem like well-established ideas (Yates 1998). New laws were in place: "sexist" advertisements were routinely criticized; schools no longer thought it acceptable to suggest that girls should limit their ambitions or only work for a few years and then rely on a husband. What was the "subjectivity" of young people who had grown up in this world? In schools too, at least in Australia, the discourse of what education was about had changed markedly since the 1970s. Then there had been a "disadvantaged schools program" with special funding for schools in poorer areas. In the early 1990s, there was a "Schools of the Future" program, with funds to reward schools who were seen to be winners. "Disadvantage" was out, "effective schools" were in, and not just in Australia; these political agendas and education policy fashions circulate rapidly and globally. What was the experience and effects for young people in poorer and richer circumstances going through school in the 1990s?

The study also emerges from our interest in some influential and contending ways of theorizing and researching subjectivity and gendered subjectivity. There is a vast array of conceptual terms and approaches for theorizing subjectivity and for characterizing its contemporary form, each with their own blindnesses and insights, and each evoking different disciplinary/intellectual traditions—discourse and the construction of subject positions; Foucauldian technologies of the self; Bourdieu's concept of habitus; relational psychology; Beck's risk and choice biographies; psychoanalytic informed understandings of desire; Butlerian notions of perfomativity

. . . and so on. In an era that Rose (1999) describes as dominated by a "culture of the self," theoretical work itself turns to subjectivity and to analyzing its formation and effects.

In the early stages of our study, we had been struck by what we saw as two different trajectories in theories of subjectivity that had been influential in work on gender and schooling. One line of analysis paid much attention to social messages in various forms, with claims about "discourse" and the "construction of the subject" largely replacing "roles" and "socialization" as a way of describing identity formation. The other line attended to developmental agendas within individual biographies, especially at adolescence, when it was argued that gender differences became particularly pronounced. Although the first way produced many sensitizing insights, it tended to create a rather linear and flat picture of the individual life being made, a picture in which a person was a cipher of discourse, a one-dimensional figure on whom social messages were writ (Hollway 1994; McLeod 1993, 2000b; McLeod and Yates 1997). Accordingly, the "construction of identity" arguments tended to reproduce many of the blindspots of socialization theory and slip analytically from discourses to subjectivity as if they were the same thing. In contrast, a central question for us has been "How do discourses turn into subjectivity?" (Nielsen 1996, 5). The pivotal issue is not simply one of generalized "identity construction," but instead one of how the social is mediated and encountered subjectively. "How does cultural discourse 'turn into' the psychological projects and desires of individual boys and girls?" (Nielsen and Rudberg 1994, 2).

We also felt that much poststructural work on the "discursive construction of identity" was glib and formulaic in its reference to the construction of "nonunitary subjects." Rather than simply repeat such theoretical propositions, we wanted to understand that theorized process empirically, to actually try to see how embodied identities were shaped in a complex, contradictory, discursive, and social context. The developmental agenda, the second way of investigating gender identities, paid insufficient attention, we felt, to the specificity of these particular times and to the varying social and educational settings in which different girls and boys were located (*Feminism and Psychology* 1994 special issue).

It was from these concerns that we planned this study to be longitudinal and recursive, to confront a flat linearity, but also sociologically framed, to keep difference and historical specificity to the foreground.

We wanted a study that would follow "biographies in interaction with schooling." When we started, we possibly hoped to produce a new theory, a new model of what that process looked like, but, as we proceeded, we became more convinced that the point is not to seek that nirvana—it is to maintain different ways of seeing, rather than to homogenize these into a single new model. (This issue is returned to in chapter 4.)

Specificity and Theory

In the years of working on this project, we have become much more self-conscious and self-critical about what we believe in as "theory." What theory looks like to a Bourdieu or a Bernstein or a Giddens or a Gilligan or a Butler is not the same as what theory might look like to a Lather or a Bordo or a Fraser or a Putnam. In part, what we feel is a tension between two different desires or preferences. On the one hand, we are wanting to find modes of showing what is happening that are powerful, that have some explanatory purchase, that have something new to say that is not already well known or common sense, and which take us beyond simply telling endless "rich stories." On the other hand, and at the same time, we share strong ongoing resistance to overarching, universal explanations and model-building. This is especially so, we suspect, because of our initial training as historians, a discipline with an orientation to specificity and context. We have been heavily influenced too by early feminist debates about the ways powerful models tend to trample over the particularity of women's experiences, as well as by subsequent insights that any claim to truth does violence to experiences and starting points that are framed as "other."

Nevertheless, we did, we think now, begin with an idea that our study would allow us to work with some existing important theories and produce a new synthesis of these that would overcome the lacks and limitations we saw in each. As we proceeded over the seven and more years, we have become more convinced that this is not what we want. For some purposes, a concept such as the Foucauldian "governmentality" or "technologies of the self" is useful; for other purposes a focus on Bourdieu's "habitus," "field," "disposition," or on Giddens's "biographical projects and reflexivity" or on re-articulations of gendered themes such as autonomy and connection is more salient and illuminating. Our chapter on class illustrates how we see and have worked with this issue. It is impossible today to work with the concept of class in any way that does not have major flaws. But, in a study such as ours, to not engage with this historically located concept would be equally flawed. We need powerful concepts to frame and test and debate as well as to deconstruct ways of seeing; but we also need to resist the old (and masculinist?) idea that the best theory is the one that looks most like a universal formula.

We do not then embrace a single type of theory or one theoretical position that is able to capture and explain the "full picture" of what we have been studying. Our approach to theorizing is shaped by feminist and poststructural methodological traditions, and is contextual and historically attuned, rather than universal and undifferentiated. It is, however, not a form of grounded theory in that we began our empirical study with some distinct theoretical questions. Theoretical concerns, as many others have shown (Britzman 2000; Lather 1991, 1994), shape the very design and conduct of any study, whether or not that is made explicit or self-conscious. As Bourdieu argues: "Every act of research is simultaneously empirical (it confronts the world of observable phenomena) and theoretical (it necessarily engages hypotheses about the underlying structure of relations that observations are designed to capture)" (Bourdieu and Wacquant 1992, 35). We see the particularity of the experiences we have been studying as in some way "speaking back" to and enriching theoretical discussions. And we have tried to foster and sustain a dialectic and reflexive relation between theorizing and research. We regard theories as themselves part of the construction of truths and knowledge about "class" or "gender" or "adolescence"—that is, theories construct at the same time as they seek to explain. Our engagement with certain kinds of theoretical work was motivated by an interest in two interrelated sets of issues. The first concerns the effects of different types of schooling on the formation of persons and the shaping of trajectories, individual dispositions, and ways of being in the world. The second set of theoretical interests involves strategies of subjectivity and the making of the self, the issue of how subjectivity takes shape and is regulated today.

In addition to these theoretical issues, other methodological and interpretive questions bedevil studies that are necessarily limited in scale. In what way can a study of 26 people add up to something more than a story about 26 lives? (Yates 2003). In what way can a study set in one specific location, Victoria, Australia, have something to say to those whose interest is in lives and schools in the United States, or

Canada, or Finland? One of the consequences for us, as researchers, of interviewing 26 individuals at some length twice a year for seven years is that the specificities and complexities of each individual become fascinating and threaten to overwhelm any ability to speak about more general patterns and processes. Individual lives do exceed the theoretical models within which we attempt to portray them. Nevertheless, our study was designed with a core intention of contributing to research and debates on schooling and inequalities—of gender, of class, of ethnicity. Our methods of selecting both the schools and the individuals, and the interpretive possibilities of comparison (of individuals from similar backgrounds at different schools or from different backgrounds at the same school; of what was said and happening according to school cohort compared with class or gender groupings) and in ongoing dialogue with the broader world of other research evidence is an important part of this study. The grounds on which we claim and construct some particular experiences and meanings as evidence of something more general is an ongoing discussion throughout the book.

The issue of who is being studied is a general problematic for all qualitative research; so too is the question of which groups of people are not being studied. This is a much-rehearsed discussion, given past critiques of all-male samples tied to claims about, for example "young people," or critiques of feminism for its focus on the cultural and social mainstream and advantaged, while making universalizing yet exclusionary claims about "all women." In relation to class, we discuss (in chapter 7) the problem of ethnographies that claim to show "working-class" women, without theorizing whether there are other types of working-class women's experiences that might be different from those of the particular group that has been selected to be emblematic. There is no avoiding such problems in qualitative work; the issue is to recognize it, both in the design of the study and what is claimed. As we have noted, our initial selection of participants was limited by the fact that, of those we invited, the two individuals who probably were from the most elite and well-off and the poorest family circumstances declined to participate. Nevertheless, our focus here was never to be primarily on those overdetermined extremes that occupy so much of the literature. Our emphasis was on more "ordinary" lives. But questions of who and what is included remain pertinent in relation to national specificity and to relevance beyond national borders.

Australia, Questions of Specificity and Theories of Subjectivity and Education

The young people and the schools we studied are Australian. But issues that we address—of self-formation, the new world, of difference and inequality, of gender, class, race, ethnicity—are not peculiar to Australia. The theorists with whose work we engage, and the theoretical and methodological challenges we explore, are ones that will be familiar to readers in the United States or Scandinavia or the United Kingdom, or New Zealand, though they are most likely not globally relevant or significant. They will not be of equal interest to readers in China or Botswana or Iran or, possibly, Germany and Italy. The social context of some countries, for example, the primacy of religion or of a different national history, may make discussions about self-formation, individualization, or gender, or class of more limited interest.

A key question is: when does local specificity matter, and where and when can we take up "findings" as if they have a more general significance? Australian high schools and Australian young people are not the same as those in the United States, but, to a very large degree, they do inhabit a common world—a common media culture, common comparative movements in school systems, some common shifts in work and family patterns. Our interviews are with particular individuals in particular contexts, but, for most of the discussion in this book, issues about "dreams of the future" or gendered pathways or the making of the self over time will also strike a chord with those whose context is America or Sweden or the United Kingdom. But in two chapters, where we focus on race and ethnicity and on class, some further comment about national specificity is warranted.

While theories and discussions of race and ethnicity (and postcolonial theory) circulate widely, and have relevance in different national contexts, the substantive form in which power and schooling inequalities are played out differs markedly according to the specificities of national history and patterns of colonization and immigration. The question of what it means to be an "Australian" is currently the subject of much public contest, and the politics of race, ethnicity, and nationalism are tightly bound together. In Australia, the question of national identity has an elusiveness that is quite different from that question in a national culture that has an historical and very explicit declaration of rights, a prominent schooling tradition of civics, and nationalist customs of displaying and honoring the flag. For a reader located in a country with a different history, a different composition, a different set of public discourses, our chapter may initially have a strange feel—why are they discussing the topic in this way? Why are they not focusing on that? However, the question of how power in relation to race and ethnicity is constructed through discourse, identity, and (national) identification is foregrounded by looking at this analysis in the Australian setting where the "taken-for-granteds" are indeed different from those in many other countries. It offers one way for readers to reflect on the cultural construction and historically shaped nature of categories and race/ethnic relations, to explore issues of "whiteness" and "otherness" from other perspectives, and to counter essentialist, universalizing, and stereotyped visions of ethnicity, race, and school inequalities.

The significance of national specificity also comes into play in relation to class. One popular way of thinking about the significance of class is to equate it with socioeconomic advantage and disadvantage, and this is a somewhat familiar terrain for studies of schooling since there is such a strong overall correlation of schooling outcomes related to SES (e.g., see Brantlinger 2003; Lareau 2003; Marks and McMillan 2003; Teese and Polesel 2003). The best-known sociological studies of schooling and class experiences of young people are works stemming from the 1970s and early 1980s such as Bernstein, Willis, and Bourdieu, in the United States, Bowles and Gintis, and Anyon; and in Australia Connell et al.'s *Making the Difference* (1982). We wanted to take a fresh look at what schools are doing on this front because we felt that too many studies had been framed to show reproduction: focusing on convergence of family and school. Our study aims to interrupt some of this convergence by looking at young people from similar class background going to different schools, as well as those from a different class background at the same school. This focus, together with a close-up longitudinal perspective, offers distinctive insight into how particular schools manage and respond to such differences. But this is an area in which the shape of different national school systems also has an effect. Australia, courtesy of government subsidy, has an unusually large proportion of its school population attending private schools. In Victoria, the state in which we conducted our study, approximately 30 percent of the secondary school population attends private schools (Teese 2000). But the strategies and patterns of subject formation that we analyze in the private school (City Academy) are translatable to other countries that have a history of elite schooling, whether it is "private" or a product of residential segregations or family cultural capital and its contribution to selective entry success (Brantlinger 2003; Power et al. 2003).

The more significant question, however, is "what does 'class' actually mean in countries like Australia and the United States, and in this period of history?" The great bulk of the population is not the archetypal male factory worker or owner of the means of production of nineteenth-century Marxism. Similarly, although there is a history of labor unions in countries like Australia and the United States, there is not a class consciousness of the type apparent in many "old world" sociological studies. Most people in both countries see themselves as "middle class" (meaning "not elite" nor on the bottom). Chapter 7 examines some ways of seeing what is happening with class analyses today. It considers the challenge of keeping class visible when talking about gender or ethnicity and of how to avoid essentializing "working class" as a single type of experience. It also examines the problem (both theoretically and empirically) of conceiving of class primarily in terms of the binary middle class versus working class, as if those categories were completely self-evident or unchanged from the 1950s or 1960s.

"Subjectivity" and "Identity"

The "making of self" in the current historical period, whether we define that as late or post- or a second modernity, is identified by a range of theorists (Giddens 1991, McNay 2000, Mansfield 2000; Rose 1999) as being of new and distinctive importance, a process that signifies the emergence of new kinds of identities and social relations. Equally, for researchers writing from the perspective and politics of social movements such as feminism, anti-racisim, and postcolonialism, the construction and development of subjectivity remains a central issue in a different way: What keeps patterns of old inequalities recreating themselves in new contexts? What kind of a thing *is* subjectivity and how is it formed? How does it develop? How might it change?

While subjectivity and identity are terms that are often used interchangeably, we aim to distinguish between the two in order to register different kinds of arguments and analyses.[1] Throughout this book, we use identity to describe how young people see themselves—their more self-conscious identifications and self-identity, as a particular kind of person. This could include how they view themselves in terms of personality (optimistic, solitary) or kind of student (motivated, indifferent, successful, struggling) or how they see themselves in relation to standard sociological categories (e.g., from the middle class). Whether (and how) people self-consciously see their gender as an important part of their identity and the identity of others is of interest here. But, as we will discuss, this is neither a simple or unitary issue (in a single interview, participants may well deny that gender is important in one part of the interview and talk about it as important in another part), nor the only way one can interpret their gendered subjectivity, as themes can emerge over the course of the interviews of which they are not conscious or are not immediately apparent to them.

The primary terms with which young people represent (or do not represent) their identities is significant to our account. But our use of the term "subjectivity" signals that those identities are not simple, given, presumed essences that naturally unfold, but rather are produced in an ongoing process, mediated by multiple historical and contemporary factors, including social, schooling, and psychodynamic relations. Mansfield (2000, 11) argues that across diverse theories of subjectivity, from philosophically and socio-politically-based views to linguistic and psychoanalytic uses, there is a consensus among theorists that "subjectivity is constructed, made within the world, not born into it already formed." The term "subjectivity" alerts us not so much to the idiosyncrasies of the individual (though this is, of course, relevant), as to how "subjects" are formed—the range of influences, practices, experiences, and relations that combine to produce a young person and young people. In this way, subjectivity refers to both general and particular processes and patterns in the making of modern lives. As a theoretical term, subjectivity has a complex and multifaceted history, and one aim of our discussion is to elucidate and work with some currently influential theories of subjectivity and think through how they illuminate our empirical study of young people. This is discussed directly in chapter 4 and underpins our discussions throughout. We also occasionally use the term "biography" when we want to capture the temporal dimension of subjectivity, to underline that subjects are not only constituted in the "here and now" but that this process is an accumulating and recursive one. Individuals carry histories within them, and the accumulating effects over time of young people's relationship to particular types of schooling is a major focus of this book.

This then is an investigation of subjectivity set against two types of temporality: the temporality of historical specificity (contemporary times), and the temporality of the adolescent or high school years (biographical life stage). By asking broad questions about "self, school, and future," we are interested in both the self-conscious and the non self-conscious ways in which young people today understand themselves and their times, and whether forms of a new neoliberal, "individualized," and "reflexive" subject override formations of the subject through more traditional themes of gender or class difference.

Researching Subjectivity in Longitudinal Perspective

There has been a proliferation of qualitative research on identity formation, from poststructuralist concern with the discursive practices of identity construction, through to life history and memory work (Cosslett, Lury, and Summerfield 2000; Haug 1987). Interviews (Kvale 1996), and psychodynamic processes and meaning construction within interviews (Hollway and Jefferson 2000; Walkerdine, Lucey, and Melody 2001), narrative and critical discourse analysis (Freebody 2003, Kamler 2001), and the exploration of "critical incidents" or "fateful moments" in individual lives are equally popular research approaches (Plumridge and Thomson 2003; Thomson et al. 2002; Tripp 1993). Much of such work tends to draw upon intensive interviews, often only one or perhaps a few, and they are often conducted within a close time frame (but see Thomson et al. 2002 for a focus on critical incidents within a longitudinal qualitative study). Elements of this range of work influenced our design and analysis of the interviews, such as asking participants to recall a particularly happy time or a period at school when they felt miserable, or paying attention to the descriptions, repetitions, or metaphoric ways in which they described themselves. But the longitudinal aspect also allowed for other kinds of questioning and approaches. We were as much interested in what participants said (and how they said it) in any one interview as we were in comparing what they said over time. But our interest in a certain passage or interview was read from an overall experience where we *could* look forward and backward, both in terms of what was being said by the person we were talking to and what we had thought about their responses at particular times. In comparing interviews over time, our aim was not to point out disjunctions or contradictions, to see when they were telling the truth, when they were fabricating stories. Rather, we wanted the interviews to work in a way that allowed us to observe how attitudes, dispositions, sense of self and future were taking shape incrementally; and to see how the narratives they chose to tell us did or did not change. Attention to distinct critical incidents, for example, or to the close analysis of a key passage in an interview can reveal complexity and nuance, but we wanted also to read such incidents in the context of others, and to compare the relative, enduring, and fleeting, significance (for them for and us) of events, memories, aspirations, and self-descriptions over the adolescent years.

One influential strand of sociological research on young people's identities, or new types of youth biographies, often constructs individual or composite case studies and typologies to illustrate an overall social trend or aspect of generational change (du Bois-Reymond 1998; Dwyer, Tyler, and Wyn 2001; Dwyer and Wyn 2001; Evans 2002). Often influenced by theories of risk and reflexive modernization (particularly the work of Beck and Giddens), the main features of contemporary youth identities are classified as "normal," "choice," and in some studies "risk." The normal biography refers to young people who pursue a relatively traditional pattern of transition through school and work and anticipate conventional gender roles, while choice biography describes a detraditionalized pathway that is evidence of and emphasizes choice and flexibility in their imagined futures (Collins, Kenway, and McLeod 2000; Dwyer, Harwood, and Tyler 1998). Furlong and Cartmel (1997, 10) also argue that "young people increasingly perceive themselves as living in a society characterized by risk and insecurity which they expect to have to negotiate on an individual level."

Again, elements of these ways of researching youth identities have influenced our interpretations: we can point to examples of how the "normal biography" persists, as well as trajectories that are consistent with the choice biography model. In chapter 8, for example, we explore traditional or "normal" forms of masculinity existing alongside retraditionalized, "choice," and individualistic forms. Such categorizations are useful for conveying a sense of the broad patterns of difference in young people's identity and future-making. However, in such typological thinking there are dangers of reifying biographies as categories, and of concentrating attention on the extent to which young people's lives conform to the available categories of identity. There is also, as Andy Furlong has argued

(2003), a danger in overstating the extent to which "choice biographies" and "nonlinear pathways" are the predominant form of young people's transitions today, and conversely understating the extent of such pathways among previous generations. In other words, a stark generational binary is established, which can simplify and homogenize the character of contemporary social times. Our own focus is not only on whether young people's pathways have changed, but on how young people arrive at their decisions, and the kind of "identity work" that entails. It is not only the choices and endpoints they make from ages 12 to 18, but the antecedents and self-narratives over time within those decisions and patterns.

Narrating the Self

"Self narration" writes Carolyn Steedman, "has come to be emphasized again and again as formative, constitutive of the subject of modernity" (2000, 26–27; see also Chappell et al. 2003). By self-narration, Steedman refers to "interpretive self-history *and* the formal written autobiography" (2000, 27). Both of these suggest the preeminence of "autobiographical thinking" in the sense outlined by Giddens, who argues that "an interpretive self-history produced by the individual concerned [autobiography] whether written down or not . . . is actually the core of self-identity in modern life" (Giddens 1991, 52–54, in Steedman 2000, 26). In planning our interviews, we imagined the self as a "remembered thing as well as a narrated thing" (Steedman 2000, 27). We sought to provide opportunities for participants to tell us about themselves over the seven years, to remember themselves when younger, and to imagine themselves in the future. While we invited this ongoing comparison, we deliberately did not begin our questions with a refrain about how they previously described themselves; we wanted to see what their views were at different stages, rather than expose "inconsistencies" or prompt certain memories that we thought were important. We were interested in the repetitions and reiterations of themes, motifs, and ways of thinking because these offered insights to strategies of subjectivity, to the shaping of particular biographies, and to the social context that they inhabit. Biographical themes can illuminate social preoccupations, and in turn we can see the traces of such preoccupations in biographies.

A key focus of the interviews was the participants' present, prospective, and retrospective sense of self and of what kind of person they were. In each interview, participants were asked to describe themselves as well as imagine themselves in the future or recollect themselves when younger. Responses to more general questions about friends, school, or family life offered insight into how they saw and imagined themselves in the world. We employed a range of different approaches to elicit narratives; we also had a fairly standard format and range of questions on self, school, and future, versions of which we asked at each interview. These questions or prompts were then developed and extended according to individual responses. We occasionally used hypothetical questions, "What if . . .?," or asked them to reflect on ethical dilemmas. At age 15 (Year 10), we asked students to make an audiotape recording about themselves for us, giving very few other guidelines. On another occasion, students brought in a photograph that was significant to them and talked about it. In the final year we gave students a compilation video of excerpts from all their interviews and then discussed this with them the following week, after they had had an opportunity to view it.

Some changes can happen over a short period of time, especially during the "teenage years" when things can shift quickly, and a seven- to eight-year period is not essential for grasping this. Interviews conducted over a shorter period, and in quick succession, can capture elements of change and might also offer a more immediate "as-it-is-happening" sense of change and development. However, the time frame we adopted allowed participants to experience some emotional distance from earlier events and recollections, and to have a sense of themself in a long view. The length of secondary school in Australia—six years—also determined the time frame of the study, with interviews concluding in the year immediately after the end of school.

A significant background methodological factor for us was that we were setting out to undertake a major empirical research commitment at the very time when theoretical and methodological debates by feminist and poststructural writers were calling into question the research enterprise itself (Lather 1994; McLeod and Yates 1997; St. Pierre and Pillow 2000). It had been long understood by interpretive and critical researchers (and by working scientists, in contrast to many positivist education researchers who thought they were acting like scientists) that the researchers' constructing activities are a central element in the knowledge they produce. In the case of qualitative research, there was a growing awareness that the embodied persona of the researcher, the way he or she enters the field, the types of words chosen are all in turn interpreted by those to whom they speak, who make their own choices about how they respond. The researcher's interview is not a window to a self-contained and static, transparent reality, but a process that calls things into being, that inscribes as it records (Bourdieu et al. 1999, McLeod 2000a; MacLure 2003, Scheurich 1995). In the fields we worked in, more and more attention was being given to autobiographical reflection and scrutiny by the researchers about their own assumptions, acts, and inscriptions (Behar 1996; Fine 1994; Gitlin 1994; Lather 1991; Stronach and MacLure 1997).

We agreed with, and take seriously, the insights contemporary researchers have raised about the research and theory-building activities of researchers, but we did not want to give up on the idea that an empirical study could do more than just tell stories about us, and find ways of illustrating what we already know (see also Fine and Weis 1998 for a discussion of related dilemmas). In our case, we both came to this project after a substantial time working on gender issues, policies, and theories, rather than from prior qualitative empirical projects. We embarked on this project because we thought that we had reached a point at which a new empirical and longitudinal study could have something to say to the types of questions on which we and other theorists were working. Nevertheless, methodological reflection is a strong part of the account we offer in this book of young people's lives today. Investigating subjectivity—how it is formed, what it "means"—requires, we argue, ongoing reflection on exactly just what it is we are trying to do when we "research" someone else. It also requires sustained attention to the broader and contending theories that we draw on in making sense of what we "find" when we interview other people. Consequently, we integrate such methodological reflections throughout the book, rather than confine discussion of them to a separate chapter.

A specific strength of longitudinal interviews is the accumulation of responses that can be read against each other. A picture can be built up of orientations and beliefs across different times, ages, and moods. Times when they felt good or bad about themselves, were interested in or indifferent to school, were having trouble at home or with friends, feeling on top and in control of things, or when they did or did not feel like saying much to us, and so on. This offers a more substantial and complex basis for writing about identity or subjectivity than does one or two interviews alone (Thomson and Holland 2003b). Issues of contingency and the construction of truth amid the power relations between interviewer and interviewee remain significant in longitudinal interviews—they are not only problems associated with single interviews. But asking prospective and retrospective questions over time about the self means that a body of reflections at different ages from the same participant is accumulated, and responses can be read and compared against each other. Of course, longitudinal interviews, as with any form of research, do not tell us the "full truth" about someone, and again, as with all other forms of qualitative research, they demand attention to local and historical context (Gordon and Lehelma 2003) and to questions of interpretation and meaning. Simply having a large number of interviews, while offering a rich basis for researching the formation of subjectivity, does not do away with such matters. Nevertheless, the range of interviews over time, and our methods for developing a prospective/retrospective focus and the comparative backward/forward readings, allow patterns, themes, and orientations to build up in a way that can counter charges of overreading the "evidence" or overstating the significance of particular responses.

In addition to the audiotapes and typed transcripts of the interviews, we made videotapes of all interviews, and these afforded a palpable and visual immediacy to biographical change. Watching and re-viewing someone tell a narrative about themselves does create a different impression from reading that narrative. Mannerisms, self-consciousness, self-censoring, times when students seemed physically to change so much that we did not initially recognize them, or, conversely, participants expressed durable and recognizable traits and ways of being and physically presenting themselves—all these images helped us to build our interpretations. Reviewing video footage prompts vivid memories, along with an evocation of atmosphere. We are easily reminded of how participants were responding to us, to times when the interview flowed, when it got stuck and the questions did not work, or when their answers were hesitant, excited, formulaic, or heartfelt. It can also take us back to the time of the actual interview, to the room, the weather, to how we responded to the milieu and ethos of the four different schools (reminding us of our schooling experiences), to what we were doing in the rest of our lives as we tried to make time for interviews amid busy schedules, how we were affected by some interviews, frustrated with others. The videos, then, captured not only the embodied responses of participants, but also the embodied responses of the researchers and the physicality of the research encounter and interview, and underlined how such experiences and memories shaped our interpretations and analysis (see also Lahelma 2002).

A Video Strategy

In the year after they had left school, we met with and gave each student a compilation video of excerpts from each of their interviews, from when they were 12 through to when they were 18. We arranged to meet up again about a week later after this interview, and to talk about their impressions of their video and their participation in the project more generally.[2] The video activity was both an act of reciprocity, giving back "memories" and a record of themselves, and a deliberate research strategy to prompt reflection on the self. How do you see yourself now? How do you recall yourself at the start of secondary school, when you were 12? Tell us about how you see yourself in the future; what was it like watching the video of yourself when younger? What kind of picture of you does your video capture? Of course, the videotape itself was only ever going to be a partial and highly selective representation of them. Yet the visual immediacy of seeing and listening to oneself, observing vivid physical change, recalling incidents that they had retold to us, all provoked intense and self-conscious reflection on how they now saw themselves in the present, in the past, and the future. These recursive, comparative reflections were both important strategies of subjectivity and methodologically significant, offering a way into understanding some recurring biographical narratives that also echo wider social themes. These too are discussed in the following chapters.

We did, we see clearly in retrospect, presume and incite a certain mode of reflexivity, via the video strategy as well as in the series of regular interviews, and this too was a distinctive and effective research approach to researching subjectivity. We have tried to make methodological reflexivity (Pillow 2003) an integral part of our account, but here we are referring to reflexivity as an ontological characteristic. Reflecting on their experiences of conducting a longitudinal, qualitative study, Thomson and Holland (2003b, 242) suggest that "the extension of this relationship [between researcher and researched] over time demands (even produces) a high level of reflexivity on the part of both the researchers and the researched, drawing analytical attention to the effects of the research intervention on both." This was evident too in our own study, and perhaps heightened by our attention to retrospective questions about the self. It could further be argued that our attention, or indeed sensitivity, to reflexivity is symptomatic of living in late modernity (Beck, Giddens, and Lash 1994) and, we would add, a characteristic of our [the researchers'] gender, class location, intellectual formations and dispositions, and the kind of work we do. We are accustomed to talking in this way, of being oriented to the self as a biographical project and casually expecting others to be equally interested in this mode of reflection. But, as we discovered, and discuss in later chapters, it was a style of questioning that suited some students more than others. We noted earlier the highly honed reflexivity of middle-class girls, and their ease with reflecting on themselves, but for many of the boys, particularly the working-class boys and boys from non-Anglo-Australian backgrounds, this style of questioning sometimes made them uncomfortable and was not always effective in eliciting the kind of narrative responses we hoped for—and we return to this issue in later chapters.

In this chapter, we have discussed some of the theoretical interests and ongoing methodological reflections we have tried to keep alive as we repeatedly visited the four schools in our study and engaged in regular conversations with participants about how they saw themselves, their futures, and the school, and other experiences they were undergoing. In the next chapter we explore these issues from the perspective of some everyday concerns expressed by parents, teachers, students, school teachers, and politicians: "What is a good student?" We explore how answers to this question vary according to school and type of student. The issues raised in the chapter about these differences are especially pertinent today, when so much emotional, economic, and political energy is directed to matters of "choice" and "success." Parents face the pressure of making the right school choices for their children, students experience the pressure to succeed, particularly at end-of-school examinations, and there is increasing consciousness on the part of schools to present and market themselves as certain kinds of institution, able to produce "successful students" who embody identifiable and marketable attributes. The following chapter tells some recognizable stories about "the good student" but also engages with the different theories—about gender, subjectivity, reproduction, and social change—that we have touched on in this chapter.

CHAPTER 3

What Is a Good Student?

When we first interviewed 12 year old Nassar at the beginning of high school, he told us he hoped to become a scientist when he grew up and left school— "get some degrees and be a professor or somebody." At lunch he often went off by himself in the playground with his scientific calculator and tried to memorize facts, such as the distance between planets. He had migrated to Australia from Sri Lanka two years ago and, in the early years of his school there, had been one of the best students. But "when I came here into primary school I think I became very unintelligent, because I thought primary school was very easy, but the only problem I had was, I didn't know English. English was what, you know, causes me a lot of trouble since I came here." He is an only child and spends a lot of time at home doing homework. He is worried about how to organize his homework and how to keep his mind on his studies; his mother arranged for a tutor to help him with his mathematics.

Over the next few years, Nassar tells us that he thinks about girls quite a bit, but worries that this is dangerous because it distracts him from his studies. On his recounting, he seems to be struggling with his schoolwork and having difficulty achieving the grades that he would like. His mother really wants him to be a doctor, but he does not like the idea of "cutting people." However, by the middle of secondary school, he has decided to please her and aim for medicine, even though his own preference would be to be a scientist. He says with pride that he works hard, but not as hard as his friend in Sri Lanka, who is a similar age and at school from 7:30 in the morning until 8:00 at night. Nassar continues to be puzzled about the expectations and requirements of school work in Australia:

> Um, I do a lot of work, but it just . . . um . . . I don't know. Sometimes I don't like, when I get my results down. I also got a B in my physics project. I worked hours and hours on that and um, it was about 12 pages and the teacher cut two points off because he was saying it was too long. I read about four books straight and everything, on nuclear energy, and the end result was disappointing.
>
> (Nassar, Suburban High, Year 10)

He complains too because he put a photograph of an atomic bomb on the cover of his nuclear energy project and was told by the teacher that this was not appropriate.

At school he is teased and has few friends (his best friend moved to another state). "I tried to hang around with them [other kids in his year] and it didn't work much, and, no matter how much I tried." At aged 15, Nassar reflects on how the other kids

> used to give me a lot of pressure and I found out the best thing I can do is to be quiet and stay as though I'm not even in the class, and not talk much. And that's another thing I found, that was good for me, but um, because most of them were picking on me. I mean another thing was in Year 9, I never leave my pencil case on my desk. Always, no matter where I go, I take it with me. Because when I come back it's not going to be there. I know. And so what I try to do is, you know, is to try to avoid all that.
>
> (Nassar, Suburban High, Year 10)

Later in that interview, when we ask about teenage suicide (a topic that had been in the news), Nassar says that it is due to the fact that they "can't cope with the pressure" and adds, "When it comes to peers, all I think about is forget about them, they are only a distraction." He believes that school is not racist, but that there are many different subcultures and cliques and this makes it difficult for those who do not fit in.

> They don't really care how, what kind of a color, what kind of a size head a person has, or anything else. Everybody sort of, in many cases, respects each other. But some people have trouble, it's more like getting into peer pressure or something like. You know, peer pressure to try to blend in with these people, and it's more like the Suburban High School society, so you have to try and blend in with that.
>
> (Nassar, Suburban High, Year 10)

Nassar continues to struggle to understand his ostracism, his not "fitting in." In a school that has an explicit agenda of inclusiveness and whose student body does value diversity and does speak out about racism (we discuss this in a later chapter), Nassar has found out that not all ways of being are equally acceptable.

> I think it's sort of, oh, the teasing makes people go really down. Because I know about teasing, I've been teased a lot. Um, not as a gay person, but ah, I'm not gay, um . . . but well at first many people thought I was different. Well I knew I was different. I come from a different culture, I have a different background. Until I was mature, I grew up completely in a different society and everything.
>
> (Nassar, Suburban High, Year 10)

Issues of sexuality surface in several of his later interviews, often in terms of repudiating being gay as the reason why he is bullied or ostracized. He tells us of his attraction to women and of his close relationships with a few men, but he does not elaborate. He represents his difficulties in making friends and being bullied as a result of his coming from "a different culture."

Nassar's own views on cultural difference in relation to Australia pivot on understandings of modernity and "fitting in." He is critical of the whipping up of racial emnities, but he also thinks modernity and technological advance are important, and that Australian Aboriginal people would not have been better served by a noncolonial history:

> Because I mean, let's say Australia, if Captain Cook and all these people never found it or cared about Australia and it was just here, it would just be primitive [. . .] it wouldn't be as civilized. I mean not as, no, a good word to say is, it wouldn't be modern, it wouldn't be technological, it would be just nothing. It wouldn't fit in.
>
> (Nassar, Suburban High, Year 10)

Nassar believes that Aboriginal people have benefited from colonization as it has rescued them from backward practices: "Australia does need a history, so they [Aboriginal people] shouldn't let go of their culture, but they should try to improve and fit into the modern world." (Questions of national identification and "otherness" are discussed in detail in chapter 6.)

Gradually as the project proceeds, Nassar, experiences trouble on all fronts—school, where he is struggling; home, where his parents have separated; and in his personal life, where he has psychological problems and many absences from school. The school directs him to counselors and other types of assistance, both in and out of school, and, after his absences from school, finds bridging courses for him. However, by the end of the project, when most of the students have completed school and are in their first year of university or work, Nassar is struggling to return to school and amass enough subject credits to continue on to a technical college, where he may complete a diploma or certificate course in computer studies.

Nassar's story illustrates a range of issues about young lives and schooling that we pursue throughout the book: issues about national culture and changes; about gender and ethnicity; about what is valued in and what is produced by different school settings. In this chapter we examine such issues through a consideration of "What is a good student?" Being a "good student" refers to both broad social definitions, often implicit, and to individuals who embody such characteristics; to judgements made by others and to judgements made by self in that broader as well as interpersonal context.

A "good student" is constructed discursively and socially and takes differing forms in different schools. Being (or failing to be) a good student is also something that is lived and managed psychically by young people as they go through school. Qualities of a good student are both explicitly and self-consciously designated by schools, teachers, parents, and young people themselves (not identically), and also, as many sociological theorists have argued, deeply inexplicit. In this latter sense, it refers to qualities, or orientations, or dispositions or knowledge that are obscure, or tacit, as Nassar's experiences suggest. The requirements may be puzzling to groups who fail to measure up, or may be ones they are not able to adopt or do not wish to adopt (Anyon 1983; Bernstein 1977, 1996; Bettie 2003; Bourdieu and Passeron 1977; Reay 1995a; Teese 2000; Walkerdine, Lucey, and Melody 2001; Willis 1977). In part, the power of schooling as a social institution, its ideological or discursive functioning, is still that it can produce certain effects of advantaging while seeming to make this appear to be an outcome of individual efforts.

Good students are judged in the here and now—how they behave, what they look like, and what they do as they go through school—and also by results and outcomes. A "good student" (what it means to be a good student as well as the identification of individuals who can be designated that way) is also produced by schooling and by one's particular school (which are not identical). A good student may be one who most successfully embodies the disciplining of the self that is said to be one key theme of contemporary times; or one who most produces the appropriate forms of cultural display (distinction, apparent superiority) that generate hierarchical opportunity in "open" societies; or may be one who is most adept at the "new literacies" that mark contemporary work and, increasingly, education. Indeed, one of the themes of this chapter is that the interplay of these issues strongly marks the lives of young people today. On the one hand, schools are highly marked by the competitiveness of schooling in the Bourdieuean sense, in which the relativities of success between schools and individuals are highly visible, while the sources of such outcomes are not equally transparent (Ball 2003; Teese 2000; Teese and Polesel 2003). On the other hand, schools are also visibly located within and responsive to social and discursive changes in work and culture that are remaking and redefining which qualities count as the embodied characteristics of a "good student." This has led to the new debates about girls' advantage and boys' disadvantage (the arguments that pedagogy and curriculum now favor feminine dispositions and learning style), as well as some sense of a school curriculum in flux regarding what matters—is it the traditional intellectual basics or is it the ability to be a lifelong learner? Is it the ability to be a nerd, or is it the ability to be a flexible portfolio person who can remake him or herself constantly? (Arnot, David, and Weiner 1999; Dwyer, Tyler, and Wyn 2001; Gee 1999; MacDonald 1999).

A central argument of this chapter is that the interplay of themes about distinction and hierarchy and themes about new work and cultural literacies characterizes the normative vision of the good student today; this interplay is encountered and realized unevenly across our four different schools. In this chapter, and throughout the book, we try to show more than one way of entering and reading the lives being constructed through school. To grapple with what it means to be a good student, we need to attend to the broad cultural discourse and social change that frames these lives, as well as to the more specific discursive milieux of school and family that is brought to this engagement. We try here, as elsewhere, to show both the social and institutional patterning of context and process and the making of lives within these patterns.

Schooling as a System of Competitive Selection *and* a Mode of Disciplining the Population

The Australian schooling system is not the same as the French system, and neither of these are identical to the organization of education in the United States, but, in a broad sense, one dimension of the world young people enter in school is common to all three. They enter a system that is competitively structured, one in which final outcomes, particularly entry to prestigious universities and courses, cannot be achieved by everyone: the system is set up to be selective. Indeed, as the form of work changes, and as certification escalates, students and their parents face heightened awareness of the competitive arena, an inflated sense of schooling's significance in mediating life chances (Ball 2003; Brantlinger 2003; Power et al. 2003; Teese 2000). Competition exists between schools and between young people in school.

In the sense that R.W. Connell (1995) described "hegemonic masculinity" as the approved and powerful form of being masculine against which being gay or short or not good at sports or female was judged inadequate, we can characterize a broad hegemonic "good student" that a culture widely recognizes. This is a student who is good at doing what examinations require; who applies him or herself to the necessary study to succeed; and who does in fact succeed. But, as a plethora of studies of class, race, ethnicity, and gender have shown, being this good student is not equally available to young people. One interest here, then, is how the four different schools in our study perform and produce the "good student" and a second is how particular students manage their own performance of this, given both the broad social system and the particularity of their local context.

The story of Nassar is one, relatively familiar, example of a student who has trouble penetrating the codes of how to be the kind of student his school values. He does not know how to navigate the peer culture or how to work out the pedagogical expectations of the teachers and the social practices of the school. Nassar brings to high school his own conception of being a good student, one that has strong emotional elements drawn from his family and his experiences of moving from one culture to another. He desperately wants to be recognized as a good student by the school and his peers. But neither his attempts to work hard at school nor his comportment, his way of being at the school, give him this designation by others. He responds with anxiety, physical and mental health problems, and by falling behind in his studies. Compare Nassar's struggles to be a good student with another young person in our study, Alannah, who is able to manage a potentially difficult situation in which the requirements of being a good student pose competing demands.

In Years 8 and 9, Alannah is falling behind in mathematics—and this is well recognized as cause for concern because being good at mathematics is part of the broad cultural hegemony of the good student. She explains that her difficulties are in part due to having had a poor teacher for two consecutive years, a teacher whom she says is not providing the help she needs. We had heard similar stories about this particular teacher from several students. Being a "good student" at this particular school, City Academy, the elite private school in our study, also means being actively involved in school associations, extra-curricular activities, and sporting teams, and this implies having good and genial relations with teachers. Alannah holds a leadership role within the school, one in which she needs to keep working with the same teacher who is not helping her in mathematics. In this case, she makes a decision not to seek a different teacher, not to push her needs in her academic work, because she clearly recognizes the consequences of doing so.

And what are the weak things of the school? The not-so-good things about the school?

Alannah: Um, just a few little things, like at the moment I, um, my maths teacher . . . This is my third year with the same maths teacher and I know he really, you know likes me, and I respect him and everything, but it's too long to have the same teacher. Even if the teacher was a really good teacher, which he is not, but even if he was, it would be too long.

Alannah: It's [the maths teacher] is actually our [homeroom teacher] and I've had him for three years for maths and I can't handle the way he teaches, but I just have to sit there. I can't do anything about it.

[later in the interview]

So is there anything else you want to say about that?

Alannah: Oh, only that . . . oh, I'm sure if I just . . . I'll try and work hard no matter how this guy's going to teach me and I'll just . . . you know because I want to do maths next year and everything.

Have you talked to your parents about this problem?

Alannah: Yeah, that . . . like mum really wants to go to the Head of Maths and say, 'Look this is ridiculous. Can my daughter change classes?' But

> the fact that it is . . . because he's middle school, he's the middle school, like principal, and I work very close with him being middle school leader, and he's the type of guy that gets very offended, very sensitive, and you know, he's a real great person, but you know that would just like destroy everything, so . . . if I get a tutor and everything.

So you're the one who is stopping your parents from going ahead with that and you would rather get a tutor?
Alannah: Yeah.

(Alannah, City Academy, Year 9, age 15)

Alannah's decision not to complain about her math teacher, for fear of alienating him and hurting his feelings, can be interpreted as a characteristically feminine response to be concerned for others and to place that sensitivity to their emotional needs ahead of one's own needs and ambitions. As we'll discuss, there are gendered variations in being a "good student" and girls remain expected, by themselves and by others, to manage social and interpersonal relations, to smooth over any such difficulties. But Alannah's moves are also a skilled social performance, and managing social situations with confidence and ease is an important element in the repertoire of the good student at City Academy. Alannah's decision to not upset the status quo and protect her teacher is especially striking because at City Academy students and their families are paying customers and have considerable purchasing power to influence staffing, as her mother recognizes.

A further theme we might note here is Alanna's self-disciplining and strategic thinking through of the consequences of her actions. She does not want to jeopardize her positioning in the school as a "good student," and with a strong self-consciousness of that, she monitors her conduct accordingly. In comparison to Nassar, she has been able to work out the implicit codes and expectations of the school and devise a solution to the immediate problem that does not challenge those codes or threaten her status. Alannah and Nassar inhabit a general culture of schooling that emphasizes certain achievements, such as good grades and doing well in mathematics, as important, and also a particular school culture that operates in distinctive ways to produce its own version of the good student—and students need to work out the codes of both. In seeking help with math outside school, Alannah addresses the demand for success and achievement in the conventional sense of results and also averts a difficult interpersonal issue. Her way of managing and thinking about what is valuable, of combining a range of demands and interests continues into her post-school life, setting up orientations to a "portfolio" working life, an orientation that we discuss in later chapters. Although she passes her final school examinations, she does not do as well as many of her school peers, nor well enough to enter a prestigious university course. But she responds to this temporary setback by devising an alternative strategy that combines a part-time university degree, another part-time qualification at a local technical college in business studies, and continuing with part-time work.

So, what is a good student today? How do different schools convey and produce the good and less good student? How do individual young people construct their lives in these contexts? We begin by looking at what young people, at age 12, from quite different backgrounds and schools, and in their first high school year, said about what their school most values.

Managing Appearance

Near the beginning of our study, we asked all our participants and the friends they brought to the first high school interview the question: "What do you think this school thinks is important?" Over and over, at the four different schools, the issue mentioned most was appearance and, more specifically, appearance to the community outside the school. These students talked animatedly about the enormous attention given to policing the correct wearing of uniforms, emphasizing the amount of time schools spend talking about the school's reputation. The clear message they were receiving was that the school would be judged by their [the students'] behavior in public: by the way they acted on public transport, by whether they were seen smoking or drinking.

A good student, they heard, behaves well by exercising self-control and self-discipline. This is hardly a novel observation. What was surprising was the extent to which the students themselves saw this management of external appearance as the one message that schools repeatedly foregrounded: not "learning," not "being a moral person," not "being a good citizen," not even "ambition" or "success" or "hard work," but rather the performance of being a well-behaved advertisement for the school:

What do you think the school thinks is important?

Lee-anne: Um, I don't know. Probably our appearance and what the public thinks. They're always saying you've got to make a good impression on the public and that.

Kimberley: And a lot of people call in and complain about things, about the school, yeah. And I was surprised because I thought the school was pretty good and had a pretty good reputation.

Julia: They expect a lot from us, because they're saying the school has a good reputation.

(Regional High, Year 7)

Nicky: I think being proper and having a uniform and everyone going home in blazers, and team spirit.

(City Academy, Year 7)

Phillip: Your appearance. We have to be good every time someone comes and looks at us.

(Suburban High, Year 7)

Jenna: The school's more strict about the uniform than anything else.

(Suburban High, Year 7)

David: Setting a good example after school if you are wearing your school uniform.

Trevor: Yeah. And he doesn't like students smoking out of the school grounds in their uniform.

Jack: In their uniform, putting the school down.

(Regional High, Year 7)

These comments reveal students' perceptions of the first and major lesson their high schools conveyed in inducting them: the need to be self-conscious and vigilant about how you appear to the public. In the first year of elementary school, schools spend much time teaching children what kind of behavior is appropriate; how to perform being a student in terms of speaking to the teacher, following commands, dressing, "sitting straight," or having appropriate facial expressions (Kamler et al. 1994). But this second induction is different. Its emphasis is not on who you are in the classroom, but on who you are, or appear to be, in the street and in the community. Students are encouraged to see themselves not as free-floating individuals but as students "badged" in a particular way, and perceived through that badge.

The foremost lesson they learnt is the preeminence of performance and appearance in the public domain. A good student is not simply someone whom teachers can easily manage because they know the rules of right conduct in the classroom. Rather, a good student is someone who works for the school as well as for themselves.

These shared understandings of what schools value and of what counts as being a good student echo some prominent themes in contemporary discussions about the "marketization of schools," a development in which schools are repositioned within a market model of choice between consumer goods rather than as institutions of public service. This is accompanied by a policy focus on performativity and outcomes and the ranking of school performance within various kinds of league tables (Ball 2000; Gewirtz, Ball, and Bowe 1995). Our four schools each had a distinct public profile, ones that could be deployed for marketing ends—some with more obvious market cachet than others—and to "niche" the school in a "choice" economy. Our interest, though, is not primarily in how schools are changed within the new emphasis on marketization and performativity. Instead our focus is on how such imperatives and school-based articulations of the "good student" become part of the self-formation and identifications of the students. The premium placed on public appearances produces a heightened consciousness about how one's conduct is interpreted through the eyes of others (and, possibly, particular social values with consequences for citizenship: heightened attention to appearing to do the right thing as compared with being a good person).

Across four very different schools, we noted that young people entering year 7 heard some shared message about correct conduct and appearance as the mark of the good student. But this does not mean that it was in fact a common message, either in its conditions of delivery or in how it was received or in its likelihood of potential accomplishment. Being a good student publicly is not simply a matter of an individual's making a decision to act in a particular way at a particular time. While the school exhorts them to act in certain ways, students' orientations to this and the ease with which they adopt particular modes of conduct also draw on their family history and the culture of their peers. Moreover, how their appearance and ways of acting are read and rated by the community is, in many respects, overdetermined, and taps into circulating histories about different schools and hierarchies and discourses of distinction, and is thus always more than an "individual" performance.

City Academy has a particularly self-conscious vision of the archetypal good student. Many of the students had fathers and grandfathers who were former students, and were part of the "old boy" network that embraced and sustained the academy's cultural and social power. Within the wider community too, this school's history and reputation combined to badge it as one that routinely produced a "good student" in the hegemonic sense of success in examinations and high-status pathways. In comparison with other schools also read in this way, as elite institutions that reliably produce success, the school also has a more particular niche and is seen as shaping an identifiable City Academy student who embodies particular sensibilities. The school's own self-publicity and our interviews with students (some of whom liked the school, and some of whom did not) all concurred that this school placed much weight on students developing extracurricular interests, pursuing accomplishments in the arts and sports, and fostering school and "team spirit." Its reputation is based to a large extent on its capacity to produce students who conform to hegemonic views of success while also celebrating the development of students as distinctive "individuals" who were accomplished across a range of interests. Community reputation, school expectations, and the weight of generational continuities provided a strong impetus for students to continue policing and performing the "academy" identity.

In response to our general question, "So do you think that this is a good school?," a group of 13 year old girls in Year 8 spoke effusively about all the opportunities the academy provided, particularly the extracurricular activities such as skiing and the debating club. One then elaborated:

> *Diana:* Also, you have to like live up to the expectation of City Academy. Like you have to be careful what you say. You just can't say whatever you want. Like you have to say the right thing to be cool and all that stuff and like even if you want to, if someone offers you to do, one of these opportunities and it's just, you really want to do it, but you sort of don't, because people will think, oh my God, what a dickhead sort of thing.
>
> (Diana, City Academy, Year 8, age 14)

In the regional city, the two schools in our study had long histories of being talked about publicly in ways that emphasized their function of binary "otherness" to each other. Regional High was one of the oldest high schools in the state, priding itself on its traditions. It had extensive buildings, including a wood-paneled assembly hall; a reputation for being academic; and with strong traditions in music and sport. Regional Tech was located in a poorer area of the city, formed from an amalgamation of three technical schools, and had a history of being contrasted unfavorably by teachers as well as parents and the community with Regional High. Parents sent their children to Regional High because it was associated with having "good standards." Many were small businesspeople. Children at Regional Tech more often had parents who were out of work, or in semiskilled, casual or short-term jobs, and who had had unhappy school experiences themselves. They hoped their children would have some opportunities and learn useful skills from the school.

In our Year 7 interviews at Regional High, the issue of reputation was central in how students thought about their school. It was virtually an obsession. Students talked about appearance and reputation not just when we asked specifically about what the school values. They also raised the issue of reputation at length, over and over, in relation to many different topics in our interviews. Regional High students spoke extensively about how their school measured up to the private schools; how it was "like" and "as good as" a private school. Every group of students we interviewed at that school answered a general question about how the school compared to other schools by mentioning that their school had a boat shed and took part in a rowing competition with private schools.

How do you think this school compares with other secondary schools?

Kimberley: It compares pretty well, like we raced in the boat race.

Julia: I raced in a boat race this year, I was a cox. Well, we came second in our finals, and I think we did pretty well to be up there with them, like it was . . .

Lee-anne: . . . all other colleges and stuff, because like . . . .

Kimberley: Grammar.

Julia: Yeah, we raced against all private schools.

Kimberley: Yeah, and all the kids from other schools have opinions about the other kids from other schools. Like we'd call kids who go to like the expensive schools, like Grammar and Cubbin Private. And we'd call them posh, and they'd call us Westies. Even though we're not, they'd just call us like Free or something. Yeah, just because like, they think that if we go to . . . because there were these kids and they were teasing me, they were saying that our parents didn't have enough money to send me to a private school. Like, I think Regional High is just as good as they are.

Julia: I think Regional High is better. Because our boat sheds are really good. Some of them college boat sheds aren't too good. And they'd say to us . . . .
Kimberley: Yeah, the boat shed is really cool.
Julia: Yeah, it's got two storeys in it.
Kimberley: It has a really nice window and everything.
(Regional High girls, Year 7)

But to be accepted as a pseudo-private school places a school like this under considerable pressure, requiring constant vigilance and hard work on the part of the students, parents, and school personnel. Maintaining this school's reputation involves much more work and effort than it does at the elite private school in our study, where there are generations of parents, and a ready community belief, who affirm with little further effort the same story—that theirs is a "good" school.

Regional High, then, performs much repetitive work to convey the message that the good student looks like a private school student, and it spends a lot of its funds to the same ends. At the time of this study, more money was being spent on the salary of the rowing master of the school than on their literacy specialist. These artifacts of appearance do have effects on the "educational" processes of the school, including its student composition, and the expectations and behavior of students and parents. Because the school was seen as a desirable and successful state school, there was hot competition from upwardly aspiring parents to get into this school as compared with the other one in our study, and so its demographic composition was skewed toward those with resources to deliberately influence where they lived. And students and parents entered the school, initially at least, with expectations that homework would be done and good things achieved by being at this school. As a result of the policing of externals of appearance, both students and community saw this school as having good discipline compared with Regional Tech, though our interviews suggested there was as much bullying here as at Regional Tech, and more complaints of unfairnesses by teachers. That is, both the students' own understandings of themselves and the ways these students are perceived by other people are framed by what their school has done, and by managing (and history of managing) its performance as a "good school."

In interviews with students from this school, we hear an intense desire by the students to be judged and regarded as if they were private school students. In order to achieve this identification, they need to discursively position themselves and their school as not like other state schools, and align themselves with the values, conduct, and "spirit" of the private schools. Many students were quite virulent in their dismissive regard of Regional Tech, and of other government schools, as if projecting on to that school the most extremely negative qualities attributed to government schools and thereby symbolically expelling such qualities from their own school. Regional Tech, "Tip Tech," they say, is "a dirty school, where there are lots of fights," and terrible teachers.[1] In the following interview extract, even a government school that achieves good results in Year 12 examinations is diminished on grounds that achievement alone is not as significant as "reputation" or as having the right kind of grounds and buildings, such as the iconic boat shed.

How do you think this school compares with other secondary schools?

Lee-anne: Um, oh well the rest, like schools like Cubbin Private, like they're more strict . . . .

Kimberley: So are we.

Lee-anne: Oh, some of them, like from schools like Central [government school], they're all a bit, you know, they swear and they're smoking, but people from Cubbin Private, you don't see them smoke as much as what you do from schools like Central and that.

How do you think school compares to the nonprivate schools?

Lee-anne: Oh, I think they're all pretty much the same.

Julia: I think our school's got a better reputation, because like Plains High . . . .

Kimberley: They might have a higher VCE pass rate.

Julia: Yeah, they have a higher VCE, but they don't have like a too good a reputation. Because all fights and stuff break out over there, and it's a dirty school. That's what a lot of people say and that. So I think we have a better reputation than a lot of other schools.

Kimberley: I think probably some of the best high schools in Cubbin are probably Grammar and Regional High, and Cubbin Private and all this. But I wouldn't want to go to Central or Plains High because they haven't got very good grounds and buildings. Some of them, oh, they have a few, but, and stuff. Oh, there's just a rumor that they haven't got very good teachers, and all of them smoke and dare other people to smoke, so they start smoking.

Julia: Yeah, it's just a dirty sort of school.

(Regional High girls, Year 7)

So at this school the good students bring to the school and learn to intensify a self-conscious marking and monitoring of status, a self-assessment in which one's physical setting and attributes are important, and in which association and behavior are modeled on the perceptions of private schools and their networks (disciplined, clean), and on marking one's difference from other students attending other state schools (unruly, dirty, lacking status).

The fact that the comparisons are not simply based on an empirical inductive measuring of the actual behaviors and conditions of different schools is seen in our broader interview evidence from the two regional schools about actual incidence of bullying, which does not seem to differentiate Regional Tech as worse than Regional High, and seen too in the flow of the girls' narratives and interactions. Their desire to be judged as good means that conventional criteria are quickly discarded if they do not achieve the right effect. This is evident in the deemphasizing of the higher school certificate (VCE) pass rates in favor of the valuing of reputation, for example; or changing emphasis as inconvenient counterevidence enters the discussion, as in Kimberley's final comment when she shifts her case from the status of grounds and buildings as the criteria, to rumors about quality of the teachers and claims about smoking. In an earlier excerpt, we saw Julia quickly counter a comment Kimberly reports about Regional High not being affluent with an account of its boat sheds being superior to those of one private school—this is offered as compelling evidence, and at this school, and in this regional city, such evidence does matter. In these narratives of "the good school" we hear reflected this school's emphasis on such relativities, as well as its desire to be "as good as" private schools, and the intense and repetitive discursive and emotional labor, and capital works, that are directed toward this and to distinguishing itself from other government schools.

Gendered Constructions of Being "Good"

Discursive constructions of who are good students (in terms of categories of people) work back from evidence and rumors about outcomes as well as from perceptions of students' behavior while they are at school. For most of the twentieth century, conventional wisdom was that girls were well behaved but also rule-following and not the best students (Walkerdine 1988). When computers entered schooling, a host of articles appeared on the theme "why can't girls be more like boys?" in their interests and uses of these. But the changing statistics on girls' overall successful school retention relative to boys (Collins, Kenway, and McLeod 2000), along with the prominent debates during the last decade about masculinity, dropouts, and crime, have produced new conventional wisdom that constructs boys and male behavior in schools as a problem (Lesko 2000; Yates 1997). One facet of this debate has been to question what schools demand from students, to criticize schools as feminized institutions both in their dominance by female teachers, and in the taking up of feminist reforms in curriculum and pedagogy (Lingard and Douglas 1999). So, at the time of our study, there was a new critical attention both to what schools were doing (how were they constructing or measuring the good student) and to how boys feel about schools (do they see themselves as inferior, as not measuring up in terms of school expectations).

We discuss the issue of gendered lives in school at various points in this book. Alannah's abilities in managing conflicting and changing demands is one we return to in later chapters in relation to other girls in the study. Similarly, the more general imperatives for a self-conscious managing of appearance as a component of the "good student" that we referred to earlier, is differentially achieved by girls compared with boys in the study. In later chapters, we discuss how a backdrop of social change is creating some different orientations to future opportunities in the girls and the boys we followed. We also analyze some different ways they handle issues of intimacy and autonomy, friendship and bullying in the course of school. But in this chapter we focus on the perceived "good student" and the issue of gender, the issue that threads through the earlier reforms directed at girls, and through more recent debates challenging discursive and institutional constructions on behalf of boys. We wanted to see how the young people now at school themselves regard this issue today.

Two things were apparent from our interviews throughout the length of the study. Students were not highly self-conscious about or concerned about gender as a component of school practices, and they were complacent about any gendered issues they could identify within constructions of the good student. Notwithstanding the media and political foregrounding of schools as a problem for boys, in our interviews the self-conscious response of both males and females when asked about this issue was to not see it as a problem, to continue to view boys as normal or the norm.

At one point, early on in the study, we asked people whether they thought there was equal opportunity for girls and boys today. Virtually everyone responded affirmatively that schools did not discriminate between girls and boys. In the past few decades, the system in this state had shifted from policies that allowed curriculum subjects to be differentially offered to girls and boys, to formal equal opportunity legislation that forbids differential access or treatment; indeed, public schools are required to have equal opportunity committees. Because explicit differentiation and direct discrimination are not allowed, students, when asked directly, see gender as no longer an issue, and this was produced as well as confirmed by the fact that in three of the four schools they were unaware of the existence of their Equal Opportunity Committee or of what it did.

When our participants were around 14 or 15, we asked both girls and boys what they thought of the current debate that today it is boys who are underachieving and in need of special attention and programs. A few students responded by disagreeing that either boys or girls today are disadvantaged or differ as a group, but the majority of young people agreed that girls were doing better work in school, and applied themselves better, but strongly disagreed that anything should be done to alter boys' ways of operating. Boys frequently gave a negative slant to girls' practices at school, even if they see these as being associated with success. For example,

Andrew: Basically they [boys] have more fun. Or try and have, you know, mess around and play up to see what they can get away with. Stuff like that. The girls more or less just get straight down to work and stuff like that and work hard. Not to say boys don't work hard, that is.

Do you think it is something that schools should do something about?
Michael: Um, I don't really . . . I think that boys and girls have got the same chances to do well in VCE, but, as Andrew said, they, boys, tend to stuff around a bit more. But you can't stop that. Boys will be boys. so there's not a lot you can really do. It's their choice.

(Regional High, Year 10, age 15)

In other words, here, as with the issue of dieting and appearance, which we discuss in chapter 8, we see a persistence of the "male as norm" assumption—in both cases with effects on the self-perceptions, behavior, and possible outcomes for girls and boys. The "good student" in this sense may now have a feminine persona—but one that is derided as much as emulated.

Paul Willis (1977) showed nearly three decades ago that, for working-class boys, it is important to maintain their difference from girls, their belief in their own ways of being. Since then, with the growing visible success of girls in education, a similar reaction is also heard in boys such as Andrew and Michael, boys who are attending an academic school, have ambitions to be successful in life, and are not conventional "school resisters." Even a number of girls in our study suggested they did not particularly like their choices in this stage of school to work rather than mess around, and spoke of their own belief that boys could turn their behavior around when it mattered, in the final important school examination in Year 12.

Gendered ways of being certainly do enter how individuals manage their school lives and how they produce, enact, or reject ways of being the "good student." When they were first at high school, for example, the working-class boys spoke in apparently contradictory ways about how they saw their new schools compared with their previous primary schools. It emerged that in many ways they missed the caring and interest in them as individuals that they had experienced at primary school; they were intimidated by the bigger boys; they were frustrated by school rules that circumscribed their physical activity at lunchtimes—but that it was important to them to assert their maturity by identifying with being a high school student and saying that that school was superior to the primary school. Later on too, for the boys spending part of their time in the workplace, they were clear that the particular disciplines of work in terms of assessment and sanctions were much harsher than those of school, but they tried to meet the former and did not care about the latter because in the workplace they felt like men, were in the company of men, rather than being disciplined as children by teachers (Brett, Regional Tech 1998). The "good student" was not a persona to which they aspired.

Curriculum Values

For most people, a good student is also a student who "does well" and achieves good grades (though they might be disparagingly seen by some groups as one of Willis's "earoles"[2]), and this raises the issue of what is currently to be successful in terms of the curriculum. In

Nassar's story at the beginning of this chapter, we see some of his puzzlement about cracking the codes: initially thinking that trying to memorize facts from his scientific calculator might help, later being rebuked for an essay that was too long, trying to be quiet and inconspicuous in class, not getting anything quite right. Is a good student someone who knows a lot or someone who knows certain types of things? Is it someone who is good at examinations, at mathematics, or at everything? Is it changing?

In Australia, and in many other countries, there is much public debate and policy formulation on these questions.[3] On the one hand, comparative standards testing (such as the International Studies of Educational Achievement, President Bush's use of Texas Reading Scores, the move to national tests and international benchmarking) gives performance in traditional intellectual tasks continued high salience, and data of this kind together with dropout data dominate discussion about groups (why are working-class students, or boys, or Indigenous students not doing well). On the other hand, considerable attention is being paid to the implications of new technologies for what should be learned, and more generally to the problematic issue of changing patterns in work and what kind of preparation is vocationally appropriate today (Bagnall 2000; Cohen 1997; Gee 1999; MCEETYA 2000).

Our study shows some of the ways such curriculum issues and the effects of changing times are being worked out and constructed in particular schools and in particular lives.

In Year 7, when students were prepared to say that the school valued something other than reputation and appearance, the curriculum area that was most commonly named was mathematics.

In the system of education we are discussing, it is not mandatory to continue with mathematics into the two senior years of high school. Also, when entering high school, most students encounter a range of new subjects, which, from our interviews in the final year of primary school, they were eagerly anticipating. Neither Mathematics nor English was one of these anticipated subjects. Nevertheless, when we talked to the students toward the end of their first year in high school, most of them indicated both that mathematics was the curriculum area that mattered most to the school and that it was one of the subjects they liked least. At the beginning of their high school years, for the students themselves, mathematics is a preeminent signifier of whether you are a good student, both in terms of intellectual ability and of being vocationally on track:

What do you think this school thinks is important?
Maths.
Maths . . . . Because if you don't learn maths, when you're an adult you'd just be pretty hopeless, because most jobs include maths.
(Jenny and friend, Regional High Year 7)

Like . . . maths and all that. All the major subjects, so it helps us get a start in jobs and all that (Andrew, Regional High, Year 7)

Well, Maths and English, I suppose, are the most important subjects so I suppose they'd think they were the best, kind of thing. They should be the most important, I'd say.
(Sharon, Suburban High Year 7)

Yeah, they sort of think them subjects [science, maths, social ed and English] are the main ones, even though, you know, most people don't like the main subjects. . . . (Keren, Regional Tech, Year 7)

Sometimes I think, what will I ever need this for, I don't want to be anything to do with maths. But then, then if you think about it, maths is part of an everyday life thing. It's going to be useful in whatever I want to be, which is, sort of, a vet . . . .
(Alannah, City Academy, Year 7)

The perception that mathematics is the subject that really mattered is particularly interesting in relation to the students at Regional Tech. These students commonly came with a family history in which their own parents had had generally poor experiences of school, left school early, and did not expect schooling necessarily to be associated with success. The school itself was well equipped with new computing facilities as well as a wide range of technological and craft facilities and options, and students enjoyed these. Some girls, for example, indicated that they did not share the Regional High focus on emulating the private school.

Christine: And then if it's like in an all-girls school you don't get to do the subject like sheet-metal work and all that. And they're some of my favorite subjects, so . . . .
Kylie: You don't have like woodwork, sheet-metal and all that.
Christine: Like there's a whole tech work you wouldn't know.
(Regional Tech, Year 7)

Nevertheless, Christine and Kylie's comments suggest that although they may enjoy and do well at such subjects, they think what the school values are "the main subjects": mathematics and English. This is an assessment that the teachers in this particular school would probably not agree with—it is a school that puts much effort into its range of technical options and pathways to work and does not expect most students to go on to university. The students' valuing of what matters, of what is a good curriculum and a good student, is as much a reflection of the broad (or hegemonic) social discourse of what it means to be "a good student" than a valuing derived from the overt practices of the school (though these practices themselves may promote mixed messages: technology subjects and integrated methods are highly promoted, but remedial teaching happens only in relation to the core subjects of English and mathematics).

Regional Tech, in fact, is very oriented to "vocational" pathways, as it recognizes that only a small minority of its students will go on to university.[4] In the senior years at this school, a "good student" might be one who has skills for a particular area of work, is well behaved and reliable when sent out on dual accreditation courses to do work experience, and makes a good impression with potential employers. Two of the students in our study—Dirk and Brett—are more committed to their workplace subjects than other subjects, and are encouraged by teachers to stay on and comfortably kept in the school even when they effectively do not have sufficient academic subjects to allow them to complete the Year 12 certificate.

However, in terms of being a "good school," the dilemma both the school and the students face is that vocational pathways are traditionally associated with a mental/manual hierarchy, and as constituting a pathway for those who are not "good students" and will want to leave school early. This deficit view of who such students are, as evident in the local comparison with the other high school and in the students' comments about "the main subjects" in the early years, overlays both the Regional Tech's and the policy-makers' attempts to institute new versions of vocationalism in schools. This involves a new ethos of what schools are about, in which VET (vocational education and training) is seen as an equally desirable goal for schools to strive for and as providing legitimate academic results and citizenship values.

Teachers at Regional Tech are very aware of the hegemonic sense of "what is a good student" and equally of the fact that this school is starting from a disadvantaged position. One day, for example, when we were sitting in the staffroom waiting for our room for interviews to be ready, a teacher started talking about changes to the procedures for applying for university courses. Previously, he said, he would take the forms into class and have the students fill them in there, giving assistance where needed. Now the system had been privatized. Instead of the forms being sent to the schools to pass on to the students, the students had to take an individual initiative to go to a newsagent to buy the form and pay at a post office to register their choices. He predicted that there would be far fewer students from this school to even apply for university as a result. What seemed like a minor change to procedures, to his mind, was enough to tip the balance in terms of the future directions these young people might follow.

At this school, the typical cohort, constructed by history, location, and parental choice, rarely brings positive expectations of school or the "academic" cultural capital and support that subsidizes school efforts to produce academic high achievers. There is a sense, then, in which the culture of both students and teachers constructs this as a school in which students will never measure up to the hegemonic images of the good student. What they try to work with is producing aspects of what is valued, such as attention to work and behaving well, or good aptitude for its vocational subjects and workplace programs; that students will impress the employers to whom they are sent for work experience, as Dirk does. But because the dominant culture of the school is not geared to expectations of high academic achievement, it militates against someone, such as Alan, who began school with such expectations.

Schooling and Particular Schools: The Hegemonic and the Local

Earlier in the chapter we discussed some common themes we heard across very different schools in our earliest interviews (managing appearance, mathematics as the measure of being a good student, that gender discrimination is not an issue)—themes that reflect some broadly shared discursive constructions of the good student today. Both with Regional High and with Regional Tech we also began to discuss how each school's own positioning picks up specific emphases that have regard both to this broader shared "hegemonic" vision, and to their own histories, cohorts, and sense of possible strategy. Local school emphases also shape what qualities are valorized, both during school and in the ways we heard students at each school begin to talk, the values they talked about, and their positioning and expectations about themselves as they proceeded from school.

For a start, we might note the displays each school had for visitors, showcasing the kind of "good students" and work that was valued. At City Academy, honor boards listed historical arrays of important people going back to the nineteenth century, drawing attention to families of prominence, well-known names who had been the top academic students or school captains; brochures and newsletters spread news of many ex-students now in important and powerful social roles as judges, politicians, along with information about past as well as current students winning awards, being socially distinguished, and socially successful. At Suburban High, the halls were filled with more contemporary achievements—impressive artistic creations by students and prizes won in creative arts and new media. At Regional High, the entrance hall, honor boards, and framed photographs announced its historical traditions, and those it honored: academic achievers, sporting teams, and those who had fought for their country and died in wars. Regional Tech also displayed photographs of those who had achieved, but in this case they were sporting identities (often those with a checkered history at the school), or clippings from the local newspaper about an event or achievement of a more minor scale in which students had done well.

The way a particular school, as well as its students, must negotiate tensions between the broad cultural/historical and local discursive constructions of desirable schools and desirable student identities is evident at Suburban High. This school was founded in the late 1960s and had forged a school identity as a place that offered distinctive pathways for students: ones that emphasized "artiness," especially the visual arts, and having a casual and nonconformist persona. Students wore casual clothes rather than a uniform, addressed many of the teachers on a first-name basis, and were at ease and articulate in interacting with a cosmopolitan mix of students. The school walls are covered with impressive displays of prize-winning art and photography produced by students; it also has well-equipped art studios and strong links with art colleges that have very competitive entry requirements, including art portfolios. However, at the beginning of our study, this school had a dangerously declining school population and its image was no longer attractive to many potential families and local primary schools.

Suburban High's orientations toward diversity, nontraditional academic curriculum and portfolios rather than examinations, and its preparation of students for occupations in communications and symbolic fields, meant that its local construction of the good student was compatible with some of the changing social agendas and new forms of work valorized in schooling policies and research literature on the new vocationalism. In many respects, the "good student" at Suburban High possessed skills and qualities highly valued in the creative industries and knowledge and communication economy, areas in which job opportunities had been expanding during the 1990s. Yet during this same period, there was increased public competitiveness and comparison between schools, associated anxiety from parents about futures for their children, and increased worries about drugs and social misbehavior. Suburban High's reputation as a school that tolerated lack of discipline, symbolized in its lack of school uniform, placed its version of the good student under threat as the anxieties of the 1990s about future jobs and the centrality of university entry took on new force. In the first year of our study, the school embarked on a campaign to change its image. It introduced school uniforms and initiated a program of public relations activities and events for students, teachers, and parents at the local primary schools. Its message was that, henceforth, it would maintain the distinctive options of its cultural directions, but within a more traditional, conventional, and hegemonic sense of how a "good student" should look and behave. The campaign was successful in reversing the declining population and, by the end of the 1990s and of our study, the school had retained strong enrollments.

The kind of developments and new agendas confronting Suburban High are illustrated in a number of recent studies in the United States, the United Kingdom, and Australia, particularly in relation to the strategies of anxious middle-class parents to secure their children's future success (Ball 2003; Brantlinger 2003; Power et al. 2003; Pusey 2003). Increased parental anxiety about work and future opportunity is projected onto concerns about the outcomes of their children's education, and these intensified anxieties stem from globalization and the changing form of jobs. In Ball's words these changes represent a "very dramatic interruption to the trajectory of economic growth and patterns of employment which provided the basis for the massive post-war expansion in the middle classes and the creation of the so-called 'new middle class'" (Ball 2003, 19). An associated global wave of neoliberal social policy has made all aspects of social life seem more difficult and more fragile (Pusey 2003), and this too feeds into parental concerns. One response to these anxieties is a greater attempt by middle-class parents to control the organization and pedagogies of the schools their children attend in ways that emphasize discipline and academic competitive achievement, notwithstanding the social values of fairness and equality to which they may also give lip service (Brantlinger 2003). In Brantlinger's study, parents juggle one set of personal liberal social values with another set of anxieties regarding their child's future and a preference for school and curriculum organization that is most likely to lead to successful outcomes (in the hegemonic sense) for their children and secure middle-class advantage (see also Walkerdine, Lucey, and Melody 2001). For parents as well as for schools, the "good student" is neither a seamless, unitary discourse, nor a wholly rational one. Anxieties about competition and the future and the role of "discipline" in relation to it, compete with other concerns about the new vocationalism, new kinds of work, and the end of a linear and lifelong career. And these come together with more specific interests about particular children and what certain kinds of school are doing or not doing to care for them.

The significance for the identity-making of young people of their local school cultures is especially apparent in the contrast between the two "middle" schools in our study, Suburban High and Regional High. The former emphasized inclusiveness, personal attention, second chances, and a therapeutic and overtly caring style from teachers and school managers. The latter emphasized competitive striving, strict discipline, an orientation to achieving tasks and goals, and a view that educational and social outcomes are a result of one's own efforts. In one part of their official discourse, such as that expressed in school newsletters, both schools explicitly take up the same sense of what it means for a student to do well—that is, they will achieve good grades and proceed to a good course and/or a good job. Yet, in other ways, they produce different conditions for the "good student" and different values for those who go there.

At Suburban High, a "good student" is one who attends well and comfortably to interpersonal interactions with teachers. The articulate and personable Daniel, notwithstanding his learning difficulties and the need for the school to devise alternative classes for him, was a favorite of some teachers and flourished in the school. Yet the school's therapeutic and inclusive mode also posed difficulties for some students who were concerned about the lack of urgency these modes allowed in relation to academic achievement. This was particularly so for two of our students who, while enjoying the social ambience of the school, often reflected on what their schooling experiences would have been had they gone to a private school. They both came from middle-class backgrounds and had had the opportunity to attend private schools, and, as they go through school, both of them dwell on what they might be missing by not attending a private school with a stronger orientation to disciplined work and competitive success. In Madeleine's case, her father constantly urged her to try out a private school, but she preferred the atmosphere of Suburban High. Marcus briefly transferred to a private school during Year 8, as he wanted to participate in more sports (and private schools have a strong sports curriculum) but returned in Year 9 because he did not like the strict discipline and he too preferred the atmosphere at Suburban High. Yet the option of private school lingers throughout his interviews, and in his senior years he laments that Suburban High was not "more academic," in the context of his own inability to be as disciplined as he would like. He, like Madeleine, is articulate and socially at ease, but had not graduated from high school when we last met him and was uncertain about what he was going to do. Yet, at the same school, some individuals who in many schools would have little chance of being a "good student" become constructed as such by a school concerned about individual life chances and assistance. Daniel, with learning difficulties, is one such example. Another is Amelie. In the final interviews, when she is taking a university degree in nursing, Amelie tells us that when she first came to the school she was so far behind in terms of her literacy that it seemed unlikely she would be able to graduate.

No school in our study disowned the academic, hard-working, self-managed good student, but, as a result of their history, their location (including their location relative to each other), their intake, and their internal organization, activities, and teacher views, in practice they value and produce different ways of being. Someone who might potentially be a "good student" in one school may not be such a student in the same way at another. Take the examples of Madeleine and Marcus, who while happy with the atmosphere at Suburban High, were in retrospect ambivalent about its deemphasis on hard work and the traditional academic curriculum. At City Academy, they may have found a different group of friends and been more focussed and successful in terms of conventional school results and outcomes. For Diana, unhappy at City Academy because it did not, in her view, genuinely value difference and was too conformist, Suburban High could have offered a more immediately congenial environment, where nonconformity was more of a "norm." At Regional Tech, Alan found the schoolwork demands easy and made little extra effort; at Regional High, the competitive agendas would have challenged him more directly. And at Suburban High, Nassar found his initial impetus to be "good" in a traditional sense positioned him as somewhat of an outcast; whereas at Regional High, whether or not he found a more congenial peer group, he could have followed David's trajectory in being approved by the school and directed his energies productively toward academic success.

Being a good student then is not just an individual achievement, but one that is constructed by the broad social arrangements as well as by the ways particular schools, formally and informally, manage these arrangements. What schools do here is constrained by their history, their community setting, and their comparative relationship to other schools. The big picture of how schooling operates means that certain groups are much more likely to be "good students" than others, and the examples of Nassar and Alannah represent, in part at least, that big picture story. But the local picture is such that individual lives are made differently, constructed differently, have different outcomes by going to this school rather than that school. In substantive terms today, schooling, particular schools, and individuals in schools are all also grappling with certain changing and competing agendas about what it means to be a good student.

Competition for academic success is stronger than ever, given the visible changes to jobs and social arrangements and the accompanying anxieties about the future by parents. It is symbolized in our study in the continued centrality of mathematics, the most hierarchically structured subject, as the measure of being academically good. It is symbolized too in the worries of the middle-class young people in our study—people such as Marcus, Madeleine, Diana—who do not want to be in that conventional academic rat race, but do worry about the consequences of not doing so. And it is symbolized psychologically in the renewed attention to discipline and school uniform as markers of the good student and the good school, signs that things are under control, signs that allay anxieties about change and a world out of control. But while traditional knowledge and behavior modes have not been replaced as markers of what matters, they compete with the entry of other symbols of what is "good," markers seen in big education policies, in school policies, and in students such as Alannah who manage successful pathways through and beyond school. Here schools are increasingly characterized by their competition with each other in a neoliberal regime that valorizes "choice." Students become part of the marketing of schools; the civic values they learn are about the importance of marketing themselves.

CHAPTER 4

Becoming Someone as Project and as Process

The passage from 12 to 18 years old typically evokes a time of dislocation and transformation, and a forging of adult identities. Regarding the teenage years as a period of rebellion and uncertainty is a common trope in both psychological and sociological traditions—the dominant lenses for interpreting and constructing adolescence. Marking the transition from childhood to adulthood, adolescence is represented as a quintessential phase of "becoming." Nancy Lesko writes: "Adolescents, like the primates of Donna Haraway's work, occupy border zones between the mythic poles of adult/child, sexual/asexual, rational/emotional, civilized/savage, and productive/unproductive. . . . On the terrain of adolescent bodies is a struggle for what will count as an adult, a woman, a man, rationality, proper sexuality, and orderly development" (Lesko 1996, 455).

The term "adolescence" itself represents a particular perspective on young people's identities, and is a term that we have in general not used throughout this book. It has, for us, a discursive association with psychological and maturational understandings of identity rather than sociological ones, though there are also national differences in how the term is used. The descriptor "youth," while more overtly sociological in flavor than adolescence can be equally problematic, and tends to have gendered (masculine) connotations and an association with studies of deviance and, more recently in cultural studies, with "resistance" (Cohen and Ainley 2000; McRobbie 1996). As we have been writing about our study, finding terms to refer to people in the 12-to-18 age group has itself proved to be quite difficult. "Adolescence" has a psychological association, "teenager" evokes marketing target groups, "youth" never seems to encapsulate women or girls, unless it is modified with a feminine adjective. When we first started working with our participants they were aged 12, and it was relatively straightforward to refer to them as girls and boys, but, as they got older, this became more problematic and inaccurate. Terms such as "young women or young men" do not always work either, and can seem clichéd, contradictory, old-fashioned, or even patronizing. Yet it has remained hard to find a single term to represent those over the course of the 12 to 18 period. Referring to them as "participants" or as "students" sometimes works, but it also risks conveying a more formal and pseudoscientific approach than what characterized our relationship with them or the style of study we conducted.

The historical and cultural construction of "adolescence" and "youth" and their gendered and normative truths have been charted in numerous studies (Driscoll 2002; Griffin 1993; Johnson 1993; Wyn 2000). Such work has been important in troubling the apparent naturalness of adolescence and situating the category in the context of broad historical and social trends. Lesko (2001) develops a genealogy of the cultural and subjective significance of adolescence as a category that is both much regulated and invested with many hopes and ambitions. We have developed different yet complementary lines of inquiry. We recognize that the categories of "youth" or "adolescent" have histories and are both inventions and highly governed spaces, but our longitudinal approach aims to explore that process of becoming as it happens qualitatively and subjectively, over and in time. Our focus has been on how youthful/adolescent subjectivity is socially differentiated and takes shape, incrementally and recursively, in a specific historical period.

The notion of "becoming," as proposed by cultural studies practitioners, has been a useful starting point for our thinking about subjectivity (Gilroy, Grossberg, and McRobbie 2000; Hall and du Gay 1996; Morley and Chen 1996). It offers an alternative to essentialist discourses of "being" and ideas of identity as fixed, and emphasizes identity as productive, fluid, dynamic yet also historically and socially located—the process of "becoming" obviously does not happen in a material or cultural vacuum. It might also be said, however, that some of the cultural studies stress on "identity as becoming" has tended to overstate the utopian possibilities this process might offer, and to neglect the losses, discomfort, and ambivalence sometimes associated with becoming somebody or of being obliged to become a different kind of person in a new or emerging political and social climate (Ang 2000) or in a particular school culture. In such circumstances, "becoming" is less hopeful, and includes the giving up of aspects of identity in order to become somebody else.

Many uses and nuances of "becoming" circulate, including ones as divergent as Deluezian notions of the "becoming subject" whereby "identity . . . is not an outcome of a process but is that process itself" (Driscoll 2002, 194; see also Braidotti 1994; Colebrook 2000[1]) and psychological accounts of becoming as the accomplishment of a series of developmental tasks and resolutions (Erikson 1968). In whatever inflection, analyses of subjectivity as a process of becoming typically sit somewhat paradoxically alongside studies of young people because adolescence has conventionally been a category tied to rigid developmental discourses of becoming. The end point of becoming for adolescence or the 12 to 18 period is usually imagined as adulthood, an identity that is inexorably achieved, succeeding in linear fashion the uncertainty and "Sturm und Drang" of adolescence. Much critical work on the history and sociology of adolescence has attempted to challenge the authority of that discourse, and to see adolescence as something other than a staging post in the journey to adulthood. Some work challenges this by showing the invention of adolescence as a category of identity and demography (Johnson 1993; Lesko 2001; Roman 1996), while other work (Wyn 2000) points to the changing empirical patterns and contemporary transformation of the age-associated markers that link adulthood to some activities (e.g., being in paid work rather than study) and adolescence to others.

There is a double meaning to our use of the term "becoming"; it refers to the project of becoming someone in particular and also to an ongoing process of subject formation. We try to keep both meanings in play. The students we interviewed were self-consciously "becoming somebody" (Wexler 1992). Here "becoming" refers to the *project* of making a specific identity, of claiming identifications and a sense of self, a process that is amplified in the adolescent years in part because of the dominance and intensification of discourses about transition and development. And "becoming" characterizes subjectivity as formed in an ongoing *process*—shaping and being shaped. In both senses (becoming as project, becoming as process), the notion of becoming is both about common processes in which young people (and all human subjects) are engaged and about ways in which social differentiation is produced; our interest is in how these two dimensions of subject-making come together. The feminist philosopher Henrietta Moore proposes that "subjectivity is both an entity and a project, an achievement and a set of potentialities, an imagined relation to self and others and an embodied one. Subjectivity is itself a linking term, a borderland product, the result of individual intention and agency in contact with social, economic and political discourses, practices and institutions" (Moore 2001, 264). Understanding the links among becoming—as project and process—embodiment, and social and discursive location is central to our analysis of subjectivity in interaction with schooling. Subjectivity is malleable, unstable, never completely sutured, yet it has elements of continuity and is constituted in and responsive to historical and local conditions and patterns of social differentiation. Interviewing people longitudinally is one way to try to capture this process of becoming, to see how this happens over and in a biographical and historical period.

Tell Us about Yourself

So how would you describe yourself now?
Keren: Oh, I thought you would have rubbed that question out by now. [chuckling]
It will not disappear! [laughing, mock stern]
Keren: Okay. Um, oh okay.
What sort of person are you?
Keren: Oh well, I still I, I hope to think that I am still you know, have grown up but, still have a, a fun, going, kind of, outgoing personality but, you know, that's my view, someone else's could be totally different, but yeah I think I'm pretty good.
[. . .]
Keren: Moving up in the world.
So you feel pretty good about yourself at the moment?
Keren: Oh yeah, I'm on a high at the moment.

(ex-Regional Tech student at 18, in first year after finishing school, and after being interviewed thirteen times by us)

"How do you describe yourself?" "What sort of person do you see yourself as?" "How do you think other people see you?" We asked a version of these questions each time we interviewed the students. It became, as Keren's comments suggest, a stubborn yet familiar moment of dialogue in the interview, something that, over the years, they increasingly came to expect. It was met variously with bemused looks, a knowing smile, a rolling of the eyes—experienced as a kind of joke between us, something both researcher and participant knew eventually would occur in our interview conversation and would draw just this kind of initial response. We watched the students, particularly in the early years, puzzling over how to answer, their nervous foot-shuffling, an embarrassed turning away of eyes, while in some we witnessed a more self-conscious deciding about which side of themselves to present in the interview. For others, a degree of discomfort persisted throughout the length of the study. There was uncertainty about what exactly we wanted to hear, and some unfamiliarity with the emotional and discursive repertoires for representing themselves in such a way. This reluctance or difficulty of talking about the self is culturally differentiated. It is not only, as we found and discuss here, that there are gender, class, and ethnic cultural differences in how readily people in our study could or would respond to this set of questions. But it is a type of question that is perhaps less familiar to mainstream Australian cultural norms than to equivalent North American ones. Nevertheless, discomfort and silence or hesitant and uncertain answers could be as revealing as an easily elicited and more overtly "rich" self-description as it told us something about them, even when they thought they did not know how to answer, and even when the question appeared to make little sense.

Keren repeatedly described herself as cheery, funny, always telling jokes. She often came across in interviews as optimistic, and told us regularly that when thinking of the future she simply "takes it as it comes." Yet throughout her school years, and particularly during the middle years, Keren is having a difficult time—with being bullied, struggling with her schoolwork, and experiencing some emotionally hard times at home. At the end of the final interview, after watching her compilation videotape, and after the audiotape recorder is turned off, we mention that she seemed to really enjoy her elementary school years. Both of us clearly remember her from the first interview as bright and happy and as speaking warmly about her teacher. We tell her this. She laughs, and says that her mother had told her back then to make sure she smiled a lot in the interview and to answer all the questions. This is, at one level, a class-related response to managing an unfamiliar situation whose significance was unknown (the research interview with women from a city university). The injunction to smile and look happy also assumed that we, and possibly others, would be judging, and possibly negatively judging, how Keren responded: being cheerful is a reliable mode of self-presentation. Keren does this for us over the length of all the interviews. Her self-conscious presentation as a "joker," her deliberately "bouncy" demeanor, her diligence—including in the interview—and the hard work she put into constructing her future sits against her self-perception as someone who "takes it as it comes."

In asking questions about the self longitudinally and repeatedly, we had an opportunity to see what persisted and what changed. Even when self-descriptions appeared to remain the same over the course of seven years, the meaning of that description could resonate differently, in changing circumstances. When Brett was in grade 6 (end of elementary school), he looked directly at us, smiled, and told us that he sees himself as a good friend, kind, a cheerful boy. This remains a vivid memory for us, one somewhat poignant in retrospect. He was sweet-faced, and slightly serious, excited about going to secondary school, which was one that had a poor reputation in the town and was known by other students as "Tip Tech," a "dirty school," where there were lots of fights. In the middle years of secondary school, he tells us again that he hopes his friends know that "I'd do anything for them." In his final year he is impatient with school and longs for the adult world of work, where he can be with his mates and be treated by others as an adult. At each of these stages, being close to his friends is important for Brett, and central to how he sees himself. But, "having mates" takes on different meanings as Brett gets older, and he becomes more obviously embittered with the rest of the world around him. As he moves through high school, the commitment to his friends is no longer voiced as a gentle expression of concern for them, which we had found quite touching. Soon it becomes part of a litany of grievances he voices about the school and the uncaring teachers and about bullies and his readiness to fight. The relationships with friends are a refuge rather than a more intense reflection of how he relates to others, as it appeared in the earlier interview. Brett leaves school without completing his Year 12 qualification, hoping to get work in the manufacturing and construction industries; it is likely that he will have limited opportunities for full-time work in the future. Doing things with his mates, being seen as a good friend becomes particularly important; signifying entry to adulthood against the child's world of school and providing a focus for activity against, simultaneously, the dull routine of school where he is labeled as a bad boy/a poor student and unreliable, and the likely prospect of unemployment.

In repeatedly including questions about self-description in our rounds of interviews, one purpose was to hear what each person would choose to say to us directly about their sense of themselves, seeing this as one layer of evidence for looking at how they narrated and presented their subjectivity. Answers to such questions were interpreted in relation to responses to more indirect questions, and to our accumulating understandings of their attitudes and values as they talked about future dreams, relationships with friends, school experiences, political outlook and so forth. We also wanted to compare how their views of themselves changed over the adolescent years, see if there was continuity or disruption, and notice any recurring tropes, metaphors, or adjectives of self-description. This included the way they said things, silences, nervous giggling, their hesitation, or their confidence and enthusiasm in the narrative they told about themselves to us, researchers from the university.

We never expected this to be a transparent truth about these young people, a straightforward revelation about "their subjectivity." It was always going to be a story in part constructed for us, in the setting of a relatively formal research interview, usually taking place in a small room somewhere in the school, in which students would be taken out of their regular classes. Sometimes they would be having a good day, other times they could be feeling flat, sometimes they were playful, happy to be out of class. At yet other times the interviews were a quiet space away from friends and teachers, where two people were happy to listen to them, to take whatever they said seriously, and not be there again the next day to remind them of what they had said. Answering the question was also shaped by the way we, as researchers, posed it, the way we paused as we uttered it, or tried, sometimes awkwardly and not always successfully, to introduce it in a way that we hoped would make it easy for them to answer. (In the first year, when the students were 12, we thought it might help them to imagine describing themselves to a "pen pal."[2] This did not work very well at all, not least because many of them did not know what a "pen pal" was—and it simultaneously managed to make the task even more puzzling and emphasized our generational difference. Many of the transcripts and videos of those first interviews show us trying to explain, at length, this "simple" question: "how would you describe yourself?," met by some tentative replies, polite but brief efforts to help us by answering it properly. Whose uncertainty did that interaction register?) All these factors shaped what was told and what was heard.

What we were told then was, of course, a partial truth, constructed from so many contingencies. Scheurich (1995) argues that: "In an interview there is no stable 'reality' or 'meaning'. . . . The indeterminate totality of the interview always exceeds and transgresses our attempts to capture and categorize" (1995, 249). Many of us who work with interviews (e.g. Gitlin 1994; MacLure 2003; Thomson and Holland 2003a, 2003b; Walkerdine, Lucey, and Melody 2001) do not enter the interaction with a naïve or "modernist" expectation of the interview as an unmediated "confession"; acknowledging the construction and partiality of truth and power relations in interviews is essential. Admitting researcher reflexivity and the contingency of the interview, however, does not negate the possibility that interviews can generate meaningful insights. The methodological issue is not whether interviews are irredeemably problematic, but how to construct and interpret interviews so that they provoke understandings that do more than reiterate the interview's essential indeterminacy. In other words, refusing the possibility of a full truth does not cancel meaning, does not remove the possibility of learning something new, of gaining insight while being mindful of the construction and limits of the research encounter.

Making the Self

Across the social sciences and humanities there has been a proliferation of work privileging subjectivity as a focus of inquiry, much of it elaborating the various ways in which subjectivity is produced and governed, and analyzing characteristics of contemporary identities (Bendle 2002; Mansfield 2000). In both popular and academic texts, there is a fascination with biographical and autobiographical writing, from locating the voice and experiences of the researcher (Behar 1996) to life history (Hatch and Wisnieski 1995), and auto/biographical methods (Kehily 2002) to fashioning new forms of creative writing that play with the boundaries between autobiography, fiction, and criticism (Modjeska 2000). Reality television, talk shows, celebrity profiles, and the metamorphosis of "ordinary" lives into "identities" also point to an "autobiographical turn." Social theorists simultaneously describe the rise of attention to subjectivity and the project of self-making as an artifact of the historical period of late/postmodernity, and propose a range of concepts and approaches for theorizing how subjectivity itself is shaped and produced. Whether one adopts the conceptual language of "narratives of the self" (Giddens 1991) or "technologies of the self" (Foucault 1988; Rose 1996, 1999), or sees the emergence of a "biographical project" (Bauman 2000) or of "shape-shifting portfolio people" (Gee 2000/01; Gee, Hull, and Lankshear 1996), or theorizes subjectivity as "performative" (Butler 1990) or as "becoming" (Gilroy et al. 2000; Hall 1996; cf. Colebrook 2000; Driscoll 2002), or as "nomadic" (Braidotti 1994), a common theme remains the prominence and the problematization of the "subject."

From this range of work, three themes emerge as particularly relevant to our longitudinal study of subjectivity. They can be summarized as: individualization and "biography as a project"; reflexivity as a characteristic of contemporary identities, of ways of being and of knowing (ontological and epistemological); and gender change and destabilizing norms of gender identity and gender difference.

The formation of the self as a reflexive biography is seen by many as a defining feature of late/postmodernity (Bauman 2000; Beck 1992; Beck and Beck-Gernsheim 1995, 2002; Giddens 1991, 1992). Prescribed roles and identities are replaced by the imperative to self-consciously construct one's own identity. The self, it is argued, has become a project to be produced and reflected upon: choice biographies replace prescribed roles and futures (Beck 1992, 135; Beck and Beck-Gernsheim 1995; MacDonald 1999). Analytic attention is focused on the decisions and reflexivity of the agent whose traditional and once inherited roles—of gender, of family, of class identity—and codes of conduct are dissolving (Adkins 2000, 2002a; Beck 1992; Plumridge and Thomson 2003). Beck argues (1992, 135) that: "The proportion of life opportunities which are fundamentally closed to decision-making is decreasing and the proportion of the biography which is open and must be constructed personally is increasing. Individualization of life situations and processes thus means that biographies become self-reflexive; socially-prescribed biography is transformed into biography that is self-produced and continues to be produced." Further, Beck suggests, such "detraditionalizations happen in a social surge of individualization" (Beck 1992, 87). Individualization refers paradoxically both to "individualism" and the obligation "to standardize your own existence" in line with the imperatives of the labor market and governmental agencies (Beck and Beck-Gernsheim 1995, 7). This double process involves an increasing tendency to self-monitoring, so that "we are, not what we are, but what we make of ourselves" (Giddens 1991, 75).

Gender identities are theorized (and not only by reflexive modernization theorists) as similarly in flux, in part because of the general cultural attention to self-construction, but also because of the impact of over three decades of feminism. In accounts of reflexivity and detraditionalization, however, contemporary gender identities and relations become emblematic, representing in a kind of idealized form the possibilities of a self cut loose from tradition and required to make itself anew.

The "detraditionalization" argument has been criticized, particularly by feminists, as somewhat utopian, exaggerating the extent of gender instability and overlooking the reinscription of new forms of gender inequality—"retraditionalized gender" (Adkins 2002a, 2002b; Kenway and Kelly 2000; McLeod 2002). Reflexivity theorists fail, Lisa Adkins claims, to "register that reflexivity does not concern a liberal freedom from gender, but may be tied into new arrangements of gender" (Adkins 2002b, 12). She suggests that:

> reflexive modernity, while certainly signalling new modes of interaction, involves not a simple detachment or disembedding of individuals from social categories such as those of class and gender, but also re-embedding process in circuits and networks in which new, yet traditional—re-traditionalized—rules, norms, and expectations are at issue. (Adkins 2000, 260)

Throughout this book we argue that the effects of feminism or of reflexive modernity are experienced unevenly, and that contemporary gender identities and relations are characterized by both patterns of change and continuity; these issues, and arguments concerning the extent of gender "de" or "retraditionalization," are discussed further in chapters 5 and 8.

One framing question throughout our study has been: "To what extent can 'macro' or grand theories of social change and of modernity accommodate the challenges of 'identity politics' or illuminate the more 'micro' and local processes that sustain difference, inequality and power relations?" Focusing on how young people make meaning, construct their own biographies, and negotiate and reshape gender relations is one way of responding to and reflecting on this dilemma. For example, we might ask whether reflexivity (as disposition, as relation to the self, as mode of thinking and knowing) is an artifact of a particular class, ethnic, or gender identity, a disposition associated more with some groups than others, or whether it is a "universal," an undifferentiated attribute and artifact of late modernity. In many respects, both accounts can be true; again it is not one story opposing another. Reflexivity is a generalized disposition, in the sense that ongoing reflection on the self is increasingly incited and normalized.[3] At the same time, reflexivity takes on a heightened form among some groups, such as the middle-class girls we interviewed and the highly honed, double-edged reflexivity they embody (see especially chapter 5), and is less evident and more uncertainly worked out by boys in the regional schools and boys from non-Anglo-Australian backgrounds.

Discourse and Subjectivity

The style of our study, interview encounters and narratives, is based at a straightforward level on the argument that subjectivities are constructed through discourse, but are not simply effects of discourse. Poststructuralist discussions (Francis and Skelton 2001; St. Pierre and Pillow 2000) about the construction of subjects via discourse frequently follow two main trajectories: one locates discourse as disciplining the subject; the other elides discourse and subjectivity. Hall (1996), for example, argues that one of the dangers of some poststructuralist work is that discourse is "centered" and seen as productive and the subject is seen as decentered and disciplined, such that "regulation" becomes the overwhelming characterization of subjectivity: one is positioned in and by discourses. One interpretation of the Foucauldian concept of "technologies of the self" is that it moves beyond an account of the self as merely positioned in or disciplined by discourse, by describing how subjectivity is formed in the interaction between technologies of regulation and technologies of the self—"arts of existence" or techniques for acting on, fashioning and governing the self (Foucault 1982, 1988; Popkewitz and Brennan 1998; Rose 1989, 1996). But there are ongoing debates about the uses and benefits of this conceptualization of subjectification (Baker and Heyning 2004; Chappell et al. 2003; Tamboukou 2003), including whether one kind of technology is subordinated to the other (Hall 1996), or whether, as feminists have debated, technologies of the self simply offer another account of disembodied socialization (McNay 1992: Probyn 1993). For our purposes, the key issue is that subjects are not simply positioned and dominated by discourse or technologies; rather, the focus of our analysis is the interaction between dominant and normative social discourses and practices of the self—including narratives of the self and self-descriptions, memories, and dreams.

In the second poststructuralist trajectory, in which subjects are principally understood as bearers or effects of discourse, subjectivity is frequently represented as a reflection of, or in alignment with, dominant cultural discourses. Yet, subjectivity can exceed or disrupt dominant discourses and, as Nielsen and Rudberg argue, psychological life stories and cultural discourses are not reducible to one another (Nielsen and Rudberg 1995, 86). Moreover, "subject position" is not a synonym for subjectivity, as the latter is cut across by attachment to different subject positions—for example, as mother, daughter, teacher. Certainly, discourses make available subject positions, provide resources for self-making, regulate normative ideals, incite certain ways of being, and can also structure the very techniques available for fashioning the self. But subjectivity is embodied and emotional—desires, dreams, ambivalence—and accumulating life histories shape how subject positions are negotiated and subjectivity is fashioned. These "nonrational" aspects of subjectivity are often poorly captured in exclusively narrative and discourse-based accounts of subjectivity or in views of subjectivity that represent it as a cluster of subject positions.

Psychosocial Subjects

A persistent dilemma associated with the discourse/identity nexus, particularly in feminist and poststructuralist work, is the relationship between psychological and sociological understandings of identity and the extent to which either paradigm offers an adequate or "full" account. There are numerous discussions of what either neglects and how one is superior to the other, as well as attempts to integrate insights stemming from both. The notion of the psychosocial subject has become influential, and proponents argue that both social and psychic dimensions of identity need to be acknowledged and built into analysis and methodological approach (Hollway and Jefferson 2000; Lucey and Reay 2000; Walkerdine, Lucey, and Melody 2001). Drawing on a longitudinal study of young women (aged 4–21), Walkerdine, Lucey, and Melody (2001) develop a persuasive analysis of the psychodynamics of gender/class identities in late twentieth-century Britain and explore the impact of such dynamics on the conduct of the research itself. They argue that it is necessary to acknowledge the impact of "transferences" within interviews and recognize the psychological and emotional dynamics of the interview as they shape both the interview text and its analysis. Hollway and Jefferson (2000, 14) similarly regard subjects as "simultaneously psychic and social," and argue for greater recognition of the psychic dimensions of the research encounter. They propose the concept of the "defended subject" to analyze participant transcripts, so that transcripts are read not as transparent texts or insights into identity, but as sites in which the interviewee's subjectivity is negotiated and defended.

Such work has been important in showing the significance of psychic and emotional dimensions of subjectivity and the interconnections between psychic and social processes. Our own approach, however, is not to develop a single coherent picture—a full picture of the subject—through the idea of a psychosocial subject. This is, in part, a result of our own intellectual biographies, ones that are grounded more in historical and sociological traditions than in psychological or psychoanalytic ones, and the particular questions that we asked of our study and the lines of interpretation we developed were shaped accordingly. Recognizing this is to acknowledge that interviews and analysis cannot serve all purposes, cannot address all possible questions. In part too, we have moved to a perspective that tries to keep different things in play rather than produce a single resolution or reading (McLeod 2003). As Donald (1991) argues, attempts to produce a full and integrated picture tend to trample over the important questions these conflicting traditions have raised. Donald (1991, 4) argues that psychoanalysis "fills the gap" in cultural studies or sociology by offering the possibility of a fuller, more complete "Theory of the Subject." But, he argues,

> Any such attempt to merge the two bodies of theory [psychoanalysis and sociology] blunts their specific insights and ignores their incompatibilities and contradictions. What seems potentially more fruitful is the dialogue in which although the two discourses remain distinct—they are always in some sense talking past each other—the questions untranslatably specific to each can provoke new thinking and insights in the other. (Donald 1991, 3)

All accounts of subjectivity are partial and incomplete, even those bearing the more inclusive title of psychosocial. The challenge is to read different perspectives against each other, not to settle for a single all-encompassing account, one "theoretical explanation" of what is really happening. In our analysis of interviews, we sometimes emphasize technologies or practices of the self and the self as a project, in others we emphasize the homologies between school ethos and dispositions and social orientations. In yet other instances, patterns of class and school type difference seem to be more salient than differences between gender. In other words, we aim to work reflexively with different theoretical explanations as some ideas and concepts allow us to see some things clearly while at the same time occlude other aspects.

Habitus, Schooling, and Becoming

Our focus on researching subjectivity is underpinned by a concern with the project and process of becoming and, equally, a concern with processes of social differentiation, with how people become particular kinds of people in interaction with school and family milieu. A major concern is "biography in interaction with schooling" and how to theorize that relation: it is not simply subjectivity in the abstract or the subjectivity broadly of young people today.

Sociology of education presumes that schools do indeed shape students and in varying degrees reproduce social relations of power and inequality. We have no quarrel with this as a general starting point, though there has been a tendency for such research to overstate the rigidity of reproduction, as if it were homogenous and static. Further, the primary point of analysis is usually the way in which schooling in general is an effect of the social structure, whereas our analysis addresses how (within this) particular schools shape subjectivities. Too often as well, processes of cultural reproduction are presumed to be much the same today as they were in the 1970s or 1950s, and to be much the same across national and regional locations. Additionally, much research on schooling and identities continues to be locked in an either/or mode, emphasizing either "reproduction" or "resistance." While in our study we can chart general patterns of reproduction and of change, we have also approached the relationship between schooling and subjectivities in another way to investigate how four different types of school shaped subjectivity in particular ways. As we discussed in the preceding chapter, the students we interviewed at each of the four schools took on (embodied) an outlook, mentality, and orientation to the social world, their futures, and themselves that bore traces of what we are calling their "school ethos." Bourdieu's concepts of habitus and social field and cultural capital offer useful lenses for understanding this relationship.

In Bourdieu's theory, individuals form themselves in social situations that create for them ways of being that are more often interpreted as individual personality, ability, choices. Their "habitus" is not simply that people copy "role models," or are rewarded or punished for doing certain things, but that in quite subtle ways, through discourse, practices, and institutions, and through interactions with others in their environment, principles are set up for the individual about what matters, what is noticed, how one comports oneself physically, socially, emotionally, and much more.

Habitus then is "socialized subjectivity" and expresses "how individuals 'become themselves'," and "the ways in which those individuals engage in practices" (Webb, Schirato, and Danaher 2002, 11). It constitutes a "system of lasting and transposable dispositions which, integrating past experiences, functions at every moment as a matrix of perceptions, appreciations and actions and makes possible the achievement of infinitely diversified tasks" (quoted in Bourdieu and Wacquant 1992, 18). Habitus is a "strategy-generating principle" (Bourdieu 1977, 72) that is neither uniformly imposed nor a fixed way of being, and is not simply a mentality. Habitus is the embodied accumulation and effects of dispositions (not unlike, conceptually, the accumulation of capitals) and "ways of being," including orientations, values, and ways of comporting oneself, and is formed in interaction with "social fields." Fields are structured contexts of institutions' rules and other relations that form a differentiating hierarchy that shapes these processes and practices and determines what counts as valuable capital.

Bourdieu describes interactions with the field as a matter of learning the "rules of the game" (Bourdieu and Wacquant 1992) yet, at least on his own account, there is space for improvization: habitus is "creative, inventive, but within the limits of its structures" (Bourdieu and Wacquant 1992, 19; 2000). There is nevertheless a fundamental homology between certain social fields and habitus. He argues that

> Social reality exists, so to speak, twice, in things and minds, in fields and in habitus, outside and inside agents. And when habitus encounters a social world of which it is the product, it finds itself "as a fish in water," it does not feel the weight of the water and takes the world about itself for granted. (Bourdieu interviewed by Wacquant, Bourdieu, 1989, 43, in Grenfell and James 1998, 14)

For our study of subjectivity in interaction with schooling, habitus emphasizes the significance of embodiment, situates subjectivity as socially differentiated, and offers a way of interpreting homologies as well as contradictions between school and self (and family). Regarding schools as, on the one hand, paradigmatic social fields, we show how the discourses and ethos of particular kinds of schooling shape the dispositions and ways of being of young people. The comparative design of the study means that we can see close-up the character of different kinds of habitus and the various trajectories and orientations specific forms of schooling cultivate. As a "social field," schools structure the ways in which people from different backgrounds fare—as seen in the examples of Nassar and Alannah discussed in chapter 3. On the other hand, schools do not simply order the habitus that young people bring to school from home. Schools themselves are formative of dispositions and produce discourses, values, orientations, and principles for what is to be noticed and distinctive: this is evident in the contrast between Regional High and Suburban High, discussed in chapter 7. It is not simply that the school itself is an inert field that either corresponds to or contradicts the habitus the students bring—the school has its own dynamic habitus-shaping strategies, as the following discussion of Gillian suggests.

The longitudinal design of our study also means that we can observe the accumulated effects and formation of habitus over time. We are developing something other than a "slice" or synchronic analysis of how habitus is formed in relation to a social field at any particular time, as if habitus is largely static once formed. Our focus is not only on the end result, the culmination of effects, but also on the evolving processes by which young people do or do not come to feel or conduct themselves "as a fish in water" in specific school settings.

In recent sociological studies of schooling and inequality there has been some renewed interest in the concepts of habitus and social fields and forms of capital (Ball, Maguire, and Macrae, 2000; Brantlinger 2003; Lareau 2003). Critical responses to Bourdieu's work, nevertheless, continue to be somewhat dominated by debates about the extent to which his concepts simply represent another version of structural determinism, with the relationship between habitus and social field signalling the guarantee of social reproduction (Butler 1999; McLeod 2005; Lovell 2000; Shusterman 1999). In terms of such debates, two particular issues for our study are the utility and limits of the concept of habitus for theorizing gender subjectivity and the capacity of the Bourdieuian framework for conceptualizing gender and social change. Habitus and field are obviously helpful for understanding patterns and continuity (or, in other words, reproduction) but are less able to account for processes of change and for how patterns of difference and inequality might take different forms in different historical eras (Arnot 2002, 49), especially for issues such as gender in which Bourdieu's central metaphor of capital does not seem sufficient.

A central question for feminist engagements with Bourdieu is whether habitus can be transposed to examine the practices of gender identity (Adkins 2002a, 2002b; McNay 2000; Reay 1995b; Skeggs 1997) or other dimensions of identity such as sexuality, race, or ethnicity. Is a mode of analysis that was initially developed to account for forms of capital, patterns of class differentiation, and hierarchies of distinction appropriate for the task of theorizing other social relations and patterns and intersections of difference? A second key question for feminist analysis concerns what habitus does not encompass. Is habitus particularly helpful for understanding the power of desires, emotions, and longing in the shaping of subjectivity? What does habitus occlude or not see?[4]

In many adaptations of habitus to account for gender, there is a tendency to render it as a form of smooth socialization. Yet, a key aspect of the relation between habitus and field is the degree of correspondence or contradiction: when is there alignment between the two, and when is contradiction also part of the story of cultural reproduction? In relation to schooling, the reproduction of class-based inequalities typically arises when the habitus of the elite and professional middle classes corresponds with that of the school—producing ongoing advantage and success—and conversely when the habitus of the working class contradicts that of the school, which is more likely to lead to alienation from school; structural differences thus become mistaken for individual deficiencies or strengths. These matters of contradiction and correspondence need to be kept to the fore and emphasized in any discussions of the usefulness of habitus for theorizing gender. To represent the field/habitus relation as characteristically one of alignment (gender socialization) is to provide only a partial account, and to overlook that, in terms of class analysis, the experience of contradiction, alienation, and disjunction is central to the field/habitus explanation (see also McNay 2000).

Drawing on themes and debates in the theoretical literature we have outlined, we conclude this chapter with a study of the experiences and reflections of one of the girls in our study entering City Academy and learning its "rules of the game" in conjunction with negotiating her own biographical projects. We try to show what we mean by keeping different theoretical perspectives in play, and to illustrate our focus on both the project and process of subjectivity and patterns and relations of social differentiation.

Becoming Someone at School: "I can always be nice"

Gillian enrols at City Academy at the start of secondary school, whereas many of her peers have been at the academy for at least part of their elementary schooling. She is the oldest in a family of three daughters; her father is a schoolteacher and her mother works full-time in the publishing industry. Gillian lives across town from City Academy and when we first meet she is highly conscious of the class and social differences between her after-school world and that of many of the City Academy students. She is also conscious that the decision to send her to this expensive school was financially difficult but deliberate, made by her parents because they were confident that it provided a good education. Gillian takes on many duties in the family—preparing meals, helping to look after her two younger sisters, house cleaning—and strives to please and be helpful and responsible: these are also qualities she admires in other people. She recalls being a reliable monitor at primary school, and dutifully engages in a range of extracurricular activities—key features of the private school experience. "I tend to always do more work than anyone else, and I've had, I'm always busy, I've always extra things, like music and drama. Other people tend to have lots of time and they can just sit around and do nothing and I'm never like that" (aged 13, Year 8).

Unlike many of the other students at the academy who have a family tradition of attending this school or one of the other elite schools in the city, Gillian is always aware of her educational privilege and the need to make the most of her opportunities. Yet moving to City Academy was initially an unsettling experience for her as she found it very hard to make friends and to feel at ease. She, more than other students, reminds us that, despite any social difficulties she might be having, it is a "good school" and she regularly articulates a kind of "official discourse" about the advantages of private schooling:

Do you think you have changed much since you started secondary school?

Gillian: I've grown up and I've done a lot of individual things since I've started secondary school and I've found new friends and different types of friends and met new types of people and just had a whole lot of new experiences that I didn't experience before when I just went to school.

[. . .] Well, I like school, and some people say that they don't like school, but I do, even though I don't like some things, I like being able to do them.

Do you think this is a good school?

Gillian: It's a very good school, like the teachers are mostly . . .

Some of them we don't really like that much. But we get a lot of opportunities here

(Gillian, City Academy, Year 7)

We asked in these initial interviews what parents thought of the school, and Gillian says that hers "both know that it is a really good school and they're happy that I'm here" and that "it would be really good for me to come to the academy otherwise I'd just go to some [State school] or something."

Gillian displays a diligent attitude to schoolwork and to acquiring appropriate forms of "cultural capital." This studied determination also marks Gillian as not naturally a member of that elite class milieu (Bourdieu 1976b), whose real members are characterized by inherited wealth, a sense of traditional ownership of the academy (and other domains of power), and a self-conscious perception of themselves as the Establishment and society's leaders. At City Academy, the forms of cultural capital most valued include a confident and casual relation to dominant knowledge, know-how and distinctions, an easiness with elite cultural forms, "good taste," a less deferential attitude to class and privilege, a kind of liberalism that values the diversity of individuals. After entering this school, Gillian worked hard to acquire this easiness, including engaging in what seemed to us a huge range of co-curricular activities. Her busyness gives some insight into the pressures and work involved in becoming a successful middle-class girl—one accomplished in many fields, with a fully rounded personality (see also Walkerdine, Lucey, and Melody 2001; Wyn 2000). City Academy has a public profile of being very strong on girls' education and equity issues and Gillian has learned well the feminist dictum that "girls can do anything." This pressure is also combined with her sense of being an outsider at the academy and produces a kind of gratitude for having so much to do to in order to maximize her opportunities.

Gillian is ambivalent about making friends—she wants acceptance and intimacy but does not initially feel very warmly toward the people with whom she would have to be friends. At the end of Year 9, she remembered Year 8 as an unhappy time because she did not have any friends, but was quick to add that "things are getting better now." She has a keen sense of the proper and appropriate narrative—about the academy and about telling a story about herself as a young woman growing up.

Do you think your personality has changed much since you've grown up?. . .
Gillian: I'm not too sure. I know like I've matured and all that kind of stuff, but I don't think like my moral beliefs have changed. What's really changed the most is I've become aware of different, like different ways of life, different, um, how my personality is different to other people, and that's mainly just because I've met more people.
(Gillian, City Academy, Year 9)

What is distinctive here is the way in which Gillian talks about "difference." Previously, Gillian had represented her difference negatively and as a source of unhappiness—she longs for friends at the Academy, and she is struck by the class contrast between students at the Academy and friends from where she lives.

Is there anything you would like to change about your life?
Gillian: I'd like to have more friends at school . . . but there's a lot of people at this school. . . , I wouldn't really care about it because I don't like them that much anyway.
So you have other friendship groups outside the school?
Gillian: Yes, and that's really good for me because I don't have many friends at school, so it's good to spend time with them. Also I live a long way away, so a lot of my group, like the things that I do . . . are different to people who live here. Different, kind of social, I don't know that sounds really bad, but different social classes kind of. Because like a lot of my friends, I live in W__ and they go to state schools and stuff and it's a lot different and I do different things with them on weekends that I would do with my academy friends, coming from, like, rich families.
Can you tell the difference between the friends who go to state school and the ones who go to the academy?
Gillian: I'd say a lot of the people at the academy are a bit more sheltered. They've never had to go without anything. A lot of people from the academy, and I'm not saying that all my friends are, like really rich or anything, but, they've never really had to struggle, life's been pretty

> easy. I mean, not, that sounds really bad as well, but um . . . a lot of my friends that go to state schools and stuff don't have as much money and that's basically the difference.
>
> (Gillian, City Academy, Year 9)

There are disjunctions in Gillian's everyday school experiences, as she goes from home to school, from old friends to new, and to new forms of social conduct. These give her a heightened sense of her position, and of the kind of person she is, and is becoming. But as noted earlier, "becoming" someone is not always an unequivocal or hopeful process. For Gillian, the prospect of becoming somebody else is approached with degrees of ambivalence and uncertainty. Subject positions are not easily taken up, nor is habitus achieved seamlessly, as if it were a straightforward process of immersion. Gillian expresses on many occasions her uncertainty about how to conduct and be herself in this new milieu. In these various excerpts from the same interview we can hear Gillian worrying over the connotations of "difference"—is it proper to acknowledge economic difference, is class a legitimate difference, is it "good form" to speak of it so openly? On the one hand, the differences between her academy and non-academy friends are plain to her. On the other hand, she hesitates and is anxious about giving the "wrong impression" about class and the academy students: "that sounds really bad," and starts to conflate class difference with personality difference.

In this same interview, at the end of Year 9, Gillian also starts to understand herself within a discourse of personal tolerance, cultural pluralism, and diversity—her personality is simply different, she respects differences in others, different ways of life are okay. Such beliefs echo the ethos of City Academy and were articulated in some form by all of the academy students throughout their interviews. For example, in interviews at the end of Year 10 we asked several questions of students concerning their attitudes about religion, racism, and sexual preference. Consistently, answers at this school were prefaced with statements about the right to freedom of speech and tolerance for other viewpoints and practices, "so long as it doesn't hurt anybody"—the epitome of liberal individualism. When asked about the causes of unemployment, however, none of the students expressed such sympathetic tolerance. Unanimously, unemployment was caused by people who were not motivated enough or had the wrong attitude (this issue is discussed at greater length in chapter 6).

Gillian's subjectivity is being shaped not only by dominant gendered discourses around girls' desire for intimacy and friendship, or by the popular discourses of youth and maturity—growing up is difficult work, adolescence is a confusing period of upheaval. It is also being shaped by her relation to a particular kind of school that offers her ways of rewriting herself whereby, simultaneously, she is taking up a powerful political discourse of (selective) tolerance and pluralism. The difference discourse is so appealing because it enables her to see her sense of being marginal in a different light. It also enables the transformation of what were for Gillian quite disturbing class and cultural differences into relatively benign expressions of social diversity.

By the senior years of school, it seems that Gillian is much more comfortable at the academy, has been making good friends, is active in its social life, and is more at ease with the overall atmosphere; this is also evident in her physical poise and confidence in the interview. Gillian less frequently positions herself as an outsider, and in many instances she expresses views consistent with the other students at City Academy—she, like the other students there, blames unemployment on "lack of motivation." Given comments in earlier interviews on political and ethical values and her overtly compassionate outlook, we found this a surprising response. It suggests one of the ways in which the values of the academy and political outlook of the other students are beginning to shape and be congruent with Gillian's own attitudes. She becomes over time, and with some emotional costs, "at home" and at ease at City Academy.

The relation between the academy's values and Gillian's sense of self can also be seen in her thinking about the future and in her self-descriptions. One of the ways in which Gillian works out how to manage her life—the many demands on her time, her sense of unease at the academy, and experiences of isolation and class differences—is to represent herself as "nice." "Being nice" is a quality she prizes, a demeanor and personality she conscientiously adopts for herself and values in others. Even in the face of unreciprocated niceness, Gillian can still be nice back.

So, if you could just start to describe your personality

Gillian: Well, I'm honest and people can trust me and if you tell me something then I won't tell everyone else. And I'm friendly and so, but even if you don't want to be my best friend it doesn't matter because I can still be nice to you.

(Gillian, City Academy, Year 7)

And, two years later in Year 9, Gillian again describes herself in a similar fashion: "Well, personally, I kind of like everyone to be good and nice to each other most of the time" (Year 9, 1996). For Gillian, being nice, tolerant, and helpful are the preferred ways to navigate social and school relations (and are in keeping with a fellow student, Alannah's, handling of her mathematics teacher, discussed in chapter 3). The alignment of "niceness" with white middle-class femininity has been noted by many other researchers (e.g., Walkerdine and Lucey 1989) and, as Valerie Hey (1997) observes, what constitutes "being nice" for girls, is mediated by and takes on different meanings according to their class, racial, and ethnic identities. Moreover, being nice evokes a normative and inoffensive vision of femininity and offers an appealing, and nonthreatening subject position for many young women. At an immediate level, Gillian presents an archetypal version of the good middle-class good girl—putting self before others, turning the other cheek, and having altruistic values and ambitions. For example, she consistently expresses a desire to teach children with disabilities when she grows up. At other times, it is a vague longing simply to help. In Year 7, she struggled to define this longing: "I just want to know, I mean I know what I want to do, I just want to be able to help some people, and I just want to know that I am going to help them."

At the end of school, Gillian is accepted into an arts-based therapy course at the most prestigious university in her city, a course with high entry score requirements. Undertaking this course fulfills her interest in helping others, and because of its selective status at an elite university also measures up to the expectations of the academy and the high performing culture of its graduates.

It would be reductive, however, to read Gillian's desire to be helpful and nice as evidence of her simply and inevitably taking up a gendered subject position of conventional meek and mild femininity. First, it is a practical response to her family situation. Gillian's subjectivity is formed in relation to discourses of obligation and responsibility and her family is crucial in this respect. Both parents have demanding jobs, she helps with cooking and other domestic chores, and so on. There are, then, strong material and emotional reasons for her investment in the girl as "selfless helper" discourse.

Second, Gillian's negotiation of the social relations at City Academy suggest that she is working through ways of being successful in that environment that run counter to the feminist reforming zeal to make girls less nice and good and more shrewd and worldly. In this sense, there is something quite strategic, rather than habitually or thoughtlessly feminine, in Gillian's conduct. "Being nice," tolerant, and considerate, thinking of others less fortunate than ourselves also represent a set of values encouraged by City Academy. It provides a position from which Gillian can speak and forge her identity in a new and difficult environment: here the ethos of the school (excellence, liberal individualism, respect for diversity) intersects with discourses of dominant middle-class femininity. City Academy prizes tolerance for all its students, for them to be nice to "others," and fosters a marketable, middle-class successful femininity for girls, encouraging them into appropriate professional careers. "Being nice" is thus a resourceful way of managing her social and personal relations and of working against unhappiness. But, clearly, it is also a gendered response—and it tells us something about the constraints on her "improvisations" and the (limited) range of subject positions available to her to survive at City Academy as a girl from the other side of town.

It is also possible to read the desire to be nice and helpful in a less literal way and to move toward a more psychoanalytic account of her repeated insistence on niceness. For example, it could be in speaking so much of the need to help others that Gillian is also speaking about her own need for help, for others to be nice to be her, a reversal of her stated feelings—her isolation at school, her work at home.[5] Or taking up an analysis informed by understandings of the psychosocial subject as a "defended subject" (Hollway and Jefferson 2000), we could argue that Gillian's insistence on niceness is a defense against, a repudiation of her own not-nice feelings of aggression or hostility to others, a reaction to being in a school milieu where she feels an outsider and in home/school life where so much is demanded of her time and her work. Such fears and losses could be interpreted more psychoanalytically, but even without pursuing that line of analysis (which our study was not intended to develop), we can see how becoming somebody, a particular kind of success-oriented, self-consciously nice young girl, caring for others while learning to take privilege in her stride, was not a straightforward adaptation of the self to a new environment—her habitus was not formed in a simple and uncontested alignment with the field. Disjunction and contradiction and change over time were part of that process as well. Nor was it a celebratory opportunity of "becoming" someone, but was marked with ambivalence, uncertainty, and some sense of loss. The contradictions and tensions she experienced are partly submerged in her final interviews, but in listening to Gillian over the course of her secondary years, we gain insights into her project to become a particular subject, her struggles to become a certain kind of person; as well as the processes of shaping, including the relations of habitus and field, in which that project is being forged and reforged.

In the videos of Gillian's interviews, we observe her becoming less physically and socially awkward over time, and watch her beginning to embody a self-assurance and social confidence in her demeanor and gaze: we see her looking like, indeed, "becoming," a private school girl. While she continues to see her future in terms of helping others, her good girl, worthy, self-sacrificing femininity is gradually being challenged by the expectations of a different kind of successful, less self-abnegating though no less sensitive and caring femininity. Her turning away from studying "regular teaching" (as not good enough?) can also be read as another sign of the way in which the professional and elite middle-class values of City Academy are being taken up by and becoming part of her. Gillian gradually learns to take on the demeanor and poise of the successful, high-achieving girl, a subject position that is congruent with both the professional, middle-class values of City Academy and with the aspirations of a "girls can do anything" equity feminism that also informs the academy's ethos. The social and political goals of one influential kind of feminism coalesce with class ambition.

Over the period of our longitudinal study, we were able to observe the shaping of Gillian's subjectivity in interaction with her school ethos, and to see how her own biographical projects (to be nice, to be compassionate) persist yet also change. In a very specific educational institution and socially powerful milieu, Gillian has moved from feeling a relative outsider to being more at home. After a difficult period of hesitation and uneasiness, Gillian now embraces not only the dominant forms of conduct (the compulsiveness of edifying extracurricular activities) but also embodies the dispositions, aspirations, physical poise, and habits of thought that distinguish both the social cachet and the market appeal of this elite Academy.

Gillian's gendered story is one that embodies elements of both gendered traditions and of "New Times"—the very deliberate project of the self. It is one shaped both by big social discursive themes and the discursive themes of a particular school environment (indeed, literally by its ways of talking); it is one where both the social contexts and also the emotional and psychological pull of the demands of "becoming" are evident. In our narrative of Gillian's passage through school we show how what happens to individuals in particular schools is part of how patterns of inequality and difference are produced and reproduced (illustrating interactions between habitus and field) and how biographical and sociological projects are intertwined. Our intervention too is part of the story: we were asking Gillian to "tell us about herself." Compared with Keren or Brett, she is relatively comfortable with this demand—and that too is part of the story of who she is and how she is "becoming."

CHAPTER 5

Dreams and Pathways: Identity-Making and Vocational Choices

Clare: Sometimes I just meet some people, and it's just like, "what do you want to do in your life?" Like, "um, I don't know."

Alice: Sometimes you just say it because you don't really want to go into it. Sometimes I feel it's like a personal thing. You are sort of working out what you want to do, and you just sort of, you're not definite, you don't know what's going to happen.

(13 year old girls, Year 8, City Academy 1995)

You just sort of have dreams, but some of them you know probably won't come true.

(13 year old girl, Year 8, Regional Technical 1995)

How young people today imagine and make plans for their futures is of widespread concern—to governments and policy-makers, to school administrators, parents, young people themselves, and to social theorists and youth sociologists researching contemporary forms of identity. To understand social patterns and directions, policy-makers commonly rely on survey-based data on what young people think and large-scale data, such as the "facts and figures" of who is now achieving what, or entering certain courses, and undertaking types of jobs. Within policy domains, answers given to such questions as "What do you want to be when you leave school?" tend to be taken at face value, and young people and students are frequently constructed as an "other" whose answers and psychology are transparent. The Longitudinal Survey of Australian Youth (LSAY), for example, is a longitudinal, time-series data-set that surveys cohorts of young people and is able to show some broad changes over time. However, it is constantly faced with the problem of what particular data means: whether the questions have the same meaning at different times; how the answers relate to the broader thinking and decisions the young people make. What 12 year olds, or 15 year olds say when you ask them questions about the future is very far from being a transparent window to their thinking and daydreaming. And, as our opening interview excerpts suggest, the actual experience of being asked research questions about "what do you want to do?" is itself an intervention that produces certain kinds of answers, and ways of representing and constituting the self. "Sometimes you just say it because you don't really want to go into it," one 13-year-old girl told us. "You are sort of working out what you want to do, and . . . you're not definite, you don't know what is going to happen." "You just sort of have dreams, but some of them you know probably won't come true."

Much research on youth futures has tracked transitions, documenting either continuities or disruptions in both the experience and meaning of transition from school to work for young people today, and examining "students' hopes and fears in the face of new labor market realities" (Dwyer and Wyn 2001, 100). For our participants, labor market options and changes were clearly relevant to their sense and knowledge of what was possible, but we began at a different starting point from most studies of youth transitions and post-school pathways. We began talking to our participants about futures when they are 12 years old, at the beginning of their secondary school years in Australia, a time when there is much talk of "growing up" and leaving behind the childhood years of elementary school. We talked to them regularly over the six years of high school about their future plans and their daydreams and hopes for their future. We listened to how their thinking did or did not change as they got older, and to how they responded to school-based and family and peer interventions to become more "serious," "rational," and vocational as they approached the end of school and the transition to the labor market or higher education. But future thinking is not only about making pragmatic transitions. In asking open questions about daydreams as well as about more explicit and short-term intentions, we tried to see the biographical subject within his or her pattern of decision-making. Our interest in this chapter is how dreams and emotional longings about becoming a particular person are intimately linked to such decisions about the future. Well-meaning, instrumental programs of "career counseling" in which information about jobs is given in the senior years, or advice that simply tries to match decisions with aptitudes, fail to engage with the deeper sense of "who I am" or "who I want to become" that leads young people to identify, or not identify, with certain careers and pathways.

Young people's future thinking combines ideas about "destinations" (what sort of job I would like) and desires about being and becoming a certain type of person—these are not neatly separable orientations. Yet in research and policy discussions about young people's futures, "daydreams," and "pathways" tend to occupy different worlds. The language of pathways and destinations is more likely to be part of concerns about vocational directions, labor market options, tracking cohorts, studying transitions, and analyzing institutional structures and supports. Attention to daydreaming and dreams is associated with a more interpretive focus on subjective meanings and evident in a cultural studies fascination with subjectivity, youth culture, and nonrational forms of being in the world. Cohen and Ainley (2000), reviewing the diverging concerns of youth studies and cultural studies in the United Kingdom, criticize these bifurcated trajectories, arguing that the "youth studies" and "pathways" variant has become overly empiricist and/or narrowly economistic and labor-market focused, while the "cultural studies" community often romanticizes subjectivity and overinterprets dreams as indicators of social transformation, with scant attention to structural inequalities. In terms of the former trend, they note that there is insufficient research examining how changes in the stages of life (e.g., from youth to adult) are actually negotiated by young people. Consequently, in the plethora of findings on pathways and transition patterns, we still do not know enough about the decision-making and motivations of young people. In terms of the limitations of the culturalist trend, Cohen and Ainley suggest that the focus on, for example, hybridity, discourse and deviance or the coolness of youth cultures has developed alongside a depoliticization of the cultural studies project and a lack of interest in questions about structural inequalities.[1] Cohen and Ainley propose a "third space" for youth studies, one that is interdisciplinary and integrates elements of these two traditions, analyzing subjective desires and motivations in relation to changing social, economic, and structural contexts.

In our longitudinal study we were attempting to do something of this kind, building an analysis that combines a focus on the structural and social context of young people's pathways and destinations with attention to the dreams and projections that animate their decisions and longings about the future and their sense of who they want to become.

The summary story of what happened to people in our study in terms of school and pathways at 18 is given in our appendixes. The numbers are small, but in this summary form, the overall story of what happened to them is in keeping with patterns that are already known well from the data-tracking studies that monitor patterns of school retention, tertiary study, occupation by SES and gender, and so on. Of the twenty-six, sixteen had completed school at age 18 (and three were still attempting to do so); and girls were much more successful than boys in completing school. In keeping with patterns of the 1990s compared with earlier decades, girls too are more represented in university courses than boys; boys are more likely to be trying to get work or an apprenticeship directly from school. In terms of occupations entered, the summary picture is slightly more sex-stereotyped than the overall statistics indicate, and is a more gender-differentiated list of occupations than had been apparent to us when we were actually conducting the project. Girls at 18 were studying law, commerce, music therapy, arts and three were entering nursing; boys were drawn to computing studies, mechanical engineering, medical technology, and work or apprenticeships in gardening and building trades. Looking at the pattern by "class" (a problematic concept, of course, that we discuss in a later chapter) and by school location and type, we also find patterns that are broadly in keeping with the big picture statistics. Of the students at the private school, at 18 only one is not at university (and that is because of involvement in drugs and rehabilitation); students from middle backgrounds at the two "middle" high schools show a pattern in which about half enter university (usually lesser ranked universities and courses than those from the private school), a few go on to training in a technical college, and others try to find work. The school and students who represent poorer backgrounds produce one who enters a low-ranked university, one who is doing some limited training, one who has part-time work, and two others who at 18 are unemployed and looking for work. But these summaries are a quite imperfect way of seeing what these young people are doing and choosing in a situation in which the meaning and opportunities of given jobs, and of given training routes, is shifting. A one-word descriptor of occupation or course at

18 only tells a small part of the story of the directions in which different young people are developing their lives. We return to this issue in our chapter on class (chapter 7) as well as in our chapter on gender and change (chapter 8). The people we followed were engaging with a world that was changing, both in the jobs that were disappearing, appearing, becoming more and less important, and also in the story that was being conveyed to girls in school about the types of ambitions they should have, the types of career they should aim to achieve.

What would you like to be doing when you're 25?
Sue: a vet or an airhostess [. . .] I want to go around the world
Jenna: Why don't you be a pilot then? Pilot's better than being an air hostess.

(Jenna, Suburban High, Year 7, age 13)
[at 18 Jenna is still trying to finish school]

Amelie: I want to go into the airforce for a while, and then perhaps go commercial or something . . . and I just think about everything that I want to do when I'm older, like travel and things.

(Amelie, Suburban High, Year 7, age 13)
[at 18 Amelie is studying to be a nurse]

In this chapter, we develop a detailed study of one young woman, Nicky, and her changing dreams and plans for her future. In part this is to illustrate the methodological and interpretive benefit of interweaving both "pathways" and "dreams," and in part to investigate from a more biographical angle the themes concerning subjectivity, habitus, and gender change that were discussed in a more theoretical mode in the preceding chapter.

Girls and young women today are frequently represented as the new success story, the bearers of academic excellence, the overachievers at school, and the beneficiaries of feminism who can "have it all." The discourses and representations of modern girlhood have been the subject of much scholarly attention (e.g. Driscoll 2002; Harris 2004; Johnson 1993) as well as the focus of many policy and professional debates in education concerning gender equity and the relative success and girls and boys (Arnot, David, and Weiner 1999; Gilbert and Gilbert 2001; Yates 1997). In the kind of gender detraditionalized futures depicted by, for example, Beck and Beck-Gernsheim (1995, 2002) and alive in popular and media discourses, girls collectively are facing futures that break with many conventional patterns and expectations. One obvious criticism of such beliefs is that success, bright futures, and detraditionalized opportunities are structurally differentiated, that such futures are not equally available to all girls, even though the representation of the ideal may be culturally powerful. Similarly, an exclusive or even predominant focus on representations of girlhood can overstate the authority of such discourses and presume a common and unproblematic uptake of those discursive norms and meanings. The association of femininity with success destabilizes understandings of the conventional successes expected to flow to men, but also raises questions about how young women will themselves negotiate the imperatives to be successful, to be their own person. Rather than look mainly at gender differences in outcomes data or via dominant cultural discourses about girlhood, we begin in this chapter from the biographical and explore the interweaving of dreams, destinations. and social constructions to illuminate how social changes and popular and academic discourses concerning gender futures, individualization, and becoming your own person are negotiated within a specific social class and schooling context.

Earlier in the book, we argued for seeing the particularity of the experiences we have been studying as in some way "speaking back" to and enriching theoretical discussions. But, equally, we were concerned from the beginning about how a study of twenty-six lives can speak to more general issues for education, how particular experiences and meanings can be used as evidence of something more general. In this chapter, we confront and explore this dilemma—how and why one young woman's narrative about her self and her future is revealing and matters. What might it have to say beyond its own particularity?[2] Most obviously, in terms of standard categorizations, Nicky's particularities include that she is a girl; that she attends a private school; that she comes from an upper professional background; that she is of Anglo-Australian heritage. In other chapters, we give some detailed attention to people in our study who would be characterized differently. In chapter 8, we provide an extended consideration of three boys from different schools; earlier, in chapter 3, and again in chapter 6, attention to those with different ethnic affiliations and experiences; and in a number of chapters we talk about Keren, a girl from a relatively poor background at the poorest school in our study. But the particularities of Nicky's experiences and the ways they are framed and reframed by her go beyond those relatively crude categorical descriptors, and that is one issue we are trying to illuminate in this chapter. Nevertheless, the specificity of Nicky's dreaming and pathways is illuminated further by considering comparisons with those other young people in our study, just as those we discuss elsewhere are being interpreted, by us, in implicit dialogue with her. In reading Nicky's story we draw out themes that are powerful for her, and that resonate in the stories of other young women in our study, as well as in popular and academic discourses about contemporary gender relations and young women. We also try to show the different readings and lines of interpretation that we can bring to Nicky's story. As we have argued, individual lives and specificities exceed any single theoretical account that seeks to give the full picture or explanation of them (see also Plumridge and Thomson 2003).

Through a close-up reading of Nicky's dreams and ambitions, we illustrate some of the ways in which cultural discourses and motifs of modernity—such as imperatives and tasks to become your "own person" along with the impact of changes associated with feminism and women's working lives—are mediated subjectively. We can observe the intersecting effects of school and family habitus, in this case when they are in relative alignment,[3] and see how dispositions are shaped in and by those milieux; but we also see how that process is not seamless—despite the correspondence between home and school—and happens recursively. At the same time, we show that decisions and orientations to the future are not simply determined by family and class habitus in a narrow economic or status or occupational strata sense—nor are they free from these influences and sense of norms and possibilities. By exploring this issue biographically, we can capture the interplay of dreams and desires with the more structured effects of school and family location on habitus. We more briefly move to consider other participants, both to contrast with Nicky's agendas and choices and to follow through some of the other ways in which dreams of the future interweave with social location, community, and class.

Nicky attends City Academy, a school that places much pressure on being a distinctive person, and where the formation of such "individuals" constitutes a significant element of the school's market positioning. In that school culture, the task of becoming "your own person" is an overdetermined and complicated struggle—how to be distinctive in the face of so much distinction and privilege—and practices of self-reflexivity are especially pronounced. Nicky's story indicates the double-edged qualities of such self-scrutiny and forms of self-management. These are much discussed generalized features of late modernity but ones that are highly intensified for middle-class young women. We draw out the ambivalence of Nicky's positioning in relation to discourses of conventional and "modern" womanhood, and especially her attitudes to motherhood and what it means to be a successful woman today.

Nicky's Story

In the early years of high school, when we asked our participants whether they thought about the future, many of the girls talked in optimistic and energetic ways about their daydreams. These were full of images of adventure and independence—driving fast cars, travel overseas, journeying into space. Year 7 girls at City Academy in particular talked at length and with great excitement about what they would like to be doing at age 25—being a part-time lawyer and a part-time model and traveling the world, for example. "When I am 25 I want to be traveling around the world . . . I just want to go everywhere"; "When I'm older I'll be a big gambler. A big card player. I love cards." And "I want to bungee jump . . . I want to sky dive". These girls spoke confidently of establishing professional and creative careers and living an exciting and independent life. However, one girl at City Academy, Nicky, after saying she thought she would like to be a photographer (she had recently been on a big family holiday and taken lots of photographs), added:

> I'm always thinking about like how many kids I want to have and like . . . I can't wait until I get married and all this and mum's going "I can't believe that you're thinking about this now, I mean I didn't think about that till I was like 20." Like I think about it all the time.
>
> (Nicky, City Academy, Year 7, age 12)

This was our first interview with Nicky, and she told us that her daydreams about her future life included photography, being a busker (a street performer), and traveling:

> But what you want to do when you're older, like I'm always thinking I'd love to travel around the world and just be taking photos all the time and then I've always wanted to be a busker or something. Be a half time busker. I've always had like an easygoing life, I can just imagine it.
>
> (Nicky, City Academy, Year 7, age 12)

At the same time as she was making plans for this creative life, she made clear that she also spent a lot of time daydreaming about who she would marry, planning the details of her imagined wedding, the sort of dresses her bridesmaids would wear, and so on.

As we talked to her each half-year over the next few years, Nicky mentioned many different careers she might take up. Later in the first year, it was being a photographer or fashion designer; the following year, a kindergarten teacher or perhaps a lawyer. She often mentioned dreaming of travel, enjoying an easy life, and having children. In the local schooling system there is a two-year final certificate, and students must make important subject and program choices at the end of their Year 10, when they are usually 15 or 16 years old. At this point, schools generally offer careers advice, and subject choice becomes an important focus for teachers, students and parents. Further, in the Australian system, different university courses require particular school subjects as prerequisites, especially various mathematics and science subjects, and this adds to the pressure to make the "right" choices. In our first interview with her in Year 10, and at a time when subject selection and future pathways were on students' minds, we asked Nicky whether she had any idea what job she wanted to do when she finished school.

> I think that every time I do this I say a different job. But I don't really want to have a job where I have to go to it every day. Like I sort of want to have my own, like do it when I want to do it, do you know what I mean. Like I wouldn't mind doing like natural healing and aromatherapy courses, stuff like that and just maybe have my own work from home just for a few people and not go into it, you know, five days a week. Just sort of do art and just not have, I don't know if that means I'm going to have to marry someone rich or anything like that, but just happy sort of, not really doing much.
>
> (Nicky, City Academy, Year 10, age 16)

By the end of that year, Nicky had decided more definitely that she wanted to do naturopathy. Her mother had taken her to a private career counselor, and she had a detailed knowledge of what this course involved and which subjects she would need to take. She even knew the strategies for maximizing results within that course.

> People who do chemistry in Year 11 and then biology in Year 12 actually go better than the people who do biology all year. Yeah. And so that's

> what she said and I sort of get both and I don't really like chemistry so I'm happy I'm only doing one year of it. I don't really like science at all, but at least I'll get a change.
>
> (Nicky, City Academy, Year 10, age 16)

Early the next year, however, Nicky had rethought this plan, and had changed both her career direction and subject choice. After talking to her friends, she had decided she is a "crafty, arty person," not a "science person."

> Yeah, I sort of thought last year I was going to become a naturopath and I was like really set that you know these subjects might be a bit boring that I'm doing, but they'll be fun if I concentrate and just do the work. You know I'll be fine and get a good TER or whatever. And now I'm just sort of a bit more focused on me personally, what I want to do. Like I have to, I'm as I said a sort of crafty, arty person and everyone's like "why aren't you doing art?" and I'm like "I don't know, why aren't I?," you know. I'm not a science person, yet I was doing two sciences and I'm just like, I can't be doing this. Sort of feeling more who I am as a person and going with that.
>
> (Nicky, City Academy, Year 11, age 17)

Nicky successfully completed her end-of-school certificate, and was accepted into a university course in fashion design. When we interviewed her in the first year of this course, she was enjoying it, though she had found it socially difficult being in a course and at a university that was not attended by many students from her previous school. Most students from City Academy went on to courses in traditional professions at a more prestigious university. She talks again about wanting to have children while she is young, and about wanting to travel and be "somebody":

> Yeah, I see myself as lots of things but as . . . I have this whole . . . I live in the clouds a bit, where I just want to be famous and own these things and, I get so excited when I see celebrities and all kinds of things and I want to be at the top kind of, but then I don't, I don't know I guess everyone wants that a bit. Maybe not.
>
> (Nicky, first year after completing school, age 18, 2000)

In looking closely at Nicky's biographical narratives over the school years, what are the particularities of her experiences and circumstances? How do they shape the way she represents herself and poses questions about "who am I" and "who will I become"? She comes from comfortably wealthy circumstances, with a father who is a lawyer and a mother not in paid employment but who is busy with social and family life, and Nicky represents her family relationships as close. She attends a private school in which almost no student fails to complete school, and where, although it is academically nonselective, the great majority of students get final results that rank them in the top 20 percent of the state. In the Australian system of education important choices must be made in the final years of school, since entry to prestigious careers largely occurs at the entry point of university rather than in graduate school following a more general period of college. There is a relatively simple and public hierarchy of post-school institutions, rather than one where students may face many choices of fine gradations of university and college statuses and profiles (as in the United States). Nicky is negotiating her life and dreaming about and making plans for her future at a particular time in history, one when there has been substantial restructuring of the economy and labor market. In countries such as Australia, many traditional factory jobs have largely disappeared and been replaced by technology or exported offshore, and the production of consumer goods (such as fashion), technology, service, and knowledge industries are increasingly important. In cultural discourse (at least in the family and school circles in which Nicky is located), "creative industries" receive serious attention (photography and fashion sit well within this); and alternative therapies (naturopathy) are increasingly popular, both with consumer choices, and with proliferating university training courses. These contexts obviously have an impact on what is going to be possible for Nicky, and for students like her, but her decisions and future thinking about what she will do are also shaped by her own emotional investments and dreams about who she is and who she wants to become.

Future Thinking and Identity Work

Longitudinal interviews offer a distinctive perspective on young people's sense of their futures by showing how plans and daydreams form incrementally and how the emphasis in ways of thinking can shift. Such shifts include revisions of plans as well as scaling up or reining back ambitions, reframing of what counts as success, and the shifting significance of antecedent influences, such as friends' judgments, or teachers' interventions. Additionally, long, relatively open interviews offer places in which issues about the self and the future are talked about from different starting points and agendas. In the case of Nicky, there is some consistency through the years in the themes she flags as important to her: friendship, family—both current family and her own anticipated children and family life—and having a good "free-wheeling" life. We can plot changes and similarities in any specific future career directions she nominates: at 12 photographer/busker/fashion designer; at 13 kindergarten teacher; at 14 "lots of different ideas"; at 15 "aromatherapy and art"; at 16 "lots of ideas"; in the final year of school silence on this issue; and at 18 beginning fashion design at university. But the methodological distinctiveness arises also from our being able to hear and be told certain things, which happens only because the contact is maintained over quite a long time. Following Nicky through the seven years of interviews, we have a chance to hear not only what she chooses to prioritize as themes, but how she successively and retrospectively constructs and repositions who she was and who she is now.

In our first year of interviews, for example, Nicky presented herself as happy and bubbly, and described the best thing about school as her friends. It is only two years later that she talks about her most unhappy time as a period at the end of that first year when she felt betrayed and accused by her friends. Now she says;

> Year 7 was a really, really bitchy year . . . there were always fights, and always letters being sent, there was just different letters from all of your friends. One page letter they told me that I'd never be able to share a real friendship with anyone. . . . It was pretty harsh for year 7.
>
> (Nicky, City Academy, Year 9, age 15)

Throughout the interviews over the seven years, the issue of friendship keeps recurring, usually in a couplet emphasizing relationships with others and struggles to be herself. She talks regularly about the importance of her group of friends, about how happy she is with her particular group of friends, and her worries about whether she will maintain these friends after she leaves school and, at the same time, she returns again and again to the question of "being herself" and sorting out "who I am as a person." In Year 10 (age 15), she says

> *What makes you happy?*
>
> My friends . . . a really big group of really nice friends. And we're not all the same. I just love it, because compared with Year 7 and 8, there's no bitching any more and everyone's just, can express what they want to express and be who they want to be and no-one is like, oh my God, look what she's wearing, and things like that . . . and everyone trusts everyone, and you're liked for who you are. . you don't have to put on any act or try hard to be liked and stuff
>
> (Nicky, City Academy Year 10, age 15)

Similarly, she explains her decision to alter directions in her final school years, by dropping science and giving up her intention to do aromatherapy, both as an issue about what kind of person she is and as a decision that comes to her through her friends' voices:

> And now I'm just sort of a bit more focused on me personally, what I want to do. Like . . . I'm as I said a sort of crafty, arty person, and everyone's like, "why aren't you doing art?" and I'm like, "I don't know, why aren't I?" I'm not a science person, yet I was doing two sciences, and I'm just, like, I can't be doing this. Sort of feeling more who I am as a person, and going with that.
>
> (Nicky, City Academy Year 11, age 16)

In retrospect, Nicky noticed how prominent her friends and family were in her earlier narratives. When she viewed her compilation videotape at the end of our project, Nicky remarked that

> I really picked up on my friends and my family being everything to me—like I talked of my family the whole time and I depended on them.
>
> (Nicky, in the year after finishing school age 18, 2000)

In reviewing the videotape, she astutely noticed that when responding to our questions she had often sought reassurance from us about whether we were following what she was saying. We had noticed this too at the actual time of the interviews, but had interpreted it in a somewhat different way. We read Nicky's concern about how we were hearing what she was saying as not simply a concern about clarity of communication. Rather, we interpreted it as her concern for how we were seeing (and judging?) her, and her concern about how we, as embodied, feeling subjects, were being affected by what she was saying. At one interview, for example, where she had talked relatively freely about a period of rebellion and deception of her parents in the middle high school years, she turned to us and said she hoped that her telling us such things would not make us worry about our own children: at the time, one of us, Julie, had a young child and a baby. In the final interview, Nicky, without prompting from us, returned to this issue, recalling when Julie had been pregnant, and at a later interview arriving with a baby in a stroller. Nicky remembered feeling concerned that what we were hearing about her rebellions and relationships with her parents would make Julie worry about her future relationships with her baby. And she wanted to know if that had been the case: had what she told us caused us any distress?

In telling Nicky's story in this way, we have touched on many of the issues that are variously taken up by theorists of modernity, of gendered identity, and of education and the new labor market. In the ways she talks about school and in the ways she talks about her future, Nicky has an intense interest in "who am I?," and is acutely aware of cultural norms and her own positioning in relation to them. In her self-monitoring and practices of self-reflection, she exemplifies the culture of the self, and the imperative to construct and regard the self as a "biographical project." We can also see that for Nicky such responsibilities for making her own life are comfortably cushioned by her family's material circumstances and the cultural authority she obtains from attending City Academy. She is, because of her social class and her access to private career counseling, knowledgeable about career pathways, and strategic and astute as to what needs to be done to pursue certain directions. Yet her thinking and choices are not simply motivated by such rational, linear, and strategic planning. She has a wealth of different fantasies about who she might be and these intersect with her and her family's efforts to determine a career. No sooner does she embark on the strategic path planned jointly with her mother and career counselor, than she decides that this is not for her. She keeps to the forefront her desire to have a family while young, even though she knows this is no longer the norm for those of her gender and class or regarded as a smart or success-oriented move. But it is a desire she embraces with optimism and excitement, and is determined to make her future one that combines motherhood and success. Although the imperatives to self-construction and making a successful life can be self-punitive and burdensome, they can also be sources of pleasure and exciting possibilities.

Gender—The Changing Meanings of "Who Girls Are"

Nicky's story and her dreams and ambitions are clearly formed in a particular school and family habitus, and at the intersections of her gender/class and ethnic positioning. Nevertheless, the energy and enthusiasm with which she spoke about her daydreams in the early years of high school were characteristic of all the girls in our study, except the poorest.

> It sounds a bit queer, but I'd love to go into space . . .
>
> Leanne and I were talking last night, like what we want to do. Like I didn't want to do bungee jumping and Lisa did, and abseiling and things.
>
> I'd like to try skydiving. I'd love to be able to fly some day.
>
> I'd like to be an architect or photographer or something like that. Yeah, and I'd like to do things like the bungee jumping and skydiving . . . .
>
> I'd like to travel.
>
> (Regional High School, Year 7 girls)
>
> I'd like to have two big St. Bernard dogs. That's what I'd like to have, and I'd like to have a Harley and a convertible, and then drive along with my two St. Bernard dogs in the back.
>
> When I'm 25 I want to get a red Porsche, drive with my boyfriend to a nightclub and eat custard tarts.
>
> (City Academy, Year 7 girls)

These images and daydreams are not simply literal objectives, nor are they unrelated to images offered in television and films depicting the good life and "exciting times." But the images (and the energy with which girls narrated them) speak to desires that are important in their lives at this time—drive to some sense of independence and freedom, a glimpse of future possibilities for a more exciting life. And these aspirations for adventure and freedom do not signify only in relation to an imagined future life. In many of these interviews, girls also expressed strong desires to be free from their own mothers, to be independent and not caught up in family dynamics. The desires for freedom in the future were also reflections on their relationships in the present, and in part projections of a desire to escape from their current experiences of confinement and surveillance.

Diana: Sometimes it's nice to just imagine if you've got your own place. It's just, sometimes you just want to get away from your family, like you just hate your family. Like you just, you just get sick of everything and you just want to be by yourself, like, oh, not by yourself, but like just have your own house, and then it's yours and you can do whatever you want. You can, no one telling you what to do, and you just, yeah, you can do whatever you want.

Nicky: I've got heaps of things I'd love to be when I'm older, but also, it's sort of, when you get older, you're more independent and that. I hate it when I go shopping when I go shopping with my mum and I'll see something that I really like and she'll say no, you're not going to get it. But when I'm older I can get whatever I want, sort of thing [. . .] Yes, I think it would be really fun to sort of having your own life, and like a good job.

(City Academy, Year 7, 12 year old girls)

Can you imagine what it will be like when, say, you're about 25? What do you think you'll each be doing, or your life will be like when you're 25?

Linda: Well, I'll have . . . I'll probably be in a house with cats everywhere and I'll be sick with a cold or something. And the dogs. With cat food everywhere and my mum coming over worrying about me . . . out on some deserted island or something. So she can't come.

(Suburban High, Year 7 girl, age 12)

At an age when these girls are wanting to rebel against their mothers, the discourse of gender reform and the imperative for girls to broaden their horizons gives an energy and optimism to their orientations to the future and quest for independence. Gender reform encourages and prizes young women's independence, and this meshes with their own desires for escape. The girls' closeness to and awareness of their mother are not simply sources of psychological strain for them, as is often presumed—such tensions are able to be channeled quite productively in many cases. These themes are particularly intense with the middle-class girls, precisely because of the emphasis on individuality and achievement in middle-class life. This phenomenon has been noted for some time and examined by theorists as diverse as Gilligan, Lyons, and Hanmer (1990) in their psychological studies of girls' struggles for autonomy; Walkerdine and Lucey in their study of working-class and middle class patterns of mothering (1989); Bernstein's (1977) work on class, codes, and control; Connell et al.'s (1982) sociological study of the connections between the practices of private schools and "renovated femininity"; and in recent studies of class and schooling by writers such as Proweller (1998), Brantlinger (2003), Ball (2003) and Power et al. (2003).

The family (and their school) are nurturing individuality, a process that incorporates some rebellion against regulation, but one that also makes sure the girls do recognize the practices needed for success, such as attention to schoolwork and appropriate career aspirations. The discussion of Alannah in chapter 3 alluded to these themes; here we found her mother wanting to secure a better mathematics teacher for Alannah, and Alannah actually working out her own way of doing this independently from her mother, managing her academic progress without damaging her school social relations, which, as she astutely realized, was as equally important for being a successful student at her school as academic performance. Middle-class girls like Nicky expressed desires to be free from their mother's control, but they commonly took up their mothers' hopes that they would do well, and concerns about doing enough school work to succeed—and usually by the final years of the project were expressing greater warmth in relation to their mothers and empathizing retrospectively with their mothers' concerns about themselves.

The dreams we heard in many of the interviews with the girls are neither about a single, coherent theme, nor do they necessarily express contradictory desires. The girls' dreams do not simply represent rational and strategic ambitions, nor are they only a product of absorbing the social messages of the day, and yet they also are not only wishful fantasies. Their dreams combine elements of all these dimensions, but are not reducible to one or the other. The girls' dreams are a conjunction of desires, dynamics, and social and emotional processes that, in contemporary circumstances, may produce new identity outcomes and shifts in gender relations and positioning.

At the private school and the higher levels of the social hierarchy, the girls are extremely ambitious and usually very successful at school, but this is not without its own pressures. For this class of girls, it is not simply that there are greater opportunities today, but that they take on the whole range of possibilities of extreme success as a burden of expectation and psychologically dwell on their inability to live up to the impossible dreams. In Walkerdine, Lucey, and Melody's (2001) study of girlhood today they discuss the experiences of middle-class girls who got outstanding A-level results and were doing prestigious courses, such as medicine at Cambridge, but felt as if they were frauds because they had to work at this success rather than feeling that it came easily for them (see also Wyn 2000). In our study, so many of the girls dreamt of the glamorous and successful life that had everything: extreme career success in more than one field, glamour, excitement, and travel, plenty of money, and only part-time work so that they were at ease and not stressed. At City Academy, girls like Nicky wanted to be in the school play and the school musical, to hold a part-time job and also be constantly going to parties, and then to be an excellent skier or dancer or horsewoman, to be excelling academically, and so on. These were aspirations that the school also fostered in its promotion of co-curricular programs. Over the middle high school years the girls' sense of themselves and of the future is developing with a sense of new openness and possibility and adventure. But in this swirling sense of multiple possibility and endless expectations of themselves and from others there is a risk that the spiral of achievement and options could come crashing down around them. Many of our participants see their parents' lives as extremely stressed, and explicitly remarked that they did not want to be like their parents. This is in part a desire for generational differentiation and individuation, but also a desire to actually not take on the way of life of their busy, "time-poor" parents. Yet, for many of these middle-class girls in particular, the cultivation of an independent and successful identity required an equally intensive amount of labor.

Ambivalence of Gender Positioning

Nicky was unique among the girls in our study because of the stress she gave to her dream of getting married and having children young and her willingness to verbalize this as her dream. But this does not mean that she was unaffected by the current changed expectations for middle-class girls. She made clear that her parents expected her to be successful; she knew that her dreams of having children young were widely perceived as aberrant. In Australia, the average age of first childbirth is over 28, and for middle-class professional women, it is common to wait until the mid-30s. In terms of public life, she is full of a million dreams of ways to achieve and be a distinctive person. Her visit to a private career counselor equips her with a customized career plan, designed to match her individual aptitudes and preferences. In more subtle ways too, her own aspirations are not simply a reiteration of stereotyped femininity. Nicky is clear, for example, that she does not want to be like her mother, who does not work in paid employment, but leads a social life, with some involvement in charity work and fund-raising for the school. Nicky describes her as a real "mum mum"—someone who does not work outside the home and whose activities are family and leisure oriented. Today, at least for this professional class and especially for those associated with this elite school, to be a "mum mum" does not count as being a full person. Interestingly, this is the same mother who today tells Nicky she believes it is strange to be thinking about getting married and having children at her age and who actively orchestrates some strategic career planning for her.

So Nicky is explicitly both not wanting to be like her mother and leading a life in which her main identity is as a mother, and wanting to have a life in which being a mother is central but in which more excitement and a more public identity are somehow acquired on a part-time basis. Nicky's thinking and dreaming about her own future are thus cut across by her desire to be a mother, but not be like her mother, a desire that reflects psychodynamic tensions as well as cultural and social changes in gender norms. Nicky's dream of being her own person and her own kind of "mum" captures ideas of the "modern woman" doing it all, and the confidence of the professional classes in which the actual material conditions for achieving such a life are not an overt worry. As Nicky at aged 16 says about her future:

> Just sort of do art and just not have [to work all the time], I don't know if that means I'm going to have to marry someone rich or anything like that, but just happy sort of, not really doing much. (Nicky, Year 10, aged 16)

Interviews with Nicky also suggest that the discursive story of gender today is not simply the backlash one that there has been too much attention to girls who are now unproblematically the success stories in schools, nor the modernist account often heard when we explicitly asked students about gender—that gender is not an issue any more. There is an interesting parallel story about what is visible and what is invisible in relation to gender.

In interview after interview, Nicky tells us that it is important that she went to this particular private school because she is the fourth generation of her family to go there. But, in fact, until the 1970s, this school was only for boys. It is her father, grandfather, and great-grandfather who went there, and she is the first female in her family to do so, but this is never noted or mentioned by her. It is only some years into the study, when we explicitly ask her about it, that we find she is not even sure which school her mother went to—she thinks it was a government high school, not a private school. Nicky's identifications of herself as a school student are thus not consciously gendered ones: she sees herself here as the same as her father and her brothers, and the pattern and power of tradition and class privilege are what interpellate her as a "City Academy student." In this way, she is both disowning her mother's history, treating that history as secondary to that of the males in her family. Yet she also wants to be a mother herself, but a modern kind of mother who is not boring. Both class and gender are involved, even if not explicitly named, in the family dynamics and identifications that are privileged in Nicky's story of herself.

We can see then how changes arising from feminism as well as some continuity in gender positioning are threaded through Nicky's story. What is absent, however, is a self-conscious or political scrutiny of gender, either in the present or in the future. In many of the narratives of Nicky and friends, there is no acknowledgment of the impossibility of avoiding the overstress they see in their parents' lives while retaining the identity, wealth, and status of that life.

Reflexivity in Context of the Gender Order

To a significant extent, Nicky's recurring concerns with the question of "who am I?," and the project of becoming your own distinctive person and true to your desires, animate much of her thinking about the future. These preoccupations also suggest how broader sociological processes of individualization and reflexivity are manifested biographically. From a methodological perspective, it could be argued that our interviewing mode incited these themes. In our focus on self-description and retrospective and prospective views, we encouraged, if not produced, certain ways of seeing and narrating the self. However, arguments about reflexivity as a "methodological artifact" (see also Pillow 2003) do not fully explain the prominence of reflexivity and self-monitoring in our interviews. The norm of self-reflection was widespread, even if such practices of the self were class and culturally differentiated and conveyed in more intense ways by girls than boys. Stephen Ball (2003, 176) has argued that "middle-classness has, almost by definition, a certain degree of reflexivity . . . a knowingness which is based on both ambivalence and a certain sort of precariousness, but this reflexivity should not be mistaken for ironic distance." Rather, Ball suggests, such reflexivity arises from an imperative to scrutinize every choice and decision, to make sure the right decisions are being made, particularly those that will ensure success and advantage. We have suggested here that the reflexivity can also be read through a feminist and psychoanalytic perspective wherein women are required to see themselves through others' eyes. And again, academic intellectual achievement, today at least, itself embeds certain elements of reflexive knowing. In the sense that Bernstein once depicted as "elaborated" versus "restricted" codes, the higher levels of secondary schooling reward an ability to "stand outside" an answer, to be self-conscious about oneself (and others) as constructors of knowledge. Taking up these different perspectives gives different ways of considering Nicky's particularity and the processes and discursive setting in which she is positioned.

Like the other students we interview at City Academy, Nicky has strongly absorbed both a habit of self-scrutiny and an agenda of needing to "be your own person," to establish and mark out your individuality. But she, like others, also comes up against the reality of how very limited the scope is for not conforming: in dress, in values and behavior required for group acceptance, and so on. It is important to succeed and be distinctive, but in very specific sanctioned and approved ways. (This issue will be discussed further in chapters 6 and 7). The way in which this particular school and this particular class location inflects Nicky's story is seen by comparing her dreams and self-narratives and choices over the years of the study with other girls.

Other girls at City Academy very much share Nicky's interest in and reflexivity about their self-positioning and modes of differentiation, and the milieu in which they operate:

Diana: Also, you have to like live up to the expectation of Academy. Like you have to be careful what you say. You just can't say whatever you want. Like you have to say the right thing to be cool and all that stuff and like even if you want to, if someone offers you to do, one of these opportunities and it's just, you really want to do it, but you sort of don't, because people will think, oh my God, what a dickhead sort of thing.

(Diana, City Academy, Year 8, age 14)

Diana: And they [parents] sort of say to you, oh, you know we don't mind what you get. You know it's just so not true, and they really care what you get and they would just die if you know, they spent this money on your education and you ended up being, you know, you know, a secretary or something. You know, they, to them, that, or to my dad, that would seem really sort of low.

(Diana, City Academy Year 9, age 15)

In these excerpts from small group discussions with Nicky's peers, themes of distinction—of the school, of self, of family—and of differentiation from others are prominent. The girls express a keen sense of how their behavior will be read through the eyes of others, and how the authority and prestige of the school, in conjunction with the expectations of their parents, compel them to become particular kinds of people. Another girl from City Academy responded with incredulity when a friend said that she was wondering about the future and "if you're going to live in a house, or if you're going to live on the streets." This possibility was swiftly dismissed and her friend told her that in relation to such futures "you can usually tell from what sort of family you come from," and that living on the streets is definitely not something she associates with people who have gone to this particular school.

Comparing Nicky's story with girls from a less elite (but not poor) background, we see a slightly different sequence and emphasis in their interviews over the years. Like Nicky at 14, they too are dreaming of their multiple possible futures. Take, for example, Stephanie, who lives in Cubbin and attends Regional High and is the daughter of a small shop-owner and a mother who did clerical work. In interview after interview Stephanie stressed her goals for the future: her dreams to have a good job, to travel. And this was often associated with talking about how she intends that having children will be subordinated to, or timed around, these first priorities.

Do you daydream or think about the future much at this stage?

Yeah, a lot. [. . .] I'm starting to. Yeah. Whether I want to get married or not. whether I want to have kids or not. I definitely want a good job and I want to travel. [. . .] I've got my mind set on that, and I'll go for that.

(Stephanie, Regional High, Year 9, age 15)

In Stephanie's case, the specificity of the particular future job or the need to have multiple possible future careers is not important. What is important is a belief about needing a good job, and having that as a foundation before children or marriage is considered. Stephanie says she does not know precisely what job she'll pursue, but she does know she wants to travel, she does want a job that pays well, and she wants to be the boss rather than work for someone.

The following year (Year 10, with still three years of high school to go), Stephanie is thinking more concretely about her immediate postschool future and wanting to move away from the regional center to the city. She is talking about deciding between University and TAFE (Technical and Further Education—lower status and more explicitly vocational) and sees clearly the advantages for herself of attending TAFE. She has decided on a career in hotel management as a field that she should be able to get into and one that will provide the sort of life and "good job" she wants. A year after finishing school, this is precisely the direction Stephanie is taking. However, in this case, her final Year 12 score was slightly less than she had hoped, and she was not able to directly enter the degree qualification that was her first choice. But she quickly adjusted to a shorter, lower-level qualification in hospitality studies, and has investigated and planned what she needs to do beyond this to reenter and complete the original goal. Through her final years of school, she has a steady boyfriend who works on the wharfs and lives in another city and whom she visits every weekend. Stephanie's boyfriend left school early and is of a lower class than her, and when she leaves school, she begins living with him. But she is not deflected from her sense of the steps she wants to take, and her future ambitions and own class positioning are not defined or constrained by this romantic relationship. In contrast to Nicky, her future dreams collided with a strong sense of herself needing to have a job (rather than a rich husband) that would make them possible. (This was a vision and a set of norms strengthened by the particular emphases of the school she attends, a school whose "enterprising" emphases and themes of responsibility for your own outcomes are discussed further in chapters 3 and 7.)

Whereas Nicky and many of the girls in the elite school defined themselves against their mothers, girls in the more middle and lower social groupings were more likely to be encouraged by their mother's example, and to be spurred on by her. Stephanie says that her determination in relation to continuing at school is strongly influenced by her mother, who has migrated from Europe, and her experiences of having difficulty obtaining ongoing employment and a "good job."

At 15, Stephanie, in a small group interview with some of her friends, describes her future plans.

Stephanie: I don't want to get married until I've actually got a good job and I'm settled down and everything, and I don't want to have kids until I'm married.

Right, so there's a kind of sequence? What about you, Sue?

Sue: Yeah, take it as it comes, I reckon.

Really?

Sue: I just want to have . . . my main aim is to get a good job and have my own house. . . .

Stephanie: Who with?

Sue: Oh, well, yeah, maybe share a house. But I want to have money, and I want to have a good job, and I want to have a car. . . .

Stephanie: and this, and this, and this. . .

Sue: And I want to have lots of fun.

What do you think of as a good job?

Sue: Something I enjoy.

Stephanie: Something that pays well [. . .] I don't want to work for anyone. I want to be the boss. I want to be the employer.

(Regional High, Year 9, girls age 15)

In the final interviews, we asked the participants about changes in their own family lives in the seven years of the study, and we found that the majority of mothers at some point had embarked on some form of study or training themselves, and most mothers had also experienced at least one change of occupation in that time. Although changes in women's lives are credited as part of the big story of individualization in modern times, the meanings of this to mothers and their daughters are often submerged rather than foregrounded in such "big story" accounts. In Stephanie's relationship with her mother, and in the experience of other participants, we see that the returning of women to work and to further study has had important effects on how their daughters in particular now see their own agendas and futures.[4] Take Keren from Regional Tech, the working-class school in our study, who struggled with school yet manages against many odds to complete Year 12 and enroll in a one-year nursing course. During the course of our study, Keren's mother, a single parent, manages to care for five children, return to study and work part-time, and do some voluntary work. Keren sees her mother finish a course and get a job in a social welfare agency. In Keren's final year of school, her mother again returns to do further study to upgrade her qualifications. During this period, Keren starts to focus more on school and shows a strong determination to complete school. Keren also begins voluntary work at an agency providing food and housing assistance. In Year 12, she decides she wants to do nursing, and we hear then that her mother is very happy about this decision as she too had initially trained as a nurse. Keren's close relationship and identification with her mother have been important in motivating her and in making a particular kind of future of independence, study, and work seem possible. Like many other girls we interviewed, Keren too desired escape from the family home, and her own financial and emotional independence; the trajectory of her mother's life—itself representing the possibility of emotional and economic independence—also made that realizable.

Keren (whose story is discussed further in chapter 8) is from a background and in a school where "take it as it comes" is the dominant response to questions about the future. In talking about daydreams, students have modest wishes of a home of their own, and also are concerned to let us know that they don't expect too much. This is a very different context from Nicky's experience at a school that so emphasizes distinction and success that two students in our study find the pressures too much and leave, and where students take for granted that a comfortable life will be gained. But both Nicky's dreams and choices and Keren's dreams and choices are defined with knowledge of their mother and, to some extent at least, in relation to that mother's achievements and lack of achievements. And, as we discuss further in chapters 7 and 8, the experiences of women studying and returning to work seem to generate different practices and possibilities for the girls compared with the boys at Keren's school—no matter how much they mutually share a narrative that they "take it as it comes."

Biography, Becoming and Vocational Rationalities

In education circles, concerns about pathways and vocational choices are perennial ones and a huge amount of data-gathering technology exists in most countries to record patterns by gender, school, sometimes SES, and to consider change over time, interventions, and so on. In this chapter, we decided to concentrate on the story of interviews with a single participant in our study, Nicky, to try to show, close-up, how her story (and that of others) over the high school years is not simply a rational and linear focus on destinations and pathways—though it is, nevertheless, part of a bigger picture of class and gender patterns and what is happening to these. We have attempted to bring both the subjective and the structural dimensions of the question "Who am I/ and who will I become?" into view, here, specifically in relation to how this identity-making draws from family and school and how it enters into choices that are taken in relation to postschool pathways. Our next chapter examines these issues of identity-making and identifications in relation to some different concerns—issues of political values and racism and how young people confront questions of national identification and the identification of "others."

CHAPTER 6

Who Is "Us"? Australian Students on Politics, Racism, Ethnicity, and Unemployment

When the people in our project were aged around 15 and in Year 10 of high school, we asked them a series of questions on political and ethical issues. Some of these questions asked them to comment about issues currently in the news; others asked for their response to hypothetical scenarios (a friend who was using drugs, or leaving school, or coming out as gay); others asked more directly about issues such as their views on cultural diversity and unemployment. In this chapter we examine themes in responses from students at all four schools to questions about racism in Australia, about Aboriginal issues and migration, and about Pauline Hanson, a prominent leader of a small party vocally opposing immigration and the special treatment of Aboriginal people.

Numerous studies have been designed to examine students' views on racism and racial and ethnic difference and identities (e.g. Dolby 2000; Nayak 1999; Rizvi 1993; Roman and Stanley 1997). Our questions emerged from a study framed differently, one in which attitudes to racism or multiculturalism were not the primary or exclusive focus of inquiry. Our interest was in the developing biographies of the young people in the study and their political sensibilities and modes of thinking within that context. We raised the questions also because, at the time these interviews took place, such questions were matters of considerable public political debate in Australia. In this chapter, we discuss things that are said in relation to relatively direct questions at a particular time, but our interest in and analysis of what is said is developed from the particular and broader interests of our project and this book. We draw attention to the perspectives on racism offered by a study whose focus is young people's identity-making over time. We consider school differences and the discursive constructions emphasized in particular school cultures and how these are heard in political positionings of the students. We also give some critical scrutiny to ourselves and our incitements as researchers as well as what is said by those to whom we talk.

A further broad context of this chapter is an awareness that our study is located in one specific national context, Australia, and that not just the details of what is discussed here, but the types of issues and literatures we give emphasis to, and those we do not take up, may seem strange to readers located elsewhere. This is part of our agenda in this chapter: to draw attention to national specificities in constructions about race and ethnicity, to see discourses not as self-evident and given, but as constructed in particular ways in particular times and places.

In a comparative study of U.S. and French "rhetorics of racism and anti-racism," Michele Lamont attempted to "reconstruct the mental maps and symbolic boundaries through which . . . individuals define 'us' and 'them'." She argued that these show how "people define their own identity and the identity of their community, or the boundaries through which they distinguish between people like themselves with whom they identify and Others" (Lamont 2000, 25). In this chapter, we try to tease out the "logic of racism" (Lamont 2000) in one national setting, and in doing so to work across essentialized or homogenized accounts of "what racism is," looking particularly at the shifting claims and effects of "us and them" discourses.

We develop a related double focus on identity here by looking at how young people position and represent themselves in relation to their views about race and national identity and exploring aspects of the construction of race and nationalist discourses in contemporary Australia. We then compare some of the students' views on race and racism with their views on other political topics, such as unemployment, in order to build up a broader picture of political reasoning and the impact of school ethos on the shaping of those views. This comparative focus allows us to better understand the distinctive logic of discourses of race and racism, as well as the subjective effects of political reasoning, and the processes of identification and identity work that such discourses entail.

The Politics of Race in Australia in the 1990s

The interview exchanges we discuss here took place before September 11, before the war in Iraq, and before the conservative Australian prime minister had (in 2001) successfully used fear of "boat people" refugees flooding Australia as a central plank in an unexpected election victory. It was also before the same government promoted a campaign against "black armband" views of Australian history (i.e., accounts that gave attention to wrongs against Aboriginal people) and instead asserted a triumphalist account of Australian history and an Australian identity based on male "mateship" in wars (MacIntyre and Clark 2003). However, the seeds of a number of these subsequent developments were highly apparent in the 1990s, in the form of a female, working-class politician, Pauline Hanson, who promoted a new political party "One Nation." The party's most visible agendas were that Aboriginal people had been given unfair special treatment in welfare policies; that Asian immigration was taking the jobs of ordinary people; that "ordinary people" were not being listened to by the political elites with their free trade policies, multicultural agendas, and attention to the big end of town at the expense of provincial and rural areas. At the time when we asked people about the issues discussed in this chapter, Pauline Hanson was getting exhaustive coverage by the press and media.

During the 1990s, a number of events signified an intensified focus on the politics of race and national identity in Australia. The High Court's ruling on "Native Title" ("The Mabo decision," 1992) repudiated the doctrine of terra nullius—that eighteenth- and nineteenth-century European settlement had been of unoccupied land—and acknowledged traditional and "continuous" ownership of the land by Indigenous people, and this drew vigorous debate and challenge from individuals, mining companies, and pastoralists. There was a national debate about the need for a formal apology from white Australians to Indigenous Australians to acknowledge past wrongs, and especially regarding the prime minister's refusal to "say sorry" for previous acts of state-supported racism such as the forced removal by governments of Aboriginal children from their families. And there were recurrent but especially intense debates about immigration and multiculturalism. The One Nation political party and its leader Pauline Hanson emerged in and helped shape this political climate.

Pauline Hanson and One Nation advocated a populist nationalism, promising to address the needs of the embattled, ordinary "White Australian" and to put a stop to what they saw as the egregious demands of the Aboriginal and multicultural "industries." Migration had to be dramatically reduced: there were too many "Asians" preventing real Australians from getting jobs, and Aboriginal people received too many "hand outs," another form of discrimination against real/ white/ordinary Australians. Ien Ang writes that under the leadership of Pauline Hanson, "who drew her charisma from an aggressively lower-middle-class, anti-intellectual and anti-cosmopolitan populism, a vigorous grassroots political movement emerged of disenchanted, mostly white, rural and working-class people who revolted against what they saw as the disempowerment of their identities as 'ordinary Australians'" (Ang 2000, 5). At the time of the interviews we are discussing here (late 1997), One Nation had established a controversial presence in Australian politics (Kingston 1999; Perera 1999). One Nation meetings had been held in many country towns, prompting fiery displays of support as well as opposition. Questions of race, nation, and identity were at the heart of their politics: the interests of real Australians, whose needs had been neglected by successive Labor and conservative governments, were seen to be in conflict with those of migrants or Aboriginal people. In such a climate, we were interested in what political attitudes were held by young people from rural and urban areas and with different ethnic and class identities, and how they made sense of and located themselves (and Others) within the overtly racialized political landscape of Australia.

Identity, Nationalism and Whiteness

Questions about nationalism, about what and who rightfully constitutes and belongs in the nation, are central to discussions about race and ethnicity in Australia. The Australian population comprises a small Indigenous population and a large majority composed of both initial invasion and successive waves of immigration—approximately one-quarter of the current Australian population was born overseas. There is a heritage of belief that Australia is properly a white nation (until 1967, Aboriginal people were not counted in the census), and a history of associated practices, such as the White Australia policy[1] and government programs of assimilation. At the same time, being white is a kind of invisible, unmarked, yet normative identity. At different times in Australian history, different groups have been "racialized": the Chinese, the Irish, southern Europeans, those from the Middle East (Tsolidis 2001), while visitors from the United States most often notice the absence of the groups they themselves identify with "race"—African Americans and Hispanics. As the recent research on "whiteness" has made clear, being white is an identity position whose history and effects require investigation.

Whiteness, it is argued, has been made invisible in the process of exoticizing the "Other," documenting their disadvantage, rather than examining white privilege (Fine 1997; Giroux 1997; Roman and Eyre 1997). Underpinning such approaches is a view of "race" as a construction, not a fixed and self-evident category. Luke and Carrington (2000) argue that "race" is a "signifier of relational identity politics, a fundamental principle of social organization and identity formation that moves people to act in certain ways" (2000, 5). In this sense, "'race' is both about 'being' or claiming an identity (self-naming) and having a historically socially constructed identity (named as other by others)" (Luke and Carrington 2000, 6).

How national identity is understood, and what the key issues and points of contention are varies across different national settings. For example, in the countries Lamont compares, the U.S. and France, national identity is linked to traditions such as school-based civics, and declaration of rights of the individual, and in France to a strong pride in and government programs to support a common "national culture". Australia does not have a founding declaration of rights, and issues about national identity are often implicit rather than explicit, and contested. "One Nation" was in part responding to moves by governments in the 1970s and 1980s to see Australia as a more independent and cosmopolitan country, a country located in Asia, rather than a colony linked to Britain or America.

The debates about whiteness and the construction of race were on our minds as we listened to the students respond to our questions. We were attuned to how they did or did not position themselves and others as white, as Australian or as outsiders, and how they variously articulated elements of the cultural logic of racial and nationalist discourse.

An important issue in research about race is the mutual positioning and effects of the embodied researcher in relation to those they study, the blindness and silences that are constructed within the direct questioning; the limited options that researchers of racism may set up for those they research. We return to these problematics of ourselves and our methods later in the chapter, but the questions that were the starting points for the responses we discuss in the next section were:

What do you think of Pauline Hanson and the debate over what she has been saying?
Do you think there is much racism in Australia?
Do you think much about Aboriginal issues? (land rights, health)
Should Australia continue to admit migrants and refugees?

They were preceded by questions about religion and whether that is important today (and to them), and followed by questions about Australia becoming a republic and about unemployment.

"Us" and "Them": Identity-Making as Belonging and as Becoming

"Us and them" binaries framed students' understandings of racism and racial discourse, but with shifting referents. Sometimes the "us" referred to those who opposed racism in contrast to "them," the racists: "Even though we are multicultural and that, there are still a few racist people around. Personally I don't agree with them" (Andrew, Regional High.) We, the researchers, were usually and overtly included in the embrace of "us" or, putting that another way, the students represented themselves to us as part of our "we." Even when students opposed racism, "Australians" were positioned against "Others," sometimes collapsing distinctions between Aboriginal people and Asians, grouping them together because of their contrast to ordinary, white Australians. However, for many students the "us and them" binary mediated a different moral and political response to the relative status of Asians and Aboriginal people, whereby Asians were positioned as "more Other."

Nicky, a student at the elite, metropolitan City Academy, positioned Aboriginal people both as deserving of pity and as having a rightful claim on Australia, whereas she positioned Asians as intruders.

Nicky: I think that Aboriginals have just as much rights as we do, if not even more because they were here before we were. And I just think it's really sad what's happening with them and stuff. . . .

I think Australia is becoming very, um, populated with Asians. I think so, because they've got Japanese or Chinese writing under each street sign. In some place I went to they did and you know, it's a bit sad, but what can we really do to stop it now?

Why do you find it sad?

Nicky: Um, I don't know actually. I was probably being racist. I don't know.

(Nicky, Year 10, City Academy)

Her description of the influx of Asian migrants was prompted by a question from us asking if she had observed racism. Nicky said she had seen racism directed at "some Asians." This leads to a comment that "Australia is becoming very populated with Asians." A comment about racism against Asians displaces into fears of Asianization. The most disturbing aspect of migration for Nicky is that she has seen these street signs in a normal town.

> It's not like Chinatown . . . that's fine . . . But it's in like a normal full city area.

She concludes, "Well, it's just that a lot of things are changing to suit them, do you know what I mean?" For Nicky, "migrants" and especially Asians, are acceptable so long as they remain in the spaces (metaphoric and literal) designated for exotics, those groups of people who, in the right numbers, make our cities more interesting and appropriately culturally diverse. From Nicky's perspective, the "us and them" boundaries are threatening to dissolve.

These issues can be also be seen in the context of other themes in Nicky's biographical making. Nicky, at the elite school whose interviews were discussed at some length in chapter 5, often expresses concerns about maintaining a life in which her privileged community and networks would continue to exist. She is drawn to be not like her mother and also like her mother; to not take a standard postschool path in an elite course, but also to continue to mainly mix with the people from her school who do. In her final interviews she talks about feeling discomforted at a university not dominated by people she knows. In the questions on race and politics, Nicky initially speaks from the school-approved discourse of pluralism and rights and recognizes when she steps over that barrier to voice her worries—"I was probably being racist," she tells us. But her liberal discourse is worried, emotionally troubled, by fears of displacement by Asian signs entering her "normal" city environment. At this point in the interview she becomes noticeably more animated and emotionally engaged.

Other students see Asians as threatening the livelihood of "real" Australians.

> We're doing to the Aboriginals what Asians are doing to us. Like taking on their jobs. (Kylie, Regional Tech, Year 10)

Kylie's distinctions place Asians as clear outsiders and Aboriginal people as having a morally superior claim to the nation. In a study of Australian children and popular racism, Fazal Rizvi (1993, 133) argued that they drew on a form of "territorial belonging" to represent Asian immigrants as aliens and therefore deserving of a moral treatment very different from that applicable to Aborigines. In the examples from Kylie and Nicky, we can see that the dilemma of differential treatment is resolved through recourse to the justice of recognizing prior national belonging to "our" country. White Australians and Aboriginal Australians thus share common ground against Asians ("them") and the threat of Asianization. Aboriginal people become highly differentiated from Asian Others, and, in this set of justifications, more aligned with, rather than opposed to, "white Australians."

Writing about national identity and multiculturalism in Australia, Ghassan Hage (1998) argues that "Whiteness" is both an historically constructed category and a fantasy: a constellation of attributes and identifications that can be accumulated, in the Bourdieuian sense, whereby one might aspire to acquire certain prestigious forms of cultural capital. In this account, there are (up to a point) degrees of whiteness and degrees of otherness, and certain forms of conduct and ways of being can enhance or diminish one's capital and claim to whiteness (Hage 1998, 20). Accumulating whiteness is linked to claiming a sense of national belonging, which in turn requires practices of exclusion and inclusion to sustain the distinctions between those who more properly belong and those who do not, those whose claims are less authentic and natural. For Hage, the "spatiality" of these practices is crucial, and consequently he argues that strategies of exclusion and inclusion are better represented as nationalist rather than solely racist practices.

In Kylie's and Nicky's responses we can see some of the ways in which they situate themselves as "spatial managers" of the Australian nation ("people should stay in their own country"), alongside, as we have suggested, a certain ambivalence about "our" national belonging. Kylie lived in a small country town and attended a regional tech in Cubbin. Kylie lived in a region that had suffered from the effects of economic restructuring, and she could observe unemployment and its consequences in her immediate environment (it was also, compared with the metropolitan city, a region with relatively few recent immigrants). Concerns about visible unemployment, as many commentators have noted (Perera 1999), have fueled the popularity of One Nation in rural areas. But Kylie also struggles to reconcile a concern about jobs with an awareness of different degrees of and claims for exclusion and inclusion—her thoughts about Asians who take "our" jobs link immediately to the history of "we" and displacement of Aboriginal people.

Like Hage, the cultural studies critic Ien Ang discusses the reception of Pauline Hanson in Australia in terms of national identity. But she casts it differently, looking from another angle at the relation between identity and nation. Whereas Hage's focus is on whiteness as an identity comprising capitals that can be accumulated, Ang attends to the emotional attachments to political positioning, and the resonance of macro national changes with subjective desires. In the 1970s and 1980s, particularly under Labor governments, there had been a proclaimed move to form a new and more confident "Australian" identity: one that positioned Australia more as part of Asia rather than as linked to its colonial history with the United Kingdom, and which simultaneously developed institutions and programs of "multiculturalism" as part of Australia's national and political makeup. Ang's interest is that this "becoming" was one that had easier intellectual and emotional resonance for the cosmopolitan elite, in which Ang critically locates herself, than for many who were less powerful than that elite in both political and socioeconomic terms.

> As a migrant who was eager to find my place in this society I was excited to notice, in the early 1990s, that a new Australian nationalism could so elegantly, and with such apparent ease, shift its identificatory allegiance from being a racially and culturally exclusionary "White Australia" to an inclusive and cosmopolitan "multicultural Australia in Asia.". . .
>
> What seemed at stake in the new Australian nationalism was identity construction rather than identity expression, the sense that "what we might become" is more important than "who we are." (Ang 2000, 7)

For people outside the cosmopolitan elites, Ang argues, the "new Australian nationalism" did not represent a moment of hope, the possibility of becoming something new and exciting. Rather the key tropes for identity were loss and longing for the past, and a panic about "who we were," tropes foregrounded by Pauline Hanson and the One Nation campaign. These issues, Ang argues, were largely ignored in the "moral(istic) critiques of racism" (Ang 2000, 5) being purveyed by the professional classes, particularly the metropolitan and cosmopolitan "chattering classes" of the intelligentsia and the press.

The "us and them" binaries are both about belonging and about identity-making, and these in turn are mediated by biographical history, class location, and school ethos. Kylie and Nicky represent different class and school locations, but both want to preserve (or, in Kylie's case, establish) some sense of their own entitlement or capital of belonging. They align their sense of belonging with historical occupancy, and see the entitlement of Aboriginal people on the same grounds and against more recent immigrants. By contrast, some other students, whose parents were themselves born in another country, align their own identity, and their discourse about Australia, with a positive sense of globalized diversity, one that is less enthusiastic about Aboriginal people, who are seen as representing old ways of being and resisting science and modernization. One narrative about this, that of Nassar, was told at the beginning of chapter 3. Nassar is marked as "Other" in his school context, not only because of his ethnicity and appearance, but because his cultural background takes religion and good behavior seriously. But Nassar himself is an enthusiast for science, technology, discovery, and innovation, and for the possibilities Australia offers as part of this. He is dismissive of Aboriginal culture because he sees it as wanting to stay backward.

Another student, Stephanie, from Regional High, is not obviously of non-Anglo background, but in the course of the interviews we learn that she has a Turkish mother. Over the period of our interviews, Stephanie increasingly articulates a sense of herself as a "multicultural person," one who strongly disliked racists, and who knew lots of people from many different cultures. "My boyfriend is actually Black [Maori] and he, he's all right actually." Throughout the interview on this topic she is animated and engaged, and the questions and topic have visibly struck a chord with her. In discussing racism, she is smiling rather than indignant, and represents her ethnic difference and friendship with "different nationalities" as interesting cosmopolitanism, as something about which she has a certain expertise and insider knowledge.

> I really dislike Pauline Hanson. I am half and half [. . .] so I'm not of Australian culture, background or whatever. Um, I'm a [. . .] citizen as well as an Australian citizen, so I've dual citizenship. I just don't like her views, I am totally against racist people. I don't want anything to do with them. I don't know, I just don't like the way she is and she really upsets my mum when she comes on TV too. I think she has upset a lot of people politically and she hasn't needed to do that.
>
> (Stephanie, Regional High, Year 10)

Stephanie gives the opinion that there is not much racism in Australia, but that "there still is racist people and those I just don't want anything to do with, because I despise them." Because of her capacity to look, in Hage's sense, "white," Stephanie could comment on racism as someone who was both relatively secure in the national belonging, and who could speak candidly on racists in Australia because of her identity, her parents' experiences and her mixing with kids from "different nationalities." She was able to move between both subject positions; to claim Otherness as well as a strong degree (she can "pass") of national belonging. Speaking of racism from experience did not indelibly or negatively mark her as an Other.

Yet, although Stephanie had a strong investment in her identity as "against racists," she expressed attitudes toward Aboriginal people that were similar to those adopted by Hanson and One Nation. She thought "they" were getting "too many rights," even though "I've got nothing against Aboriginal people." Stephanie's critique of racism is most finely tuned when it affects her life experience directly. In her reasoning, Aboriginal people, not migrants, are the true Other. She repositions herself here as an authentic Australian with a history of belonging to the nation, compared to her earlier self-description as "not of Australian culture, background." Note the repetition in the next comments of "our ancestors," the expansiveness and authority of the "we" and "us," encompassing us as the researchers and as presumed managers, like herself, of the white Australian nation.

> I think they get too many rights over us and it's always we have to apologize for what our ancestors did to their ancestors. I think it's a totally different generation now, and we're totally different people and we can't keep apologizing for what our ancestors did to their ancestors. I think they get way too many rights over us now and they're talking about equal rights, well, it's not equal.
>
> (Stephanie, Regional High, Year 10)

Stephanie identifies as a non-Australian who is "at home" and naturally belongs in Australia. Her casting of Aboriginal people as more properly Other secures her position in the white Australian landscape—Indigenous Australians are less "white" than migrants. Compare this to the views expressed by Kylie and Nicky, both Anglo-Australian girls, who position migrants as more Other, "less white," than Aboriginal Australians.

Stephanie's reference to "our ancestors" constructs an historical affiliation to Australia, giving her an (imaginary) past Australian identity. The past is invoked not to vindicate the legitimacy of white authority, but rather to signal the possibility of a different kind of nation, a new generation—"we're totally different people"—and a positive future for herself as someone "not of Australian background." She positions herself as a cosmopolitan subject who experiences cultural and ethnic difference not as negative Otherness (as has been the experience of her mother) but as a positive and interesting attribute of identity. In the provincial, predominantly Anglo-Australian town where she grew up, Stephanie can lay claim to a certain exotic, but not threateningly different, status. Attitudes to race and Other do not always fall into a neat binary logic. Here they are also intertwined with Stephanie's forging of her identity, of becoming both Australian and not Australian, and a future-oriented, "multicultural" person impatient with Aboriginal claims of "prior" racism.

The notion of identity as a process of becoming features in much contemporary cultural studies, in part due, as Ang argues, to the influence of Stuart Hall's work. Ang suggests that

> Hall rescues the possibility for 'identity'—that is, the way we represent and narrativize ourselves to ourselves and to others—to be a resource of hope, to be the site of agency and attachment that energize us to participate in the making of our own ongoing histories, the construction of our continuously unfolding worlds, now and in the future. (Ang 2000, 1)

Our reading of Stephanie's representation of herself echoes with such accounts of identity. Her identity as a "multicultural" person is discursively linked to a sense of herself as becoming, and as having an optimistic sense of future possibilities defined against a backward-looking race politics. But, as Ang argues, the emphasis on becoming in cultural studies is also utopian, and tends to neglect that identity processes can be shaped by apprehensiveness about change and fear of the future (some elements of which can be seen in Nicky's concerns about street signs and Kylie's about jobs). Celebratory accounts of identity formation as a project of "becoming" can also neglect class and gender-differentiated possibilities.

Discoursing about Race in Interviews

In interviews at all four schools, most of the students were quick to identify themselves as "not racist," to separate themselves from the politics and opinions associated with Pauline Hanson. There was an implicit and shared sense that racism was unacceptable in polite or public conversation, especially when being asked about these issues in an interview with white, professional women in a school context. This was evident in both what they said and how they responded and engaged with us on the questions. There were nods and serious looks of recognition, assuming an air of gravity; an impression, on occasions, of their responding to "current affairs" questions (or teacher questions), as if there had to be a "right" answer. In most cases we were positioned and included in the "we" who oppose racism: "Well, like especially the rest of the population I don't agree with what she's [Pauline Hanson] saying, because I don't think money should be taken away [from Aboriginal services] or migration should be stopped" (Andrew, Regional High, Year 10). In such statements, students represented themselves as expert commentators upon, rather than as perpetrators of racism, and included us in this liberal gesture.

What is meant by being "racist" is not necessarily clear or agreed upon, even though much discussion proceeds as if there were taken-for-granted criteria for determining racism. This was also the case in our interviews in that neither we, nor the students, really explained what we, or they, meant by the term "racism." On the one hand, a shared commonsense understanding was presumed, but, on the other, students were explicitly concerned with trying to work out the protocols and form of race discourses and when they were or were not being racist. These were ongoing tensions for us as well, in terms of how we formulated and posed questions about racism, analyzed responses, and wrote about young people's discourses of race and racism.

Like the students we talk about, we struggle with protocols and problems of how to talk and write about this: what is proper, what is at issue, what is not appropriate to say. In this project, we two researchers have done all the interviews together, and have spent a lot of time discussing what we are doing and trying to "make sense" of it. Our process in writing is normally to begin with a discussion, then one of us will do an initial draft, followed by exchange to the other who will comment and do a second draft, and this continues, sometimes including further meetings and discussions. But no aspect of writing about the project has proved more difficult for us than attempting to write about race, racism, and the issues we discuss in this chapter. An attempt to write an article on this[2] continued for over three years before it was produced, and included long periods when we avoided even trying to talk about it. The topic seemed to produce for us much deeper tension than intellectual disagreements about which theorists and recent writings could help make sense of material. To take one example, in an earlier version, we were trying to discuss some of the themes we have raised earlier in this chapter and to discuss the type of struggles about how to voice answers that were evident in the responses, one of us used the phrase "the etiquette of racial discourse." To the other, this phrase was viscerally shocking in what seemed to be its depoliticization of the topic. Yet it also captured something of what seemed relevant about the particular perspective available on this topic from the type of interview-based study we had conducted. The phrase had been intended to convey the intense anxiety and uncertainty that participants expressed in trying to work out what was the right way to speak about racism; what language was available, what was it possible to say in this historical period and political climate? This was also a concern being played out in media commentary, amid the explosion of debate about race, identity, and nation. Our guilt and our own desire to say the right thing, our ability to avoid the issue if we wanted to, or to make the easy cosmopolitan judgments about racism in others, while at the same time knowing how much we too could be judged wanting, is similar to the tensions we analyze in others.

For many students, a central dilemma was how to respect the rights of the individual (in this case, Pauline Hanson and others who might wish to speak out) while not supporting racism. For students at the metropolitan schools in particular, responses to questions about Pauline Hanson were usually couched in terms of respecting "freedom of speech," alongside a statement of personal disapproval.

> She's horrible. Well, that's my opinion anyway. She's racist. . . . Like I believe in freedom of speech, but you've got a certain extent, like a certain fairness that you have to go to . . . it's hard to explain. And so once

> you reach that line, it's pretty horrible if you go over it, because like there are a certain amount of things that you can say about certain races.
>
> (Helen, Suburban High, Year 10)

There was a pronounced concern with establishing and policing discursive and political protocols, and a self-consciousness and uncertainty about what was the correct way for them [the students] to speak about race and racism. Was it ever possible or appropriate to express racist views? Was there a "proper" way to talk about "race"?

For some students, particularly those at the country schools, Hanson was seen as "going for it the wrong way" (Peter, Sophie, City Academy, Year 10; Andrew, Regional High, Year 10 all used the phrase) or as being a "bit harsh" (Keren and Kylie, Regional Tech, Year 10). These students admired Hanson's forthrightness and independence in speaking out—consistent with a tradition in Australia of admiring populist political mavericks. But there was concern that she could offend others and that her views would be misinterpreted. Hanson's right to speak openly in public was defended, but there was criticism of her for transgressing public space protocols ("going about it the wrong way") rather than her views being censored because they were "racist" per se. Others expressed sympathy for her views, even as they noted that she was "a bit rude." These judgments of Pauline Hanson also need to be placed in the context of her reception as a political leader who did not fit the usual mold for politicians. She was a working-class woman, a single parent who owned a fish and chip shop, who spoke with a broad Australian accent, and was often criticized in the media for speaking too stridently and acting inappropriately. In some respects, the students were picking up on what were dominant themes in public and media debates about Hanson, a debate that in its criticism of her for being racist, often denigrated her in fairly traditional sexist and classist ways (Kingston 1999).

> [Pauline Hanson] has been a little bit harsh. I know what she's getting at because it's not, like I know, it's not our country exactly, we didn't pay for it, or anything, but I think they should, people should stay in their own country . . . maybe for holidays and stuff like that, but it may be racist, but it's just the way I think.
>
> Yeah, she has a got a point, but she might, I think she's a bit rude just coming out and saying it like that.
>
> (Kylie, Regional Tech, Year 10)

While Kylie maintains a clear view of national insiders and outsiders, she has a sense of the ambiguous claim "we" have on rightful ownership ("it's not exactly our country"). There is also a sharp degree of reflexivity in Kylie's responses, a capacity to articulate her views, and then to acknowledge and reflect upon how such attitudes might be perceived by others and by us. This form of self-consciousness was evident in answers from several students, particularly those who were more ambivalent about Hansonism and were struggling to work out their opinions in relation to a highly tuned sense of how their views could be received

School Ethos and Political Positions

Another perspective on the rhetorics and subjectivity effects of racial discourse is to compare its forms of reasoning with that underpinning other kinds of political beliefs. Here we compare students' attitudes to race, racism, and nationalism with their views on unemployment and religious tolerance, looking at one school cohort in particular to consider this from the perspective of schooling as a form of habitus that creates its own dispositions and discursive constructions.

City Academy is a large elite private coeducational college with a public reputation for having a mildly socially progressive agenda. When in an early interview we asked students at City Academy "what do you think this school values?", it was common for them to compare it with other elite private schools in the same city as being more diverse (specifically in the arts and sports and being nonselective) rather than directed to narrowly focused academic aims. This rhetorical commitment to diversity is a key element of the school habitus, expressed in the school's publicity brochures and its presentations of itself to parents and students. For example, it actively supports equal opportunities for girls, is seen to have ecumenical and culturally pluralist ideals, and, as the students readily tell you, the school values "diversity" and promotes tolerance for different groups in society. In many interviews at City Academy over a range of topics, students at this school spoke effusively about the value of cultural diversity and the obligations and freedoms of the individual. Interviews were peppered with the rhetoric of pluralism, difference, tolerance, and individualism. All the students understood and represented themselves as "individuals," as somehow standing out a little from the crowd (the social class positioning inherent in this is discussed further in the next chapter). Alannah declares: "we are all multicultural . . . maybe there is racism . . . but there is no racism at school." She offers as confirmation of this point the academy's partnership program with schools in China and Japan, waving her arms around to convey just how expansive and inclusive it is. In many interviews, students tell us repeatedly that the school encourages its members to "think outside the square" (Peter, City Academy, Year 11), and is committed to valuing diversity in individual thinking. Despite such declarations and aspirations, we observed a striking homogeneity in students' opinions and outlook, and fairly normative codes of personal conduct. The restriction on what conduct was acceptable, particularly in relation to achieving and being distinctive, is discussed in other chapters. Here we want to focus on how an experience of being Other was felt by a boy of Chinese appearance in this setting.

Lee had a Chinese mother and an Anglo-Australian father, and while at City Academy he rarely acknowledged his Chinese heritage or presented his identity as "Chinese." His father was a lawyer, his mother a teacher—occupations not out of place at this school. They lived in a leafy middle-class (but not elite) suburb and Lee thinks he has "got every opportunity possible. . . . My parents really gave me options to do what I want" (City Academy, Year 10). In the early years of interviews, Lee conveyed social poise in speaking with us, and seemed at ease with the forms of reflexive discussion, as well as the cultural capital appreciated by students at City. He was in a band, had a cool demeanor, and was probably more arty and self-conscious than many of his peers.

Lee's constant theme in interviews over the first two years of our study was that "this school prides itself on its diversity, but it expects conformity." He never mentioned ethnicity in this context, but dwelt on his interest in rock music. He seemed to have trouble in this period forming friendships, and to be rather unhappy. The experiences intensified Lee's sense not simply that the school was narrower than it boasted, but that he was different—and he channeled this not into issues about racism but about being a rebel. In the middle years, he becomes increasingly ill at ease at the academy and represents himself as an outsider, not fitting in with the social scene and skeptical about the values the school espouses. Lee's parents arranged to transfer him to a different type of private school. It was a small, "alternative" school located in an old mansion, with a curriculum that was much less structured and guided by student interest, strongly focused on the arts. Students did not wear uniforms, and a lot of time was spent discussing the meaning of life. In our first interviews with Lee following the move, and not prompted by any change of direction in our questions, he talked at length about his family, especially his Chinese grandmother. He seemed more comfortable with the privilege on his father's side, and took up the opportunity to travel with his grandfather to England.

We draw this sketch of Lee to make two points about the ethos of City Academy. First, despite the overt commitment to diversity, it was experienced by those who were in some sense Other not as a place that really welcomed embodied diversity or could tolerate much difference (we also discuss this further in our chapter on class). This extended to Lee's not speaking of his ethnicity or claiming otherness on non-White grounds: in the first three years of our study, the people we followed each brought along two friends for their interview—so what was spoken of to us was also being spoken to peers. Being a rebel, a chosen form of difference that was an extension of what the school valued, was a more acceptable basis on which he could deal with being Other. Lee had much of the veneer of appropriate cultural capital, and evidence of a habitus formed within the milieu of the comfortable, intellectually trained professional classes. But it was a cultural capital not sufficiently coded White. In this case, City Academy sustains both class and ethnic privilege: its mode of cultural (re)production is not only about ensuring the authority of class elites, but also ensuring the currency of White capital. And, in a Bourdieuian sense, one of the effects of the "diversity" ethos was to make these structured differences appear to be the result of individual effort, failure, or idiosyncrasy.

Lee had left this school by year 10, the time when we were asking the students about race and racism. At that point we were struck by the similarity in the ways students at that elite school talked about race and racism, and some differences in their modes of doing so compared with students at other schools. There was a strong commitment to the rights of individuals and to freedom of speech. "I think she [Hanson] is awfully racist and she's going too far with some of her views, but I believe she has a right to be racist if she wants to be" (Sophie, City Academy, Year 10). "I strongly believe in freedom of speech . . . but she's racist . . . and I'm just totally shocked that so many people in Australia can back her . . . and agree with what she has to say" (Gillian, City Academy, Year 10). Their condemnation of racism is mediated by a commitment to pluralism and complicated by a concern to respect the rights of individuals, even to admire people whom they judge to be thinking "independently" (a quality the academy admires).

> She's said a few things wrong . . . but she's entitled to say what she wants and um, I don't support her . . . she had a lot of guts to get up and say what she did . . . about the Asians and immigration and whatever, but you know, I respect her for courage and everything, but I don't agree with that, I think, you know, she's offended, I think she should may be think a little bit more carefully what she's, cause she can offend some people.
>
> (Alannah, City Academy, Year 10)

In Alannah's comments there is a concern for hurting others, for speaking carelessly, but also a degree of admiration for speaking out, for "thinking outside the square".

While racism was condemned, the students themselves reported that they had not come across much racism or directly witnessed or heard racism. Gillian reflects that "I'm not really associated with much racism, but I can imagine that there is still, um, it's still around . . . I'm pleased to say that with more older generation rather than with, um, definitely not with people my age." Peter has "heard people say things, not to people, but about people, racist things, but not that often." Sophie does not think Australia is a racist country:

> Just people around me, I've never experienced as being racist. Well may be not never . . . I mean it's just immaturity with some people that things that they know will annoy them. I don't believe that they are truly racist.
>
> (Sophie, City Academy, Year 10)

Being "truly racist" would be out of step with the pluralist and tolerant beliefs of those around her, and those she shares.

Alannah reflects on the question of whether Australia is a racist place and responds with a "melting-pot" view of multiculturalism.

> Well I don't know. Because, well there's no, there's not really such a thing as an Australian because we are a multicultural country and we've got settlers from, oh, God knows where, everywhere, and we are all in here together. I mean there are jokes going around about all sort of things, so may be there is racist people, but they are not necessarily Australians.
>
> (Alannah, City Academy, Year 10)

Alannah's statement can also be interpreted as an aspiration, a way of defining racism as "not Australian"—an imaginary repudiation of racism as part of national identity. At this school, the students also unanimously articulated a socially progressive and pluralist discourse on religion as another artifact of cultural and ethnic difference. In common with many private and elite schools in Australia, this school was founded as and is still formally a school associated with a particular Christian denomination, but none of the students in our study described themselves as actively practicing a religion. Indeed there was a remarkable absence of knowledge about religion, other than a belief that religion was "okay for some people" and that the school embraced a broadly ecumenical position: one that did not discriminate against others. Many students said that they found religion "interesting." "Interesting" here was used as a standby adjective, a handy response to convey that you know the topic is significant, but you personally do not have much to say about it, even though you know you should. (One student tentatively said that she was baptized Anglican (Episcopalian), then looked at us quizzically, asking, "would that be right?") In the spirit of pluralism and of encountering other perspectives, different religions are studied in Religious Education. However, none of the students could recall much of the detail of these different religious traditions, and several could not tell us the name or anything about the religion they were currently studying. As Nicky said, "Well, we have religion and ethics as subjects but we don't really learn about religions." The majority of students were not active believers, but they asserted their respect for those who were. According to Peter, the academy promotes religious tolerance and understanding by talking about the holidays associated with different religions and "they try to make like the chapel services and chaplain doesn't talk like in Christian type ways". Referring in part to the Jewish students at the school and to the school's acceptance of non-Christian students, he says confidently that "nobody takes much notice of them. Of them being Jewish or different religion" (City Academy, Year 10). In this formulation, not being discriminatory is defined as passive tolerance; religious tolerance means taking religion as not being significant.

Students' views on religion offer a clear example of the school's formal commitment to diversity and tolerance and the relative superficiality of that approach. At City Academy, religion is represented as an aspect of cultural identity, a collection of festivals, religious holidays, and interesting beliefs and practices, but not something that is an active presence in everyday identity. Students have taken on the rhetoric of religious freedom and tolerance but have very little knowledge of religions.

While simultaneously expressing a rhetorically socially progressive view on race, religion, and social diversity, the students articulated a politically conservative view on unemployment, one more in line with the kind of individual responsibility promoted by the politics of Pauline Hanson. In response to the question "What do you think are the causes of unemployment?," students replied that it was due to unemployed people's lack of motivation. "It's probably because people perhaps aren't as motivated as they might be" (Gillian, City Academy, Year 10). In the tone of voice, there was a strong punitive sense that people just had to try harder.

> Yeah, I think there's not enough motivation to get jobs either. I think they need more motivation to get up and look for jobs. Like even if it means going into every store along your street and asking if they have work, but not just living off the dole or stuff like that.
>
> (Peter, City Academy Year 10)

The operation of "us and them" logic persists here as well. "They" need to get more motivation. In this individualizing worldview, unemployment is largely not a problem for "us." When asked if they knew anybody who was unemployed, most answered plainly, "No." In Peter's case he had heard about some parents of friends not working, but it was not clear if this was voluntary. Other students extrapolated from their own experience of finding a part-time job as a student living in an upper-class suburb to argue that others were just not trying hard enough.

Alannah: Like people, anyone of the lowest of people can get up and find themselves a job and . . . some people try every now and then, but not try hard enough, and I think they're the people who shouldn't get our help because they're not trying either, they're not going to try and help us either. . . .

With unemployment in Australia, what do you think are the causes of it?

Alannah: Um, I don't know. I sometimes think, oh, it's just because people are really slack and because they don't have top qualifications and they're not even going to try. But I mean all my friends at school, we'll just walk into a place and say, "oh, excuse me, do you have any work," and you know about three out of five times they'll get a job, and that's how I got my job. And you know it just seems really strange.

(Alannah, City Academy, Year 10)

Students at City Academy were familiar and, in most cases, at ease with the language and concepts of pluralism, diversity, and the rights of the individual. However, during the interviews and in reviewing the transcripts, we were struck by the shift in discursive style and degree of sophistication when it came to discussing unemployment. There was a lack of familiarity with the appropriate liberal, socially progressive discourse on unemployment compared to the ease and fluency of responses to racism and defense of freedoms and difference (suggesting the relative invisibility of class as an issue in countries like Australia, the subject of our next chapter). The lack of ease in talking about unemployment was also evident in how they responded to what was said; responses became much less discursive, brief, often a single word or sentence. Tolerance, respect for others, and sensitivity to different backgrounds and beliefs quickly and markedly disappeared and was replaced with a much less sympathetic and Hansonite view of individual responsibility.

In this elite school, cultural, ethnic, and religious diversity is rhetorically valorized as an expression of individuality, while unemployment is derided as a failure of individual enterprise. There is a stated commitment to multiculturalism, but in the form of it being a nice idea about diversity and one that does not really penetrate the hegemony of particular kinds of cultural capital. In this school, the right cultural capital and forms of identity that really matter are understood to be fundamentally "White," despite frequent gestures to valuing diversity.

In the other schools in our study, we heard some perspectives on political values that are different from those articulated at City Academy. These differences relate both to the location and makeup of the individuals and families in that school as well as the specific discourses and ethos favored by each school. The particular agendas and politics of two of these schools, the two "middle" high schools in our study, are discussed in more detail in the following chapter. Here we want to mention briefly the values at those three schools as they were expressed in relation to our questions about race and immigration on the one hand, and unemployment on the other.

Following our interviews on race, unemployment, and other issues, a patterning of answers by school that we immediately noticed was not one according to race but on unemployment. At City Academy, in relation to a question about what they see as the causes of unemployment, every student answered with some variant of locating responsibility in the attributes of the unemployed: lack of motivation or qualifications, not trying hard enough, people not presenting themselves properly.

At Suburban High, in the same city, every student answered the same question with an answer that located responsibility for unemployment with social factors rather than those concerned primarily with the individual: the impact of technology and automation, factories closing down, immigration.

> Well, there's not enough jobs, and then people get discouraged because they can't get a job, so they give up. And some people are just lazy.
>
> *Do you think that long-term unemployment will have any impact on your life?*
>
> Um, probably, I don't know really.
>
> *And what do you think are the causes of unemployment?*
>
> Things being closed. Not enough, like jobs within a job, like just say in a factory there's not like, there could be more people working. Like they're just making excuses [. . .]
>
> *What do you think are the causes of it?*
>
> Probably people not being qualified and you know you need, more and more you need qualifications to get jobs, so people, say, are getting a bit older and are unqualified, and it's much harder to get a job because so many people are looking for them.
>
> (Students, Suburban High, Year 10)

In City Academy, both the class background of the families and the ethos of the school valued and promoted individualism, rights, and pluralism. In Suburban High, the culture was one of left-leaning progressivism and a valuing of nonconformity. This school was more visibly diverse in its enrollment than the other schools in our study, it prided itself on its inclusiveness, and students themselves talked about its diverse student body as one of the distinguishing features of the school culture. The school fostered an ideology that was sympathetic to losers (it constantly gave students second chances, for example), and was attuned to social patterning. From the stories they mentioned in interviews, students here noticed and spoke out about racism outside the school. They talked readily about power, discrimination, and forms of unfairness in relation to both racism and unemployment.

In terms of political orientations, the two metropolitan schools—City Academy and Suburban High—consistently articulated two recognizable political ideologies: liberal rights and individualism in one, and a more socialist and social movements perspective on power and social disadvantaging in the other. The two regional schools in our study fitted less neatly into such types of political categorization. At Regional Tech, which Kylie attends, the perspective of those with a lot of knowledge of the unfairness of life is most evident. They try to hang on to whatever fragile possibilities arise—to "take it as it comes." Kylie recognizes, with some fellow-feeling, how things have been unfair for the Indigenous population, but has no worked-out general political approach either to race and ethnic difference or to unemployment. When things annoy her at school, she leaves. She begins an apprenticeship but, when things start to go wrong on her work placement, she leaves that too. However, when we last interview her she has found a job in a fast food outlet that not only offers regular employment and congenial work colleagues, but opportunities for some further advancement. The boys at Regional Tech too have less ideologically pure views on how unemployment works, and point to individual as well as social factors. They know that individual effort and skills and qualifications or references do matter, but they also know that a lot of jobs have disappeared—that jobs are not necessarily there for those who want them.

Our other school in the regional town, Regional High, fosters a view of students as enterprising individuals, and promotes an imperative to keep on working hard along with a recognition of work and social outcomes as the result of individual effort. This was evident in students' answers to the questions on unemployment and on a range of other matters, as we discussed in chapter 3. When we ask our general questions about unemployment, they talk with firsthand knowledge of seeing factories that have closed down—but firsthand knowledge too of people they know who do not want work and avoid it by turning up for interview in the wrong clothes.

> I think everyone should be able to get a job because then they get responsible and they have to, everyone has to learn how to be responsible, how to be reliable, how to do things, because that's just the way society is, that's the way life is, that's the way everything goes. And the world runs like that. So for people that aren't employed and don't want to be or are finding it hard to get a job, I would try to encourage them as much as I could because you've got to, it's important and it's good for you, you'll benefit from it.

> *What do you think causes long-term unemployment?*
>
> Um, sometimes people's attitudes. . . .
>
> *And do you think it's likely to have any impact on your life?*
>
> No, I've got my goals. I'm going to go for them. I'll do the best I can and hopefully with my qualifications I'll get a good job at least. If I'm not getting the one I want, at least I'll get a good job. That's you know, that's fine.
>
> (Stephanie, Regional High, Year 10)

This student, and the others from this school, accepted the message that one's outcome in life is a result of schooling and hard work. But they are also conscious of the relevance of social distinction (e.g., how one dresses) and the limitations of location and job availability. There is considerable stress on individual responsibility, an awareness of the lurking possibilities of a difficult and competitive environment and that they will have to work hard and be alert if they are not to fall prey to this.

> I see it as a huge issue because my brother has finished school and I can see how hard it's going to be to get a job
>
> Probably one of the biggest things is dropping out of a school and not having an education to get a job over other people who have stayed in school.
>
> Some of them I don't think want to go out and work.
>
> A lot of people that have been out of work for a while, and that sort of thing just leads to alcohol and drug use in the, ah, how would you put it, lesser richer populations of [this city].
>
> *What do you think are the causes of unemployment?*
>
> Probably the way they think about themselves, or the way they dress, or, um, yeah, the way they think because of where they live. They don't have much self-esteem. [. . .] They sort of don't think they can get a job. If you think like that you won't get a job.
>
> (Regional High, Year 10)

David at Regional High was one of the most politically informed participants in our study, and was very insistent on the power of individual effort and responsibility for getting a job and familiar with the political debates about racism and the rise of Pauline Hanson. He had attended a One Nation meeting with his family, and smiles wryly when we mention Hanson's name, looking at us in a slightly bemused and awkward way, anticipating our views on the topic, and aligning us with urban political correctness.

> It makes sense [what Hanson is saying] . . . even though it's not politically correct, it's all been blown out of proportion by the media [but] when you go there and listen to them . . . you find that they've never been racist . . . they've never said anything racist, they've just been misquoted.
>
> (David, Regional High, Year 10)

In his exchange with us, it is clear that David suspects we might disapprove of his view and he recognizes that his views will mark him out as different, as an outsider in his cohort. He forcefully articulates the economic agenda associated with One Nation, and makes the case for needing to protect small businesspeople. His parents both work in small businesses (his father manages a transport yard and his mother does part-time clerical work at a local business) and the small business economy and culture is very prominent in Cubbin and important in regional Australian cities generally.

> One of her [Pauline Hanson's] things is to stop migration until, um, the country's unemployment rate is back to zero, and, um, another one is to abolish all . . . those Aboriginal things [political organizations]. To restore all tariffs and get all the exports and imports going again. Cut out, I think, the red tape in industry and small business and everything like that.
>
> (David, Regional High, Year 10)

The majority of students in this school seem to have little direct knowledge about Aboriginal people, and more limited contact with immigrants than those in the metropolitan schools. Many may reject Hanson's style, but they are her potential constituency: they fear the changes they see in terms of immigration and of work, in part because they fear where they will be left in relation to those changes.

In all four schools, the school "habitus" works to mediate the values, orientations, and biography of its students, and this happens in interaction with the specific cultural and physical geography of the schools' different locations. The sense that what we are seeing here is some specific school mediation of ways of talking and thinking, of constructing self and other, not simply family values, comes from our interviews with these students over time. How they talked about certain things came to take on certain differentiations by school as we continued the study; this was particularly evident when we asked about the issues discussed in this chapter and also when we discussed retrospectively and prospectively how the students now saw themselves in our final interviews in the immediate postschool year, discussed in chapters 3 and 7.

Researching Racism and Constructing the Other

At City Academy, with the exception of Lee (who was no longer at the school when we embarked on this set of interview questions), students seemed comfortable talking about race and racism. Those in our project were self-avowedly not well informed about, or deeply touched by, religion; they were less articulate in relation to unemployment and class, though again calling on a binary "us and them" around motivation.

A different kind of response to racial discourses in Australia was offered by a student from Suburban High, Talik, who was born in Australia, has Turkish parents, and is identified as "ethnic" by physical appearance and accent. He attends weekend school to study his family culture and language, he mixes socially and at school with kids from the same background. In interviews, he is often reticent and sometimes awkward with our style of questioning, but he keeps coming voluntarily to all the interviews, even those conducted after he finishes school. Throughout he positions himself as someone who comments on racism, rather than someone who has experienced racism

What are your views about her [Pauline Hanson] and the debate that she's generating?

Talik: I don't like it.

Have you talked about it much with your friends? Does it come up at home and do you talk about it at home?

Talik: At home? It has come up a couple of times at home. Um, not with friends.

Do you think there is much racism in Australia?

Talik: Um, besides Pauline Hanson, no.

You think not?

Talik: No.

(Talik, Suburban High, Year 10)

One possible explanation for Talik's reluctance to say more and his description of there not being much racism in Australia is that it locates him less as an outsider. Or it might be that Talik is simply conforming to rules of polite behavior both in his own family and in mainstream schools: he is avoiding making us feel uncomfortable by not insisting on racism being associated with those of Anglo background.

But Talik's responses also raise methodological issues about the effect of asking questions in particular ways, and of unintentionally inciting and producing certain responses. In retrospect, and in listening to and reading the interview transcripts, it was clear that our mode of questioning made it difficult for Talik to respond in other ways. (Here too we need to acknowledge the accumulated history and effects of our interviews over the preceding four years, in which two white women came twice a year to conduct social science research interviews with him at school. In these interviews, Talik is polite and cooperative but also a little uncertain as to what we actually want and what kind of responses he should be giving.) His responses to our questions in this interview are noticeably briefer than usual, often a couple of words, and he appears uncomfortable, pausing in responses, laughing nervously, looking away from us, and is obviously relieved when the questioning stops. During the interview, we too felt awkward, and unsure of how to manage the silences and uneasiness. We could see that he was uncomfortable, but ending the interview early did not seem the right thing to do either, as that too could be another form of silencing.

In retrospect, it is evident that we asked questions about Pauline Hanson and migration as if he were an expert on the experience of racism (an Other) and he responded in a way that showed his mastery of polite and proper discourse about racism when speaking with white women in a relatively formal setting. It is possible as well that his responses reflected a sense of (or desire for) national belonging as an Australian. He does not assume the position of "discriminated-against Other" who might tell us as researchers some truth about racism. This was the position our line of questioning, unconsciously perhaps, wanted him to speak from. We did not regularly ask other students if they spoke about Pauline Hanson and One Nation at home, but by posing this question to Talik ("the ethnic family must have encountered racism, tell us all about it") we betrayed our own desire for him to speak as, and be positioned as, the Other. In his answers too there was another kind of second-guessing of our desire to hear certain answers (that multiculturalism works? that Australia is a tolerant society?) and to not offend us as white Australians. So the dynamics of the research interview simultaneously produced a form of official multicultural discourse and an Othering of the research participant; they also revealed some of Talik's reasoning about the context-specific and appropriate way to respond to questions to racism and some of our own complicity in discursive constructions of the Other.

In reflecting on their experiences of interviewing black adolescent girls as part of a study of girls "at risk," Jill Taylor, Carol Gilligan, and Amy Sullivan write of the silences, of what is seen and what is not noticed when white researchers interview black participants. In one telling example, they describe the failure of a white researcher not to notice or to follow up when a young black woman introduced a "race" topic into an interview. The young woman refers three times to "a racial comment" when describing an exchange between herself and a teacher, but the researcher does not return to this in any of her follow-up questions (Taylor, Gilligan, and Sullivan 1996, 233–235). This occurred in a study explicitly and self-consciously concerned with relationships, and with developing a "relational method of inquiry." It was a study attuned to the effects of the researcher, to the dynamics of the relationship between researcher and researched, and to the significant methodological effects of social and power differences in that relationship. Yet, it was only when they were on a research retreat to discuss the transcripts with an invited group of black and white scholars not directly involved in the interviewing, that the silencing of the "racial comment" was noticed by one of the black women.

In the example from our interviews quoted earlier, the methodological and political effect was not so much one of "not noticing" but of wanting to hear, to incite a particular response that would satisfy our curiosity about the experience of racism. In both examples, however, the question is raised of how racist and "othering" practices enter the research scenario even when there is a heightened sense of researcher reflexivity, and even when questions about race are raised directly. In our case, posing questions about race and racism to young people who are likely to be routinely constituted as Other, did not at all remove the risk of "othering." In wanting to hear the voice of the Other, the interview worked paradoxically to produce what Talik judged we wanted to hear and what he thought was the right thing to say.

Concluding Comments

We have looked at how young people negotiate racial discourses and political reasoning in the context of intensified public political debates about race, ethnicity, and nation in Australia, and a heightened attention to whiteness in that politics and in the research literature. In exploring some of the relations between political discourses and self-positioning, we have pointed to the significance of desires and aspirations as well as fears in these forms of political and self-identification. One of our concerns was to understand something of a particular national cultural logic of racism. We have argued that although "us and them" binaries are shifting and unstable, focusing on their deployment within young people's discourses helps us to see the identifications and contrasts with which they are working, and to situate these in the context of becoming and identity-making on the part of young people of this age.

In her comparative study of the rhetoric of racism and antiracism in the United States and France, Lamont interviewed white and minority (African American and North African, respectively) working-class men in both countries and found that both white majority groups expressed racism "largely though a moral critique of the values of racial minorities, particularly concerning self-reliance, individualism, and family values" (2000, 44). Deploying similar universalistic and moral arguments, both African Americans and North Africans described their "own culture as morally superior to that of majority groups." There were, however, significant national differences in "the cultural tools" available for rebutting and demonstrating racism and racial inequality. In the United States, "interviewees more often explain racial differences with reference to biology, history, and psychology, and use market-related arguments" [in the sense that performance at work and in the labor market is seen as an equalizer of racial difference] (45). In contrast, French workers "exclusively refer to specifically cultural and religious explanations in accounting for racial inequality"(45). In our discussion of Australian young people's negotiation of racial discourses, we have drawn attention to the salience of logics of belonging and national identifications in framing their reasoning and their constructions of difference.

We have also explored the impact of school habitus on the shaping of those forms of reasoning, showing how the authority of distinctive school cultures tended to orient students to particular constructions of "us," "them," and social differences. And here we have argued that students' views on race, ethnicity, and racism are also part of a repertoire of political reasoning, and that comparing attitudes to different issues—such as unemployment and immigration—can reveal both the character and distinctiveness of political positions. As such, this works against essentialized or universalizing perceptions of what the "race" debate is about by showing national and local cultural specificity. Additionally, this provided a close-up analysis of how a school's habitus infiltrates subjectivity and becomes a part of how students understand others and the making of their own subjectivity.

Finally, we have drawn attention to some reflections on our experience of trying to research racism, both in relation to how we as researchers share similar difficulties about how to talk about this topic that we identify in those we discuss, and also in terms of the methodological dilemmas of the embodied researcher, and of researching and constructing the Other. As white middle-class women, our presence provoked certain kinds of responses and reflexivity from the participants. For some, there was a finely tuned sense of answering in the right way, of anticipating our views, and tailoring answers to satisfy, please, or shock us, or of reflexively censoring or commenting on their views. But our presence and mode of questioning also silenced or made it difficult for some to speak. In the example of Talik, the dynamic of the interview worked to produce him as an Other even as we sought to speak directly and openly about racism, to give "voice" to what we imagined was his identity and experiences. Research interviews can construct what they set out to investigate, and researching racism requires us to be attentive to the identity positioning and investments of both interviewees and interviewers.

CHAPTER 7

Class in the New World and the New Economy

Many people know the classic British *7 Up* television and film series, a series that has spawned national copies in many countries around the world. In that project (begun in the 1960s) the filmmakers took a range of seven-year-old children from different social class backgrounds and interviewed them to show their different ways of talking, thinking, their bodily comportment, projections of their future selves, ways of interacting with others, and their behavior in different types of school and home settings. In successive seven year intervals (at ages 14, 21, 28, 35, 42), the filmmaker, Michael Apted, returned to those he had interviewed at age seven and made a new film about who they now were: what they were doing, how they now saw themselves, retrospectively as well as in the present and future. The project is fascinating: it shows individual biographies over time, and it also depicts enduring markers of difference, not just in where people end up (there are strong patterns of difference, but not invariant ones), but in the ways they see themselves, and how they notice or deny the way social differentiation works. The project began in a place and at a time when it seemed clear-cut to many academics, as well to those filmmakers, that "class" was the major differentiating feature that shaped people's fate and opportunities, both at school and beyond school. The *7 Up* project assumed this centrality of class in its selection principles: it included relatively few girls, and only one non-White seven year old; and it dwelt more on those who embodied the most extreme contrasts of background (the elite and the poor) than on those who in some sense were in the middle.

On the other side of the world, in Australia, some two decades later, the filmmaker Gillian Armstrong made a short film when she was at film school about three "working-class" schoolgirls from the city of Adelaide. She made another film about them when they were 18, with two now being mothers; another again at 25, when the third of the trio was about to get married; and another when the women were in their early thirties, and two of them themselves had 14-year-old daughters. This later film includes a lot of footage from the earlier films, and it shows in the background some broad changes affecting what might be seen as the same "class" of people two decades apart. In the 1970s, the working-class teenagers dressed and spoke in broad, recognizably working-class ways, dropped out of school early, had babies at 18. In the 1990s, both they and their daughters are less distinguishable by accent or dress as belonging to a particular class—possibly as a result of the influence of television, mass fashion, and different general patterns in school retention. This is not to say that the film shows nothing of the themes the literature has classically associated with "class"—such as continuing hopes for education combined with dashed experiences of it or problems of managing expectations about housing—but it does, more so than *7 Up*, bring important changes in the social backdrop to the fore. Looking at the two film series relative to each other, one is also aware of location and its specificities. Being a "working-class girl" in South Australia [a state with a history of working-class migration from England, with particular employment patterns, along with a history of concerns about public provision in relation to housing and education (Thomson 2002)] is not an identical thing to being a working-class girl in the English midlands, or even in other parts of Australia such as Melbourne or Sydney.

Why talk about "class"? And, even if one wants to talk about class, is it possible today, and in countries like the United States and Australia, to do so? Just considering these film projects shows some of the problems. Is "class" a meaningful concept once you try to put race, sexuality, gender, and ethnicity into the picture? How do the changing times, the changing cultural forms, and the changing structure of the labor market affect the utility of a concept built from nineteenth century industrial England and Germany? If "class" is not a category the young people themselves think with [and by and large it is not, even in England—see Phoenix and Tizard (1996)], if they do not see it as part of their world in the way that they in some ways see gender, race, sexuality, and ethnicity to be, then what are we to make of that? Is "class" about relations of production, exploitation, and class conflict, or is it a shorthand for socioeconomic hierarchy, advantage, and disadvantage? Is it a term that describes deeply formed processes of psychological being in the world, a concept that helps make sense of individual subjectivity, desire, and educational biography? Is it a concept that insists on the importance of labor and capital as linchpins for understanding individuals and social relations? Or do attempts to categorize and identify using "class" as their mode inevitably misdescribe and misidentify modern forms of being in the world? The slick answer to this series of rhetorical questions might be that "all of the above" are pertinent, and that there are different histories of what people are trying to work out, and work with, when they use this term.

To name what we attend to as "class," or to talk about what we find as class, or to designate someone as "working class" or "middle class," is to inscribe it (and them) in a particular way, to relate what is said and observed to particular types of wider connections and particular patterns. To use "class" as a focus and interpretive marker is to address issues of social distinction, hierarchy, power in individual identities and in the patterns of social relationships between individuals. It is also to attend to the relationships between individual formation and subjectivity, especially in the context of family and schooling, and to patterns of work, including the form of work and of different jobs; the structure of what types of jobs people from different backgrounds enter; and the dispositions, capital, power, lack of capital and power that pertain to different kinds of jobs.

In Australia (and in the United States and other "New World" countries), and in contemporary times, either working with the concept of "class" or attempting to do without it or to replace it with something else, all seem deeply problematic. In terms of self-conscious subjectivities, as Julie Bettie writes, "Class is largely missing as a category of identity offered by popular culture and political discourse in the US" (Bettie 2003, 195). Race and gender are the more visible, and deceptively natural, markers with which both individual identity and political analyses work. In Australia too, while there has been a more central history of class-based union politics than in the United States, contemporary self-identifications do not usually speak the language of class. And many of the archetypal working-class jobs (factory work, mining) are no longer as evident; they have been exported. Many of the low-paid jobs that do exist (cleaners, part-time workers of various sorts) have less visibility in the gendered history of class discussion. And a great many other jobs of the new economy—in the service, entertainment, and knowledge industries and in the professions and semiprofessions—have less immediate impact in schemas of how class is at work.

At the same time, an enduring interest of education sociology, and of this study, is how family-formed individual identities interact with school to produce the patterns of "who gets what." In Australia and indeed, in all OECD countries, a very strong relationship to socioeconomic status persists, whatever the problems in trying to operationalize that concept adequately. (Connell et al. 1982; OECD 2004; Teese and Polesel 2003; Thomson 2002) Class difference might be hard to pin down or categorically define. But in terms of studying the lived experiences of young people at school, it is hard to do without some shorthand concept that draws attention to the different ways young people who live in particular types of communities and families, with particular material resources and particular cultural orientations, encounter schools and begin to develop the routes of differentiated achievement and self-belief that are visible in the databases about retention, participation in higher education, and the labor market.

What we are drawing attention to in this discussion is that "class" is both a concept, an explanatory schema or way of marking difference used by researchers and theorists, and something that might be recognized by differing degrees in the people and social discourses we study. And both as concept and as lived experience, it is troubled by the new forms of contemporary times. In relation to schooling and young people, "class" has normally been drawn on to explain how and why certain patterns and outcomes persist; but a mantra of these times, and one starting point impetus of our project is that the circumstances of work, culture, and social life as well as theoretical agendas have changed.

It is now over a decade since we commenced our own project, and in this period there has been a visible change in the literature in relation to class, a new re-engagement with it, but this re-engagement itself has taken some different forms. Some of it is specifically attempting to engage with a sense of how class is being lived and how it is operating in "New Times" in terms of social formation and school choices. Other work is attempting to engage with a specific sense of how gender-class is lived; and some is attempting to examine new forms of work and class in relation to that.

Partly as a reaction to the influential work of Giddens and Beck on seeing this period as one of "individualization" in which young people make their own biographies rather than enter into inherited roles, a number of writers have explored how certain old patterns of advantage and disadvantage appear to be being reconstructed. In the United Kingdom, for example, some recent important studies (Ball 2003; Gewirtz, Ball, and Bowe 1995; Power et al. 2003;) have returned to the old story of what happens in schools' production of inequalities to study what the "middle class" are doing. They look at the "advantaged" and not just the disadvantaged, particularly in relation to new institutional forms of education that have made choice of schools a more central issue and have broken down a simple opposition of private and public as modes or pathways to advantage or disadvantage. Their accounts emphasize both a Bourdieuian story of cultural capital—the knowledge and attributes that the middle class (meaning professional or upper middle class) have that enables them to work the system to their advantage—and a story of how entry to jobs is now more mediated via education than simply directly by class advantage, and that the competitive attention to education has consequently intensified. In the United States, Brantlinger (2003) captures some similar elements in her study of how teachers and parents of different class background take up schooling issues today. Her account argues that members of the affluent professional classes "put forward members of their class as models to emulate" (10), and that their class advantage is mostly invisible to them. Such parents are caught in some contradictory positioning, she suggests, in that they value "liberal" and progressive practices, yet also are concerned to ensure the advantage of their own child, for example, by demanding advanced classes. She argues these parents "displayed a dissonance between their class epistemology and desired liberal identity." In other words, it is important ideologically, as the sociological reproduction literature of the 1970s used to argue, that schools appear to be arenas of equal opportunity with outcomes appearing to be the results of students' (and families') own efforts. But within the shifting forms of policy we find related moves by families to ensure that the model of the good student does remain consistent with that of those who already have advantages, and to prevent funding and curriculum regimes that might affect the outcomes of the disadvantaged at the expense of those who were previously successful. (Teese 2000; for this argument in relation to the relative advantages of girls and boys, see Yates 1997).

One legacy of the history of studying class in relation to schooling was to focus on how advantage and disadvantage happen relationally, and examine hegemonic practices of schools as class-preferential.

One of our interests in this project was in how such relationships and practices were being lived in students' biographies; we have explored this in previous chapters, especially in chapters 3 and 5.

Another interest in the new re-engagement with class has been how to go beyond the story just outlined, a story whose basic form is a binary characterization of "middle-class" advantage and "working-class" disadvantage, and to develop an account that does not homogenize "working-class" experience, and not make race, ethnicity, gender, sexuality, and place invisible. We started our study with an intention to follow some young people with backgrounds that might be classified as similar, but who lived in different places or attended different schools, to try to untangle (class-based) family and school as a homogenized couplet. We also wanted to focus as much on individuals and schools "in the middle" as those who clearly represented the two ends of a binary account about class and school advantage. Terminology here might be ambiguous. We meant "in the middle" as distinct from "middle class" (i.e., advantaged, professional, or "new" middle class); we meant schools and individuals that were not overdetermined winners or losers in education pathways.

In Australia, a major recent study by Michael Pusey (Pusey 2003) has also offered a re-engagement with class by a new focus on "middle Australia."[1] Pusey's focus was on how people are living and perceiving the raft of changes associated with neoliberalism: intensification of work and the dismantling of many centralized industry awards and systems to protect working conditions; increased focus on private and individual responsibility instead of state funding of public institutions; the normalization of women's participation in paid work. Pusey argued that there was widespread unease about the extent of the intensification of employment and spread of job insecurity on the one hand while simultaneously an apparent declining quality of publicly supported institutions such as health and education. Stephen Ball captures some similar anxieties among the middle class in England (Ball 2003). Our interest was in young people and their perceptions of their current situation and their prospective future. How do they construe changes to the social fabric and social patterns; how do they think about advantage, disadvantage, power, and education? (for an interesting comparison of how French people regard such matters, see Bourdieu 1999).

One of our interests in choosing to do a study in four schools rather than an ethnography in one school was to see how young people, living in what might be externally categorizable as different class locations, themselves construed who they were relative to others, and how they constructed their own trajectory and thinking about social patterns. Here we are trying to convey an idea of "class subjectivity" in two senses: self-conscious identifications and placements about "who I am;" along with the not necessarily self-conscious orientations and dispositions that are acquired in family settings and begin to differentially mediate schooling experiences and orientations to one's future. Looking across a range of schools and backgrounds, and not only at the most advantaged and disadvantaged, also highlights the changing social and economic backdrop to what is happening in schools, as the four schools in our study convey a different sense of employment and career possibilities, and what will be effective in the face of the changing world.

Yet another wave of interest in revisiting class has been seen in feminist attempts to understand this in gender-specific terms. (Bettie 2003; Hey 1997; Reay 1995b, 1997; Skeggs 1997, Walkerdine, Lucey and Melody 2001; Weis 1993, 2004). Much of the work here focuses on what it means to be a working-class girl or boy today. Bettie (2003) has explored different ethnic/gender/sexuality forms of working-class femininity in a Californian high school, denoting this in terms of habitus-based orientations and also "performance." She explores ways in which backgrounds and "performance" of working-class or middle-class positioning in the school context are not perfectly correlated, pointing both to ways in which individuals do take up their own lives, and ways in which perceptions of others mediate what is achieved. In Bettie's study, girls from Mexican-American backgrounds and those who were gay were likely to be positioned as "Other," even if they drew on "middle class" backgrounds. Some girls from working-class background in an academic stream could more successfully "pass" as middle-class because they could understand "the structures of exclusion at work in ways that vocational track students did not" (Bettie 2003, 192).

Valerie Walkerdine, Helen Lucey, and June Melody (2001), in a longitudinal study of girls in England who were first encountered as five year olds interacting with their mothers, provide a critical psychological perspective on class difference in the context of education. Walkerdine et al. argue that it is not only that the girls from working-class and middle-class backgrounds have been socialized differently by their mothers, and that a school consistently looks for signs of achievement in one group and of lack of achievement in the other. But, they argue, girls also have desires, drives, and emotional relationships to the school situation that run deeper than the more sociological concept of "dispositions" or "cultural capital." For working-class girls, the fears associated with entering the unknown world of the university are not necessarily conscious (or self-conscious) but are offered as one explanation for why when some of these girls do become pregnant they find having the baby a preferable option to continuing with study. For the middle-class girls in that study, as we discussed in relation to Nicky's story in chapter 5, the combined drive of home and school habitus creates desires to be impossibly successful, and constant anxiety about not measuring up.

Class Identification Compared with Class Subjectivity

In Australia, even the Labor Party, founded to promote the interests of the workers, no longer uses the language of class and oppositional class interests. In our interviews, when we wanted to ask participants about whether and how they saw different social groups at their school or in the community more generally, we had trouble phrasing this. Trying to avoid naming the issue of class in a particular way (so as not to be too leading in our questioning), we ended up asking more vaguely and inadequately, "Do you think you can judge people by how they look or the way they dress?" Not surprisingly, this produced varied responses, with most answering in the negative, and a few delineating the subgroups in their school who were identified by different choices of fashion. Similarly, when in each year's interviews we asked people to describe themselves, they invariably chose to talk about physical appearance and personality traits rather than naming themselves as belonging to a particular social category. But despite its absence as a concept to speak with, differentiated class-based subjectivities, particularly in the sense that Bourdieu and others have written about as dispositions and forms of cultural capital, can be seen in our participants and in the ways they encountered their school. And for some of these young people, a more self-conscious sense of social positioning, a form of class identification, was highly salient to their own sense of who they were and where they were going.

In our very first interviews in the project, we were struck by the different comfort levels of participants with the interview situation, their different "know how" and facility with words and with us, alongside their different orientations to the future. At the richest school in our study, City Academy, the students talked fluently and at length, skating over vast realms of possible future scenarios involving various professional occupations, glamour, and success. At a semirural primary school that was a feeder school for Regional Tech, we were more clearly encountered as unknown adults in a scenario whose import was unclear, and that made some of the poorest students distinctly uncomfortable:

What do you think your life will be like when you leave school? Do you think about that much?
[silence . . . all three girls shake their heads]
What would you like to be doing, Jackie?
1st girl: Maybe babysitting . . . and play for Australia in netball.
2nd girl: Babysitting.
3rd girl: Same.
What about when you're 25. Any ideas?
1st girl: [shakes her head]
2nd girl: [taking on a serious expression] Help look after Brendan when he has asthma.
What about if you could have a wish and do anything you really liked. What would you like to do when you're 25?
2nd girl: Live with sister—the oldest one—. . . in Cubbin.
3rd girl: [who has virtually said nothing to this point in the interview] Get a job.

The way the interviews happen, the ways the girls relate to us and we to them, is as important in understanding subjectivity and class as is the literal content of what they say about themselves and the future. The entire interview from which this extract is taken was filled with silences, monosyllabic answers, and an overwhelming sense of unease. In contrast, at interviews held at roughly the same time at City Academy, the girls displayed not only a comfortable easiness in the situation but also an ability to self-monitor and adjust the impression their answers might be having on us—to add stories about caring for the less fortunate to a narrative primarily about hopes for a glamorous and successful future.

And how we react is also part of the story of class subjectivity and the workings of "distinction." In Australia and the United States, class modes and accents are not as obviously marked as in the Old World countries of the United Kingdom and France with their historical hierarchically differentiated education systems. But this does not mean they are not present. After the first round of interviews, we talked to each other about the verbal fluency and self-assurance of the students at City Academy and how this contrasted with the interviews in the other three schools in our study. We were surprised to find, however, when we transcribed the tapes that in strict grammatical terms, those interviews and self-narratives were no more fluent than a number of others. They too were marked by pauses and the grammatical infelicities of oral speech, as indeed were our own questions. The impression we had gained was not a response to the "objective" superiority of the language that had been delivered, but a reaction to the style and situation and our own expectations. We had ourselves been schooled in country high schools and each time that we entered City Academy to do our interviews we were struck again by the grandeur of the surroundings and the sheer expensiveness of that education. On the table in the reception area were glossy brochures for the school's latest money-raising activities. Prizes, all donated, included first-class travel around the world. Fund-raising activities included lavish cocktail parties and dinners; the brochures were full of stories of the achievements of alumni now taking a host of leading positions in the world of commerce, politics, law, and the arts.

In terms of class-based subjectivity, the characteristics of those in this school who come from the more wealthy and professional groups here bring experiences (of travel, cultural pursuits, or equipment in the home), resources and networks, assurance, orientation to being a successful person, and expectations that not continuing to the most prestigious universities or courses would be an anomalous trajectory among their peers. They not only want to have a certain sort of life (one that repeats the advantages of their parents yet with none of the disadvantages) but to be a certain type of person: one who is successful and distinguished. But it is also, ideologically, part of the subjectivity of this group to not attribute outcomes to class advantages, but rather to individual efforts. It is good form, good manners, to say that everyone is equal: to not be "racist" or "sexist." At the same time, there is a consciousness that the school you go to does matter, that networks matter. And there is a very high degree of reflexive self-awareness about how one should present one's self in interactions with researchers; this was discussed in more detail in the chapter 5 through Nicky's story.

But while people such as Nicky might display class subjectivities—orientations, values, desires, modes of speech, dress, and comportment—that differentiate them from those of less elite background, the participants who were most ready to discuss social differentiation and their own ambitions relative to that were not those at the extremes [(upper) middle-class kids in (upper) middle-class schools, working-class kids in working-class schools]. They were instead those students from a background that was more "in the middle" and attending one particular school in our study—Regional High—or were individuals who in some sense were aware of a dissonance between the dominant class positioning of their school and their own class position. "Class identification" is not the same thing as "class subjectivity."

Take the elite school. Three of the students we studied—Lee, Diana and Gillian—were self-conscious about the fact that in their own eyes they did not fit the normal profile of the school. In the case of Diana, this is not so much a result of the socioeconomic profile of her parents (her father is a doctor and mother a nurse who now manages her husband's practice) or of wealth, but more a matter of the distinctions and differentiation of place. She lives in a suburb which is recognized as a good place to live, but it is on the edge of a wealthy suburb and she feels it is not one of the areas favored by families attending City Academy or regarded as having sufficiently high social status. These feelings were further exacerbated for Diana as she attended her local government elementary school, rather than junior school of City Academy. Her sense of not being part of the school and peer values was combined with frustration that the core girls' group at the school formed a coterie that she did not fit into. She was also consumed with academic anxieties about whether she could live up to her parents' expectations for her at the same time as she expressed frustration with what she saw as a hypocrisy in both her parents and the school:

> I know, and it's so full on, and I just think about it sometimes and it drives me crazy. You know, that really upsets me, how they're just so full on, and you know, you're only acceptable in life if you are a doctor or a lawyer or something else. My mum's not so much like that, but my dad is because he's always been a high achiever. But like when he was younger he had no social life, you know, he just spent his life in the library. . . . He was dux of the school and everything *[she knows this in detail, which tends to confirm her story of the pressure of expectations that has been built up]*.
>
> He went to St. Bernards and even if they say you know we don't mind what you get, you know it's just so not true . . . and they would just die if you know, they spent this money on your education and you ended up being . . . a secretary or something . . . to my Dad that would seem really sort of low, when it's just not.

Do you think that they would specifically like you to be a doctor rather than something else?

I think Dad would be really happy if I got into medicine because I could work the surgery and stuff. But they wouldn't mind as long as it was something big and huge and important.

With high scores to get into?

Yeah, exactly.

(Diana, City Academy, Year 9, age 14)

Diana in fact leaves City Academy midway through Year 10 and completes her schooling in another state. When we interviewed her at age 18, she is less visibly angry and depressed than she was in the earlier interviews. She remains firm in her view that the problems she experienced at City Academy were due to it being a particular type of school in which she did not fit:

Diana: If you go to City Academy, it's really hard to not be a "City" type person. It's really different if you've got "City Academy-ish" parents and go to that school and just live that life. . . . It's the same little groupie thing, but they just get older, and it just keeps going round . . . values are just pumped into your head. I think if I didn't have to spend all my time trying to work out firstly what it was, and then trying to see through it like, maybe if I was at a different school. I could've spent more time, firstly learning and secondly, learning other things about life.

What do you see as the characteristics of City Academy people?

Diana: Rich, snobby, everything on show. The school heroes were the people who won all the events, got themselves in the brochure. Everything was all outward appearance; who they acknowledge at assembly; put things on blazer and you'd have these people walking around with these pockets full of these stupid things. . . . I know so many people who have actually achieved, and this is just . . . this is just a joke . . . they'd put in all the photos of all the glamorous people and I wasn't in it once—and Mum said—look, this is just City's view of achievement, it's not yours . . . I think that is really one of the struggles at that sort of school, especially when you're that young. Firstly you have no self-esteem anyway. And then when you're sort of warped with these strange ideas, I don't think it helps.

What was about it that meant you couldn't be an individual?

Emphasis on uniform, nail polish, no choice of subjects up to Year 10, no options, everything under control, so strict on uniform, assemblies, old school songs.

> I can't see where they're getting this diversity thing from, because you've got to play all this sport; you've got to get up on Saturday and play your sport and you don't really have that much time to open up to anything else . . . but you know, it's a nice thing to put in the brochure . . . I don't think it's really that genuine when it comes down to it.
>
> (Diana, first year after finishing school interstate)

Lee, like Diana, railed at the conformity of the school during his interviews there, and he too left the school for another midway through his secondary schooling. Again, like Diana, his sense of displacement at the school was not due to his family's occupation or class positioning (his father was a lawyer), but derived in part from his self-consciousness about place and the distinctions of location and social hierarchy that were so important to many of his fellow students at City Academy. He lived in a leafy, comfortable area but it was not as high in status as the suburbs in which many of the students at City Academy resided; in some respects, he feels this positioned him as an outsider. But there were also other factors shaping his self-positioning (and constructions by others) as not being part of the academy crowd. While he is at the school, he never mentions his Chinese heritage, but talks freely about it and his balancing of different hopes for his future once he has left. In later interviews after they had left City Academy, both Diana and Lee indicated in a retrospective sense that although they had been unhappy at the school, they could see that during their time there they were being disciplined to a certain type of class conformity. In reviewing her compilation video at age 18, Diana mentions that when she watches herself in the early interviews she sees herself coming across as a bit "City Academy girly." But although Diana was unhappy at the school—at the time and retrospectively—the ways in which she is living her life at 18, the ambitions she expresses—to become a lawyer, to do something special and interesting with her life—are well within the trajectories and destinations encouraged by that school. Indeed, when we ask her whether she would send her own children to a private school or a government school, she finds it difficult to answer.

A third "marginal" person at this school is Gillian, whose story is discussed at more length in chapter 4. Again, Gillian feels herself differentiated by the place where she lives and her previous schooling at the local government elementary school as well as by parental occupation (her father is a teacher, her mother a journalist). Unlike

Diana and Lee, Gillian's self-consciousness about the class values of City Academy becomes muted as she conforms to its modes and begins to succeed in them. For Gillian to take on the new ethos and aspirations was part of an upwardly mobile journey, which was not the case for either Diana or Lee who entered the school from families whose culture was more homologous with that of the school, and whose rebellion from the school does not threaten or challenge their class status. By the end of school, she is taking a leading position in organizing the school formal, and has somewhat adapted her initial career expectation (teacher) to one that meets more of the expectations of being a distinctive person (therapist).

From the group of students at City Academy, those who were most self-conscious about their own and the school's class positioning were those who felt marginal in some way. Similarly, at Suburban High, two students who were offered the option of private school by their parents were those who most dwelt on the class location and implications of their choice to remain there.

In general, self-conscious consideration of class and social hierarchy was not common among the students in our study, but in one school, Regional High, it was a central agenda. The ethos of Regional High has been discussed in chapter 3 in relation to school-specific norms of the good student. At Regional High, school relativities were ever-present, a constant interest and point of reference. Students would often mention that the school was "as good as" a private school, and, as evidence of that, referred repeatedly to the participation in rowing and the quality of the boat shed. Both for the school, and for a number of the students we interviewed, social hierarchy was of intense and enduring interest, especially in terms of the relativities of school status and the status of different residential locations within the town. At this school, unusual in the Australian context, there was thus a preoccupation with actual class *identification,* not only with tacit dispositions or class subjectivity.

One of the students at Regional High, David, frequently talked to us about his being bullied in the early high school years and of feeling somewhat of a loner in the school environment. He constantly explained and named this as an issue relating to his superior social location—that he lived in an impressive house in the best part of town—and of (class) envy on the part of others. Postschool as well, he maintains this explanatory framework about his history at school:

David: I was sort of, I was different to most other people there so that's a problem.

How do you see yourself as being different?

David: Oh [I am] just totally different person, totally different likes and interests, um, just being brought up differently to most people there, you know so, you know, 'cause I, there was sort of, sort of this class you know, this class system you know 'cause it's "Regional High School," it's sort of in the middle of you know the rich area and you know there's the poor area, it's just such a wide variety of people go there.

And how do you think that made it difficult for you?

David: Oh, you know just, stereotyped as rich kid or something like that or, you know. But yeah, I, I think one of the things, um, that isolated me was because of my interests and stuff like that were totally different to other people, um, like I didn't care about them and I didn't want to have anything to do with them like on the weekends, like if they were wanting to go off to parties or whatever and act like idiots, you know I was too busy I was off doing other things that were more important to me, you know, so that obviously affects how people treat you.

(David, first year after finishing school, Regional High)

David's subjective sense of his superior positioning in the social relativities of the town in which he lived contributed to some assurance that he would in fact reproduce this superiority in his post-school life. David repeatedly locates himself firmly as upper class, wealthy, and morally superior in many ways. Yet his parents do not have high-status professional jobs—his father manages a transport yard and his mother does part-time clerical work. But there is inherited money in the family (from farming at one stage) and this has enabled his family to purchase a home in a very visible and well-established desirable part of town. David's powerful sense of his own class superiority derives from the politics of place and the social geography of class, not from professional occupation or the kinds of cultural capital associated with and that define "upper class" for students at the elite and middle-class schools in the metropolitan areas.

Another student at Regional High, Andrew, also felt that he lived in a superior part of town and went to a good school. These were very important to him and to the way in which he represented his relationships with others; they remained prominent themes in his interviews after he had finished school. During high school, he had wanted to be a doctor or a lawyer, but his Year 12 results were not strong enough to gain entry to these courses so he ended up having to settle, initially at least, for entry to a course in medical science at a lesser university. He nevertheless retained his plans to return to his original ambitions following his first degree. He saw himself as a doctor in the town he grew up in or in a similar place. Like David, Andrew's parents had occupations that are not conventionally categorized as middle class—his father managed a car mechanic repair shop and his mother worked part-time as a nurse. Andrew's parents had moved to enable him to attend Regional High. In his final interviews, Andrew recalls that when the family moved "they copped a bit of flak" and that it provoked a certain amount of envy from his parents' friends. By moving they were perceived as "more wealthy" than their friends and as "climbing up the social ladder." For Andrew too, his understanding of social relativities, hierarchies, and distinctions—especially spatial and educational—and not only parental income or occupation, was an important part of his sense of who he was and who he wanted to be.

Living in a town such as Cubbin remains appealing for him, even at the end of school, when it is not uncommon for young people to want to break ties and move away from family and local community. Andrew finds the city, where he is studying, a little overwhelming, especially because he does not know many people and thinks that the city has much more of "an ethnic flavor" than his hometown. Reflecting at the end of school on why he would like to return to live his adult life in Cubbin, he says:

> *Andrew:* Um, just it's sort of good just sort of being able to walk down the street of Cubbin and knowing a few people rather than just sort of walk around here and just another face in the crowd so, I guess yeah I've just really been brought up in Cubbin and so that's where I'm most comfortable.
>
> (Andrew, age 18, first year at university)

Andrew has experienced a sense of close community in Cubbin and he wants to recreate that for his own future. That same community closeness—of being seen and known—also gives rise to the intense attention to class positioning, to micro distinctions in where you live (compared possibly to what you do). Neither Andrew nor David's parents hold elite or even middle-class occupations, yet they maintain and project a strong sense of high social status and class identification—confirmed by the envy of the others. The social status of jobs is not the means for mediating class distinction; in this country town, it is residential location and school attended.

Regional High, as we discussed earlier, itself constructs social differentiation as something that is extremely important. Its relation to private schools and lesser government schools is endlessly discussed; its attention to the appearances that mark the school as superior (boat shed, fine buildings, playing fields, good position) and to the behavior and appearances that mark its students as superior is repeatedly emphasized. Other students at this school do not necessarily share Andrew's and David's picture of being and aiming to be a superior person, but they too often muse on social differences and distinctions. Stephanie talks about the difference she notices when staying in the working-class suburb where her boyfriend lives, where men work on the wharves, and in her view young people do not take school seriously enough, compared with the town and the school she lives in.

The *subjective* awareness of and interest in social differentiation and social hierarchy is evident in these young people who are living in a smaller city, where the markers of social differentiation are encountered as part of an everyday lived experience.[2] In this setting, families and individuals connected with the different schools saw each other frequently; stories about the kinds of people who inhabited the different schools circulated through multifaceted rumors and gossip. When we asked questions about markers of social differentiation, the young people in this town could talk very readily about them—but the differentiations they were attuned to were local hierarchies, ones that would be categorized differently by sociologists working on a broader canvas. For example, none of the young people in our study in this city came from solidly middle-class or upper professional backgrounds. The norm in the city was that most people worked in (or owned) small businesses, and that most worked in occupations that would be classed as "semiskilled" or "manual." Social differentiation here related to relative wealth and family history and especially to location and style of housing, much more than to occupational categorization, though people who are "bosses" or self-employed tradespeople are accorded status and are considered important in local politics and sporting clubs.

In the last chapter, we commented on the assumptions we were bringing to questions we posed to Talik about racism. Attempting to study "class," we became aware of our own class experiences and current position entering the story as well as the interpretations we tend to make. It is no accident that a lot of the literature on class and education does import, often explicitly, an autobiographical thread naming the working-class roots of the writer. One of our starting-point decisions about the design of the study was a frustration that researchers too often read one set of experiences (their own particular background) as the story that they rediscovered in those they studied. In our study over the seven years, we were both revisiting who we had been (in our reactions to City Academy) and recognizing who we are now: urban dwellers who eagerly left our country towns and communities to embrace life at university, and whose daily lives and interests reflect the cosmopolitan becomings discussed by Ien Ang and referred to in our previous discussion about Pauline Hanson and One Nation. As metropolitan people now, we did confront some disjunctions between the classifications of hierarchy and distinctions that we have become accustomed to and those that are lived by the country students and permeate their own sense of self and orientation to the future. In our daily lives, different things are taken as markers of taste and sophistication and superiority than those that are the currency of Cubbin. And in our intellectual work too, we are familiar with the SES ways of classifying where jobs stand on the social hierarchy. It came as a shock when we revisited our notes and discovered that David and Andrew, so sure of their superior place in the hierarchy, were from families that in the city would be classified much lower, both occupationally and residentially. The subjective resonances of class identification are important in our own identities and in those we study at Regional High, but we have also shown that this is not a universal experience, either within the participants at a school (City Academy) or when comparing young people attending one school and geographical environment (Suburban High) compared with another (Regional High). As we have suggested, everyone has "habitus," and everyone forms dispositions in the context of family and place; but for only some people are markers and relativities of class identification and relationships significant as a formative and emotional part of who they are and who they want to be.

Schools, Class, Class Mobility and "the New Worker"

Considering young people in schools from the perspective of "class" puts on the agenda issues of identity formation in relation to school contexts, but it also raises the issue of work patterns and work characteristics in the society beyond school. Two issues in particular continue to resonate in the contemporary literature and for our project: issues of change in the nature of work and how work is entered, along with issues of relational positioning of schools and individuals.

The literature on the "new worker" signals some of the changes that have been widely observed and also projected about changing forms of work in countries like Australia. These include the idea of lifelong learners who will change jobs a number of times and will construct their own career identity (Chappell et al. 2003) as well as the workers who discipline themselves to produce correct behavior rather than being controlled by overt sanctions (du Gay 1996; Rose 1996). There has been much attention to "new literacies" and to the "shape-shifting portfolio person" who understands that aesthetic and communicative knowledge is important, that certain representations of self are the capital with which one succeeds in the workforce today (Gee 1999; Chappell et al. 2003); this has happened in the context of the increased prominence of service jobs and knowledge work compared with manufacturing jobs. How are both the schools and the young people constructing themselves in these particular times?

The distinctive characteristics that were emphasized over time in the two "middle" high schools in our study, and which we read in the people we followed at each school, continued to influence student identities in their postschool years and to shape identities and orientations to future work in quite different ways. At Regional High, the enterprising self is emphasized, whereby the self is constructed as a CV, where one becomes a planner who plots education and job relationships, who works hard, who projects the steps that will be needed in the next five years, and who believes that outcomes will be the result of one's own efforts. At Suburban High, the self as a project dominates: this is the reflexive self who is most fascinated with questions about "Who am I?" and who wants to extend the period of self-exploration well beyond the period of school.

At the end point of our study, the destination of the seven students who were our initial focus at Suburban High school were: one boy left school in Year 10 to take up an apprenticeship, but dropped out before completing it; one boy had hoped to get into a university course in an information technology area, but got a disappointing VCE result and is doing a TAFE one-year course in a similar area; two (one boy and one girl) are still at school because they had dropped some of their studies in what would have been their final year (in one case, medical problems were involved); one boy took up an overseas exchange in Year 11, and has not, as he had originally planned, returned to finish his schooling (though he has returned to Australia); three girls began university courses, and, of these, one had dropped out within three months of commencement, one was considering dropping out at this time, the other was continuing and had found a subject area she enjoyed (Women's Studies).

In her year after finishing school, Madeleine, who dropped out of her university course, reflects on the influence of her school on her future decisions.

Do you think the school had much or any influence on where you ended up in terms of your course decision?

Madeleine: Not really, no. It was sort of a spur-of-the-moment decision. I just read the VTAC guide and it looked good, so I put it down. I didn't really look into it properly. Um, my careers teacher just pushed me to do whatever it was I wanted really. . .

Do you think much about the future?

Madeleine: Um, I try not to. . .

What would you really like to happen for you in the future?

Madeleine: Um, I'd like to find out what it is that I want to do and go do it. I'd like to travel. Yeah, I just want to land on my feet, just sort myself out. Not make that same . . . Uni mistake again

[she had started a university course, but dropped out after about a month]

(Madeleine, in first year after finishing school, Suburban High)

The characteristic response from somewhat diverse students at Suburban High was that they did not feel highly driven to get on the career track and were unlikely to express a strong commitment to a particular job or field of study. (There is an extended discussion of one of these students, Marcus, in the next chapter.) Many conveyed a feeling of aimlessness, a sense of uncertainty about their immediate and distant futures. For some students, this uncertainty caused some concern, for others it was understood as part of growing up, of finding yourself, but most did not convey a strong sense of work-related ambition to get on in the world.

At Regional High at the same point (five months after finishing their final examinations), all except one of the students we began with now seemed firmly on a vocational track. Three of the students—two boys and one girl—were at university (all in directly vocational courses); one girl is taking a technical college course in her chosen field (hotel management); one girl was accepted at university but is working prior to applying to join the police; and the only person on a different trajectory is one boy who left school as soon as he was old enough (Year 10), and when last we made contact was doing casual work in a supermarket. (John's experience of school is discussed in chapter 3.) The impression we had of these students at the end of school (we were not able to interview John who had left earlier) was that they all had clear plans about what they were doing and where they were going. Indeed, in most cases, they were not only taking a vocational course or path but had further plans about what they were going to do next, and were taking steps to make that happen: going to the gym regularly to pass the police fitness test; applying for a scholarship with plans of completing nursing within the armed forces; finding out options for continuing beyond the current degree to do a graduate degree in medicine. As one of the students confidently asserted,

Do you think much about the future?

David: Yeah, the future's . . . you've got to have, got to have a goal . . . because otherwise you just, you're going to university and you think, oh, what's the point you know, so you've got to be focused on the end.

And what would you really like to happen for you in the future?

David: Oh, get a job that I'm happy with and enjoy, and get paid a nice amount of money [. . .]

(David, first year after finishing school, Regional High)

The themes in these final interviews reflected a picture of the ethos of the two schools that had been consistent throughout the previous six years of interviews and that we discussed in chapter 3.

Regional High generates a sense of a world in which individual effort and hard work bring rewards, and constant effort and vigilance are needed to keep up with those at the top of the social hierarchy, who are always an explicit point of comparison. In many respects this school fits the habitus and dispositions of the community it draws from: small businesspeople who themselves try to make their way using their own efforts, and in which hierarchy is measured much more by relativities of economic success within the local scene than on any larger scale. The outcomes for individuals are positive in terms of the types of things parents and policy-makers worry about: attachment to career routes, taking action, and being strategic, hardworking, and energetic. Students who make it through to Year 12 here acquire a strong sense of their own responsibility and efficacy to take action to shape their own future. At the same time, the students are accepting a view of life as a "rat race" in which they compete at a disadvantage. These students are also being nurtured into individualist ways of thinking that put the responsibility for one's fate on the individual, and carries with it relatively little empathy for victims of bullying or racism.

Whereas Regional High was a school whose central motifs were concerned with distinction, hard work, and winning; Suburban High was a school with some pride in a tradition of being a bit alternative, inclusive, and pastoral, and of looking after the emotional well-being of its students. From students' comments over the years of our study, we had a sense that this was a school that paid a lot of personal attention to students, tried to help them and give them second chances, and one where there was genuinely less racism than at other schools. (Of course, all the schools in this study formally declared racism and sexism unacceptable, but in Suburban High it actually carried through into students' broader answers about incidents and social issues related to difference and racism in and out of school and in their own judgments about what they thought the school valued and what they thought its strengths were.) Students spoke very warmly of teachers—both in general and in relation to particular teachers, and reported one of the strengths of the teaching as being its ongoing commitment to "giving you another chance." For individual students, the result seemed to be that they felt nurtured, treated therapeutically, but not highly pushed. Though drug-taking was present and talked about by students at all the schools in our study, at this school it seemed more normalized. Students found it easy to get involved in drug-taking—and also easy to talk about—but found it difficult to stop, even when they wanted to do so in the run-up to the final Year 12 certificate.

When students at Suburban High made comparisons with other schools, they did not focus on social hierarchy so much as the style and the culture of this school. As individuals, students felt less pressure, and one consequence seemed to be that in this immediate postschool year many have not advanced along the educational pathways to the extent that they might have if they had been at another school.

Do you think the school was a good one, or do you think it was the right one for you, the school?

Madeleine: Um, I think I might have done better if I was at maybe one of the private schools Dad wanted me to go to, but I was happier there, like I think it was a good school, yeah.

(Madeleine, in the year after finishing school, Suburban High)

Madeleine continues, saying that a private school would have been "more disciplined" and "stricter," but that at Suburban High she liked her friends and she liked the teachers, and, by comparison, when she went on to university "it was so daunting there was just so many people and you didn't know anyone" (and she dropped out of that environment within two months).

Regional High, at least as reported by the students, was not highly attuned to differences in sociocultural identity and background, but was greatly sensitive to the public circulation and markers of social distinction, and highly directed to an individualist view of progress and possibility. Suburban High, at least as reported by students over seven years of interviews, was highly sensitive to individual and group difference, and nurtured a sense of the value of having good relationships rather than being materially successful or pursuing traditionally high-status occupations. We have previously discussed in chapter 6 the different political views of students at each of the schools. We noted especially the difference between Suburban High's attention to the changed social and economic context and how that was affecting people's opportunities for work and Regional High's emphasis on the need for individual responsibility and hard work (a view somewhat influenced by immediate local knowledge of factories closing down).

Students at Regional High, in retrospectively assessing their school, judge it to be a good school, one that measured up in a competitive environment, but they did not feel particularly warm about it. For the individual student, it had generated (or at least enhanced) a striving to work hard, to hang in there as much as possible, a drive to self-improvement but a willingness to be realistic about aspirations. In terms of orientations to a more long-term social whole, it was producing a sense that the unemployed deserve little sympathy, that outcomes are the result of individual application and effort. The existence of social distinction might be recognized, but there was little railing against unfair distribution of starting-point advantages and power; wistful envy rather than resentment framed their attitudes toward the advantages of private schools. In contrast, students at Suburban High responded to our questions with a more distanced reflection on the shape of social change, in ways much more in tune with a "leftist" view of the world. Social change has happened; it creates problems—employers eliminate jobs. Students at Suburban High do not take unemployment as a personal reflection on the unemployed, but just as something that happens for reasons outside their control. In relative terms, this school was doing well in cultivating positive and respectful social relations but, at least at the immediate postschool stage, was doing distinctly less well in helping students achieve in the conventional pathways through further education and work.

Recent feminist debates about "social justice" have attended to the interaction between the politics of distribution (who gets what) and the politics of recognition (how groups and individuals are respected or marginalized, advantaged or harmed) (Fraser 1997; Gewirtz 1998). Like Nancy Fraser (1997), we assume that "distribution" and "recognition" are not antitheses but intimately linked when it comes to studying what schools do to produce fairness and unfairness, advantage and disadvantage, and lesser and greater forms of social equality, including class-related dispositions and outcomes. Issues of social justice relate to what happens to individuals and groups in that school and also to what is being developed through them as orientations to the social whole. As Gewirtz suggests, there is a "relational dimension to social justice" and this includes the "formal and informal rules which govern how members of a society treat each other" (Gewirtz 1998, 471).

In both these schools in the middle, issues of distribution and recognition are entwined, even though there are different emphases, motifs, and practices of distinction. In the case of Regional High, in the short term at least, the school is not producing an overly sympathetic orientation toward issues commonly associated with the politics of recognition. The students appear to be not highly sensitive to, or interested in, issues of group marginalization and inclusion, of recognition and respect, of violence—issues that have marked the new social movements around gender, race, and culture. But they are aware of some of the class-based forms of recognition and the stress by this school on how one's individual future might be advanced. The sense of self-efficacy that the school also generates contributes to greater individual opportunity for these students than they might otherwise have had. Their future sense of themselves as capable and responsible for their own outcomes is enabling, both individually and in terms of social patterns, but it also feeds how these young people see and relate to others, including some lack of sympathy for those who are disadvantaged or targets of bullying and racism. At Suburban

High, students are more successfully schooled in a broad range of "social justice" concerns, and, in our final interviews with them in the year after finishing school, were carrying their sensitivities and willingness to speak out about racism and sexism into their postschool social relations. But, at least in the immediate postschool phase, they appear to be placed in a more uncertain relationship to the labor market than students at Regional High. The production of immediate distributional outcomes is one part of social justice but not the whole. What schools do to and for the students in those schools is also part of it, but not the whole. The values that those students acquire and take with them in relation to other individuals and social groups--what kind of society the schools are helping to produce--are a significant part of any consideration of the relation among class identification, class subjectivity, and schooling.

In this section, we have been discussing some patterns in the trajectories of identity-making in two schools. Discussions of "class" and schooling have often been framed by a static sense of what class is, and read mainly in terms of how patterns of academic success and failure are created. By looking at these two groups in the middle, we can see some new orientations and values being formed. For one of these groups, distinction and social differentiation are a salient means of reading the world and their own place in it—but it is a rather "Old World" and circumscribed reading of social relations. For the other group, located in a more ethnically mixed urban setting, understanding and accepting difference are important. The time-scale of our study contains a limitation in seeing the effectiveness of either orientation in relation to postschool work. At 18, the people raised with traditional values of working hard and planning are most clearly on track (and it may be that their orientation to being strategic, finding ways to continue when initial hopes are disappointed, continue to be important identity foundations in the new work order). The self-development, self-as-a-project orientation of Suburban High is not proving a fast career track foundation for these students at 18, and we don't know how these students will be in their mid-twenties, but they undoubtedly have a rather different basis for approaching who they are and who they might be. And, compared with Regional High where John is simply abandoned at the minimum leaving age, Suburban High does well for those who have learning problems and are most in need of encouragement and structured support.

What we have also been trying to do in this section is show that "class," because it is one way of attending to family, school and work relations, opportunities and changes over time, is useful for focusing not just on what happens to groups in school and from school, but also for examining how social relations of a certain type (political, ethical, and social values) are reproduced or modified.

Gender-Class Differentiation

If we were to summarize the type of comments about the future and agendas for the individual that we heard in our interviews, we could do this in a way that roughly held true for three different types of social location for both girls and boys. For those of elite background being educated in the elite school, the themes were about being a "somebody," a distinctive person, successful in some field. For those attending the middle high schools, who came from a range of SES locations, the wish was to have a good life. In the case of students at the poorest school, the wish was to have a comfortable life, but the repeated mantra was to "take it as it comes." We could also summarize outcomes both by school and by gender (as we have in the tables in Appendix 2a and 2b, and discussed also in chapter 5). Our numbers are small, but the broad patterns are in line with the ones the databases show: those in the private school more often go on to "good" universities and professional courses; those in the middle to lesser universities and courses and technical colleges; those from poor backgrounds are less likely to finish and more likely to be doing casual work. In terms of gender, the courses and occupations the people in our study were in at 18 also seem quite gender-stereotyped: nursing, arts, music, fashion, law, and commerce for the girls; mechanical engineering, medical and computer technology, gardening apprenticeship for boys. However, another reading of our seven years of interviews would show that there is gender-differentiated subjectivity within the comparison by school or by SES background, and that the meanings of the pathways and outcomes by gender are not simply replicating a historical gendered job segregation but have new meanings in new times.

There is a sense in which many girls in our study, across their class differences, experience this as a period of opportunity, while their male friends experience the future in terms of uncertainty. At 12 to 14, the girls talk about their daydreams of the future: dreams of energy and travel, of speed and daring, of glamor and independence. At the same time, boys are not thinking about their long-term future:

their interest is sporting triumph in the short term. At 15, many girls say they are "optimistic" when asked explicitly how they feel about the future; boys more commonly reply, "mixed."

In the group with least family history of school success, "take it as it comes" may be the mantra, but it hides different and gendered ways this is being lived. Keren and Kylie are at 18 doing relatively traditional things for working-class girls: working as a registered nurse and working in McDonald's. But both see themselves and their possibilities as projecting forward with new opportunities. Keren has found a career she enjoys, is setting up her apartment, feels appreciated in her work. Kylie is working full-time at McDonald's but happier than she has previously been, and is taking on new supervision roles, attending training courses, and finding new networks for social and sporting events. Brett and Dirk, from the same school and comparable family backgrounds, wanted apprenticeships or work in a factory. Both are unemployed and neither has completed any recognized training. The differences here between the two boys and the two girls are both subjective and material. Keren's close relationship with her mother who has herself been returning to study has engendered a persistence that belies her expression of "taking it as it comes." With Kylie, there is a pragmatism and flexibility about her ability to continue in work, and objective opportunities to explore in an industry that is expanding in this town, while the traditional jobs the boys seek are closing down. What we see with these young people at 18 is not so different from what we hear in the interviews about their mothers and fathers. Stories of mothers who return to work and study, take on new types of work, embark on new directions, are surprisingly common across the people in the project. At Regional Tech, common too are the stories of fathers who become unemployed, or are on pensions, or are struggling for work. What is happening for the young people here is both a material reality in terms of the changing job structure and a psychological trajectory seen in the dreams or lack of dreams of futures, taking us to the intertwined relevance of the focus on class as explanatory concept and class as lived experience.

Concluding Comment

"Class" is not something you can pin down once and for all, but it embodies concepts and discussions that remain highly important for studying young people in the context of schools and in the context of coming from (family) and becoming (a type of person, a type of worker). In "New World" countries, social differentiation in the form of class is often denied or invisible, particularly for those who most benefit. The somebody you were being directed to becoming at the City Academy in this study was different from the one you were becoming at Regional High, even though the latter would dearly have liked to be the same as the former. The fact that Regional High had to keep talking about social hierarchy, while City Academy did not, was one aspect of their difference. Place and cosmopolitan/provincial distinctions as well as family occupations and histories in the two locations were also part of the story. These stories of school differences and class-based inequalities are familiar ones, but what we have tried to do here is give close attention to what happens to those who come with different backgrounds to a particular school, and what schools seem to be doing to hone particular ways of being across different types of students who attend them. Discussions of "habitus" and schooling are often taken up as if schools were some hegemonic or monolithic backdrop against which those from working-class backgrounds experience dissonance and rejection and those from middle-class professional backgrounds find affirmation. This is, still, part of the story, but attention to four schools and the students who attend them suggests that schools (as distinct from schooling) are a more differentiated and active constituent of the social patterns beyond school than are often recognized. In Australia, there is a recognition of this in relation to particular elite private schools who have long marketed a particular identity. We have suggested both that the marketed identity is not to be taken at face value (our discussion in chapter 6 of the practices compared to the rhetorical commitment to diversity and ecumenical support at City Academy) and that the overlooked ordinary high schools, here Suburban High and Regional High, are forging directions that are noticeably differentiated in relation to discussions of the new worker.

One issue that is apparent from a close-up perspective is that both individuals and schools are forging identities relationally. We have not in this chapter tried to develop a typology or a model of what class is; we have attempted to show ways of focusing on individual lives and their meanings, and to what schools are doing and achieving now, to explore lived and embodied subjectivity at a particular stage of important engagement between family formation and public institution.

An important but submerged background in our discussion is the issue of "the new economy." Here we show some differences in the lived experiences of two working-class girls and working-class boys at the same school, and in the ways their experiences of family and gender are shaping orientations and outcomes different from the ones their parents experienced. "Class" is a useful concept in studying young people in Australia today, but what we are examining is not a story of reproduction against a backdrop of change, but a story of change and reproduction within a context of change.

CHAPTER 8

Gender Themes in a Changing World

As we conducted the final interviews with our participants in the year after they finished school, debates about the education of boys seemed to be everywhere—in media reports, in commissioned policy research, in academic research, in the announcement of a Commonwealth government inquiry into the education of boys. Evidence was frequently cited indicating that, on average, boys were not performing as well as girls in examinations, and that they experienced particular problems with literacy and those aspects of the curriculum, such as group work and communication, in which girls were "naturally" more successful. Numerous postfeminist scenarios painted an alarmist picture of gender instability, with boys confused and struggling at school, emotionally at a loss (the new symbols of social anomie) and girls on an inexorable and selfish path to success. This was a scenario that had, and continues to have, a strong grip on public opinion. We had both worked in the "gender and education" field in relation to the education of girls and feminist reforms, and had also participated, via policy debate and research, in discussions about the education of boys and the relative academic performance of girls and boys (Collins, Kenway, and McLeod 2000; McLeod 2001; Yates 1997, 2000; Yates and Leder 1996). These are complicated and important debates, easily simplified in the media to a winners and losers account of schooling, with boys the new losers. Such views remain difficult to dislodge, despite the massive amount of research that documents the postschool pathways of girls and boys (where girls' success at school does not easily translate into labor market advantage) and the differentiation within gender groups once other social categories, such as class or ethnicity and race are added. At one level, debates about boys' education involve schooling outcomes, curriculum reform, and pathways. But on another level, the boys' debate is also part of a more widespread cultural concern with the meaning and effects of gender difference and the consequences of feminism, especially regarding the character and apparently changing form of gender identities.

One starting point for our study was to see what had been the effect on schools and students of more than two decades of feminist and gender reform. The debates about boys' difficulties and girls' new advantages thus had strong personal and professional connections for us, and they echoed loudly as we listened to our participants reflect on their school experiences and plans for the immediate and long-term future. We heard stories of great ambitions, tales of strategic and enterprising planning to get a life in order, as well as stories of resignation, a sense of things not working out. At the end of school, and as students looked back and reflected on their adolescent years, we also wondered whether there would be some evidence of change in gendered ambition, or differences in themes and preoccupations in their biographical narratives. What kind of changes might we see in the forms of femininity and masculinity? How were shifts in cultural discourses associated with gender difference and gender relations being negotiated by young women and men?

Throughout this book, we have considered debates about gender detraditionalization, arguing that many theoretical accounts tend to overstate the extent of such processes, neglect the ways in which new forms of gender traditionalism are being reinscribed, and fail to adequately acknowledge the unevenness and social differentiation of such change (see also Plumridge and Thomson 2003). This is not simply to make the argument that abstract theories do not sufficiently attend to the level of the micro, local, and empirical,[1] but to make an argument for theorizing the unevenness of change and integrating difference, embodiment, and subjectivity as more central concerns in theoretical accounts of social (and feminist) change. In this book, we argue that the uneven impact of feminist and gender change can be illuminated by exploring the interaction between biographical and sociocultural processes. The following discussion thus neither presents an argument about a utopian transformation of gender nor a pessimistic account of the reproduction of gender; it also is not an attempt to produce new gender typologies of young people today—boys are like this, girls are like that. Such arguments would be sociologically overstated and historically naïve. Change and reproduction characterize gender relations and gender identities today.

Researching Gender and Change

In scholarly work and in everyday talk, the term "gender" is a multivalent, overdetermined signifier that denotes many aspects of social relations and subjectivity. As a key word in contemporary culture, it is usually represented as a commonsense, self-evident category. In the previous chapter, we asked what kind of "thing" class is, and similar questions should also be posed about "gender." For when we, and other researchers, write about "gender" it can refer to many different things and there is often unacknowledged slippage between types of meaning and referents. Gender can refer to differences, to clusters of attributes, to identities or subjectivities, to relations, and is also often used in an abbreviated form, such as "gender reform" or "gender change" when social reform and social change are implicit. "Gender change" can denote changing discourses and imperatives about identities and relations between men and women; it can also refer to changes in how people perceive themselves as a "gendered" subject; and it can also, of course, refer to what particular individuals do to their bodies and how they act in social presentation and performance. Gender can also refer to counterposing group differences, a theme in cultural discourses, a social structure, a valuable category of statistical studies and of populational reasoning. Second-wave feminism made much of distinguishing between gender and sex, such that the former usually referred to the social arrangement and sex to biological identity. Since then, there have been many debates within feminism on the possibility of making so neat a distinction, of working out what such analytic distinctions mean and whether they are sustainable, particularly in relation to embodiment and sexuality (Butler 1990; Gatens 1991). Connell's (2002) definition of gender captures a common sociological usage. Gender describes not only differences and contrasts between male and female, he argues. It refers also to relations between people and to a social structure that deals with different kinds of human bodies, ascribing different social meanings to them; which, in turn, have ramifications in personal and public life (Connell 2002, 10).

While we share this very broad understanding of gender as a social relation and system, in this book we have pursued a more subjective and biographical focus to explore the shaping of individual students as gendered (and classed) subjects. In analyzing our longitudinal interviews, we have been aware of what Harriet Bjerrum Nielsen calls "unacknowledged gender" (Nielsen 1996). We did not explicitly ask students to talk about how they thought of themselves as a girl or a boy, or to respond to questions about their "gender identity" in direct and immediate ways. Rather, we interpreted gender subjectivity from the ways in which students responded to the full range of questions and issues—even when gender was not for them an obviously foregrounded issue. Nielsen usefully suggests that

> The gendered subjectivity is the gendered "being in the world" which consists of unacknowledged and to some extent unconscious gender (unconscious images/discourses and feelings attached to gender). Unacknowledged gender is the way gender is present as background when one reflects on something else, for example what kind of person one is, what kind of desires one has, what kind of feelings one experiences as having. (1996, 11).

Questions about young people, changing gender relations, and the form of contemporary gender identities have been investigated from many different angles within educational and feminist inquiry. Many longitudinal and tracking studies, for example, have identified themes in generational change, locating young women and men's choices and life patterns in historical, policy, and comparative contexts, and identifying the emergence of new forms of youth biographies (du Bois Reymond 1998; Dwyer and Wyn 2001). Other longitudinal studies have looked more closely at critical incidents, and at gender and class formations in transitions to adulthood (Thomson et al. 2002; Walkerdine, Lucey, and Melody 2001). Another popular strand of research has examined the cultural, social, or discursive construction of gender identities within current and "postfeminist" times. This encompasses ethnographic work embedded in cultural studies traditions (Bloustein 2003; Hey 1997; Kehily 2002) and close-up studies of gender discourses and identifications in schools and the intersection of gender, class, and race in processes of contemporary identity construction (e.g., Francis and Skelton 2001; Gordon, Holland, and Lahelma 2000; Reay 2001; Weis and Fine 2000).

A number of feminist and educational studies have directly tackled the question of what is distinctive about gender relations today compared to a generation ago (e.g., Dolby and Dimitriadis 2004). Taking Paul Willis's *Learning to Labour* (1977) as a landmark ethnographic study of youth, masculinity, class, and schooling, Dolby and Dimitriadis argue that the sociological moment Willis so richly studied has now passed. The close relationship he describes between the state, class (national), capitalism, and schooling has been "replaced with a story that is more complex, and in many respects, more troubling" (Dolby and Demetriadis 2004, 8). They point in particular to the impact on young people of structural changes in work and the proliferating effects of globalization (see also Kenway and Kraack 2004). Similarly, Madeleine Arnot, whose early work on the reproduction of gender codes was circulating at the same time as Willis's (1977) study, has recently argued that the "modality of gender reproduction has now changed" (Arnot 2002, 16). Arnot analyzes the "recontextualization of gender relations" as arising out of what she, along with others, see as the dual impact of processes of individualization and globalization (see also Arnot, David, and Weiner 1999; Dillabough and Arnot 2001).

For Arnot, and for us, a key aspect of such processes of recontextualization is that its effects are uneven for girls and boys. In the following discussion, we pursue this line of argument in two main directions. First, we consider responses to some relatively direct questions about gender equality as offering one way into understanding how cultural and social changes in gender discourses are being differently negotiated by particular groups of young people today. Second, we explore, via case study analysis, themes of community and autonomy in students' retrospective and prospective narratives about their futures; and we analyze some of the gendered inflections—conventional, contemporary, and reconfiguring—of these themes of autonomy and community.

The discursive signs and subjective experiences of autonomy and community/connection have been central concerns of feminist inquiry across philosophical, psychological, and sociological traditions. This has been in large part because femininity (and women) have been conventionally positioned problematically in relation to autonomy, with the gendered chain of signifiers locating the exclusion of women from autonomy and privileging their immersion in relationships with others. One fundamental political and philosophical move for feminism has thus been to secure autonomy for women. But the quest for autonomy can itself be double-edged with young women placing themselves under greater pressure and scrutiny to achieve their autonomy and its linked successes (as we discussed in chapters 4 and 5). At the same time, the cultural themes or tropes of community and autonomy have taken on a particular significance in contemporary social and political theory in ways that are not overtly connected to gender differentiation. These include concern about the decline of community life and social capital (e.g., Putnam 2000) and discussions of individualization and the production of autonomous subjectivity (Beck and Beck-Gernsheim 2002; Rose 1999). The convergence of these streams of thought regarding autonomy and connection frames our analysis of how young women and men in our study represent themselves, their futures, and their relationships with others. We draw out some emerging themes and new gender configurations in what we see as young men's attachment to community and relationships and young women's embrace of autonomy and independent futures. How are emotional and ontological dilemmas typically aligned with and discussed in relation to women, realized and negotiated in the lives of young men? And how do the subjective concerns with community and autonomy work out in relation to what Rose describes as a broader "culture of the self."

We now turn to consider some of the ways in which students at all four schools talked to us about gender equality, as one means of showing some of the complex and contradictory features of contemporary, postfeminist gendered discourses.

Retraditionalizing Masculinity, or "Most males are just normal"

Participants' perceptions of gender equality conveyed some significant tensions in that they mostly declared an official discourse that sexism did not really exist any more and gender was not an issue in schools, but also maintained in other ways that masculinity was "normal" and that it was girls who were in need of changing, not boys, and that femininity remained problematic. Compared to 20 years ago, in the state in which our project was located, girls and boys today are more likely to be studying much the same curriculum subjects in secondary schools and to be familiar with the formal language of "sexism" and "equal opportunities." All the students in our study expected that women as well as men will be in the workforce for much of their lives, and they all say, initially at least, that there should be (and in most cases assert that there is), equality between boys and girls. When we directly asked students about some of these matters, all of them were quick to tell us that boys and girls today have "equal opportunities," and they were confidently able to identify practices or ideas they thought were sexist and speak fluently about sexual harassment or antisexism. But sexism was a term they commonly used to describe any practice that drew attention to gender differences, rather than a term of negative discrimination or stereotyped assumptions about capacity.

When we asked students in the second year of high school about the policy and media discussions that suggested boys were losing out and needed some special programs, there was little sympathy for the idea—either from the girls or the boys. Boys saw what they were deciding to do (such as "muck around") as simply a matter of their choice, and they regarded special or sex-based programs as a form of discrimination or sexism. Additionally, while all the students were familiar with the official language of "antisexism," and certainly know that it was the right thing to express to interviewers and teachers, they continued to differentiate between what was "normal" for girls and boys on quite conventional "sexist" grounds. For example, both girls and boys thought that it was "okay" and normal for boys to muck around in schools, and that it was equally normal and rather embarrassing for girls that body image was much more important for them than it was for boys.

Contrary to popular concerns, many boys continue to do well at school, but many are rather ambivalent about competing with girls. While many boys told us that they believe in equality, many nevertheless showed a distinct resistance to doing subjects or activities in which girls are doing well. If girls are performing well at school, some boys react by boasting about the way boys take it easy in terms of school work, sneering at girls who work hard. In response to questions we asked in the early years of high school about whether they thought that girls were doing better at school than boys, or if boys needed special programs, girls and boys unanimously answered that girls did work harder, that boys played around a lot in class, but that there was really nothing much to do to help boys. As we discussed in chapter 3, boys reported that it was their choice to be like that and it was "just the way they were":

Andrew: Well, most of the boys sort of piss, stuff around. Yeah, they stuff around and they don't do a real lot in class and that.

Do you think it is something schools should do something about?

Andrew: Um, well, there's not a real lot you can do about it, um, 'cause if you send them out then they are only going to get further behind.

As Michael reflected, "I think that boys and girls have got the same chances to do well in VCE, but [. . .] but boys tend to stuff around a bit more. But you can't stop that. Boys will be boys. So there's not a lot you can really do, it's their choice." (Year 10 boys, Regional High)

One group of girls at the same school thought that boys' mucking-around behavior did not necessarily impede later academic success.

> Yeah, they seem to, like, they [boys] take out all the prizes in year 12 and stuff, but they don't worry about it from Years 7 to 11 or whatever, because it doesn't seem important to them until they get to year 12. Because they then, then most of the boys got all the maths and science prize and stuff. And like, oh the Dux wasn't a boy, but usually it had been.
>
> (Year 10 girl, Regional High)

This observation was reported in a matter-of-fact manner, and as evidence of boys making fairly sensible choices in terms of managing their schooling and future outcomes. Although the statistical evidence indicates that more girls than boys are doing relatively better at school, from the point of view of students in our study, there is nothing obviously damaging about boys' attitudes to schooling. There is still a persistent belief among them that boys can be successful, regardless of how much they "muck around" in the junior and middle years of schooling.[2]

Boys' and girls' representations of conventional masculine behavior as natural and sensible was also evident in their discussions about body image and dieting. Both girls and boys interpreted girls' concerns with body image and being slim to be stupid, pathetic signs of their vanity. In contrast, boys generally talked about body image as something they did not really care about and, if they did, it was because of a reasonable concern with weight and fitness:

Is body image important to you?

Andrew: No, if they say something to you, you just don't listen, just ignore them.

Is it different for girls?

Andrew: Yeah, they have to like . . . if they're fat or something they have to go on a diet, whereas males wouldn't really care. They don't really

> care how they look. Like if they were really fat or something, they'd have to try and go on a diet or something or exercise, but most males are just normal.
>
> (Andrew, Year 8, Regional High)

Masculinity continued to be regarded as normal and as neither open to nor needing to change. This is not an unusual perspective, but it is significant in terms of social change, job opportunities, and gender equity reforms in schooling. While masculinity was regarded as innate, and as not influenced by social norms and changes, femininity and girls were seen as open to change and needing to undergo some reshaping as we enter a different social and economic period. They carried the responsibility of feminist and social change. It was girls' futures, their decisions, their choices that were subject to more scrutiny and greater expectation for change. Earlier gender equity reforms to extend girls' opportunities assumed that girls were capable of making different choices (e.g., to stay at school longer, to do mathematics) because their current choices were not helping them to enter a wider range of occupations or offering greater chances for personal fulfillment. For boys today, the issues appear to be different, with fewer peer and policy expectations that they need to make changes and different choices. In the context of changed economies, labor markets, and changing social and interpersonal expectations, such gendered differences in views about choice and change are significant. In the case of many of the boys, there was less of a sense of their relating to a period of change. The contemporary concern with boys and schooling reflects the differences we have just noted. Much of the earlier gender reforms directed to girls was about changing girls (and also changing schools and teaching to enable this). The current discussions about boys frequently presume that boys or masculinity is set, and the debates are thus more about how schooling needs to change to allow for that.

Making a Modern Life

We have argued that the impact of feminism and associated gender and social changes appears to have had a much stronger effect on girls than boys. Additionally, recent social changes and associated expectations that individuals need to change, to become flexible and adapt to new circumstances, appear also to have had a stronger impact on girls' sense of their futures. The cultural imperatives to remake oneself, to reflexively construct a biography, to "be your own person" register differently for women and men, and intersect with feminist calls for women to make new choices. We turn now to a more close-up study of some of the girls and boys we interviewed, in order to explore in more detail these themes alongside those of community and autonomy in the making of modern lives. We begin with two young women from Cubbin—Keren from Regional Tech and Julia from Regional High.

After many difficulties, Keren completes secondary school and achieves her goal to undertake nursing. (We have discussed aspects of Keren's story in chapters 4 and 5.) She does not do well enough in her Year 12 results to get into a university course, but she knows alternative routes (from her mother and her teachers) and enrolls at the local Technical and Further Education College (Community College). This will qualify her to work as a nursing assistant, but is a step on the path that she has planned for herself. From the outside, her decision to enroll in a one-year certificate nursing course looks like the result of the low and gender-stereotypical aspirations of a girl from "a tech school." However, what appears on the face of statistical data to be evidence of the reproduction of gender and class futures, if read from a different angle, can show the subjective significance of how that life was put together, a future assembled and strategically imagined in the context of materially difficult circumstances. Keren perceives her future as one of emotional and financial independence, and a quest to become her own person. When we first met Keren, she wistfully described her future in terms of having her own house, but this is, she reflects, "imaginary, very very imaginary." In Year 10, when she imagines herself working in the future, she cannot see herself "in a big, big, place, my own building, my own office; I see myself working, but not that kind of work. . . . Just a small business, don't know what kind, but just a small one" (aged 15). The kind of future that would make her really happy is one characterized by both conventional fantasies of wealth and very modest expectations: "If I get the job I want, I win Tattslotto [the lottery], basically just to have a good life . . . well, I don't want to be a millionaire, but good wealth, a house, a car that runs" (aged 15). At the end of school, a happy future for Keren would be a "stable one," "not too rich, just comfortable"(aged 18). She is at that stage saving money from a part-time job to move into a small apartment of her own, and enjoying gathering together all the furniture and appliances she will need for her independent life.

Keren tells us with excitement that she has already collected many household items. Since she was about 14 she had been preparing her "Glory Box [Hope Chest]." The "Glory Box" is not a term much heard today, but in preceding generations it referred to the collection of household items—sheets, towels, dishes, cutlery—that young women gathered in preparation for marriage. It was a simple form of dowry, signifying women's orientation to the domestic and private world of homemaking, and happened in an era when many women stopped work (or were required to stop work) once married. The Glory Box was probably more common among families of modest means, as it offset the expenses involved in setting up a new home, and was evidence of careful domestic economy and planning—good housewifely virtues. The Glory Box is a remnant of older practices of domesticity and classed femininity, but for Keren it represents freedom and control, and a sense of opening possibilities for her, and not preparation for marriage and dependence.

Keren's sense of the future, her experience of school and of what she is doing at 18 reflect strong class patterns of difference and inequalities—which are plain in the comparison of Keren's life at 18 with that of Nicky from City Academy whose story we discussed in chapter 5. But, again, neither is this evidence of any simple story of gender/class reproduction. Much of the contemporary writing about girls and success and new work futures is tied to the ambitions and pressures of the middle class. But, for girls like Keren, whose ambitions remain modest, there seems limited language available for writing about achievements such as hers that does not sound patronizing. Keren's pathway through school and on to further study is neither a story about working-class escape through university education and the professions, nor is it about failure and thwarted ambition.

Compared to her male working-class peers at Regional Tech, Keren's trajectory is significantly different. The influence of her own mother returning to study, the broad impact of feminism on what is possible for women, and new education and work opportunities are creating a different set of options and dispositions for Keren than for her male classmates. They continue to demonstrate the historical contempt for schoolwork as feminine and school as a place that tries to treat them as children, and look to "manly" jobs that are rapidly disappearing (this is discussed later in this chapter). While Keren is undertaking further training at the end of school, earning money in an occupation where jobs are plentiful, and enjoying it, her male classmates of equivalent background in our study failed to complete their Year 12 certificate, and both are unemployed and uncertain about what their future holds or what they might expect to become.

Julia is not from an identical demographic background, and not at the same school, but she too is confronting and actively planning future options in today's world. Julia attended Regional High and, as noted earlier, this is a school that emphasizes being enterprising, working hard to succeed in a competitive world, and keeping up with the private schools. In the first year postschool, most of the participants from here are in fact actively "on track" in educational and vocational pathways. Throughout school, Julia is always busy, taking dance classes, playing basketball, and working at a part-time job and, like many of her peers at Regional High, she is very goal-oriented. A recurring theme in her interviews is the importance of working hard, of getting work done, and of planning to make things happen. At 15 she tells us:

> Right now I think this is where you start to find yourself and who you are and what you're going to be and you start to wake up a bit to real life and it's not just an easy road with people paying your way. You've got to make it, you know, you've got to make a future.
>
> (Julia, Regional High, Year 10, age 15)

Julia also enrolls in a nursing course, but in a degree program at the local university rather than the one-year diploma Keren takes on. Julia did not get the results she had hoped for to enter her first preference, psychology, but she has definite and confident plans for how she will work her way in to another field of study. Like Keren, and many of the other young women we interviewed, Julia is enterprising and strategic, with a clear orientation to getting on and constructing her future. For many of these young women (except for those at City Academy), planning and being strategic were less about making a stellar successful life and more about ensuring that they had plans in place, goals to follow, and a record of hard work. Cultivating an enterprising subjectivity signals an ease and sense of purpose in the world, a capacity to imagine and present oneself as "can-do," as able to imagine and make a life. What school curricula and workplaces value today (flexibility, knowingness about oneself and the impression one needs to make) has changed, at least in part, and this produces different consequences and accords different significance to ways of being conventionally associated with femininity and forms of gender difference. For young women in particular, such strategies of self-making represent new possibilities for autonomy, as well as dangers in the potential for punitive self-scrutiny and feelings of never being the "good enough" woman.

But the account here of the impact of largely sociological changes provides only one dimension to Julia's enterprising self. Toward the end of elementary school, her family moved to Cubbin because her father had to leave his respectable and responsible government job due to a case of misconduct in his workplace. In Cubbin, the family lives in a middle-class and comfortable area, her father takes up unskilled nightshift work, and her mother works as a hairdresser. Throughout her interviews, Julia refers briefly to her family's move, to her father's not being happy and his belief in hard work and the importance of education. But it is only when she is 16 (Year 11) that she talks at length about her father and the family story of dislocation. This knowledge offers us another perspective on her determination and hard work. Her extended response is prompted by a question from us asking her to reflect on some of the important things that have happened to her since we started doing the interviews, when she was 12. She answers: "There's a lot of bad things that have happened. There's a lot of bad things that are going around now still with my family."

Our question came after she had showed us photographs of her "doing the deb" that she had decided to bring to show us at one interview—it was not something we had asked her to do. "Doing the deb" refers to debutante balls that are undergoing something of a revival in Australia. They resemble the American high school formal or prom but with echoes of a much earlier time when girls were presented publicly at a formal dance for the first time—a "coming out." For the "deb ball," girls are dressed expensively and formally in white, like a precursor of the traditional bridal gown, and they spend weeks with a partner and the rest of the group rehearsing formal dance steps. At the ball, formal portrait photographs are taken that are similar to ones at university graduation or at weddings.

In the photographs, Julia is very beautiful, a little like Grace Kelly in her film star days, and her family looks on proudly. The idealized "happy family" image in these photographs, and of Julia as the optimistic "girl most likely to succeed," cut across the story she tells of her father's disappointment and the family's unhappiness. We learn that her older brother dropped out of school when he was 15, has been living at home, not working, smoking a lot of dope, fighting with her parents, and making life miserable for her. Julia's father regards her brother, as she does, as aimless and not working hard enough. Her busy extracurricular life offers distraction. Looking back on that time, she says, "I think I tended to do a lot of things because I didn't have to think about home; so I guess I, in a way, I really did use those things as an escape . . . I used a lot of it to not be there" (retrospective interview in first year of university). Of the final two years of school, when she seemed to us in interviews to be happier and more in charge of her life, she subsequently reflects that: "It's kind of strange because, um, I felt so stressed at those times. I don't really remember a lot of those years. When I think about them, like I remember just like, um, either really hating me at home or something like that, but I don't remember a lot of happy times" (first year university).

The disjunction between her memory and retrospective telling and our interpretations at that time underline, immediately, the contingency of interpretation. But it also underlines the value of a longitudinal and retrospective approach that allows for the telling and retelling of incidents and times, and for our initial readings to be recast. It is not simply that our account was wrong and Julia's was true. This disjunction in accounts also led us to wonder about the intense emotional investment Julia had in presenting herself to us in a particular way. Her bringing in the "deb photo," her representation of an idealized time, all this ran counter to what she now recalls of that time, but created a powerful narrative for us, and for her, about herself at that time.

Another possible analysis of this scenario is that Julia takes on the responsibility of work, of trying to make her father happy, and of compensating for her family's social and class dislocation, a gendered story, of women taking responsibility for the emotional well-being of others. Julia's ambitions and hard work could also be motivated by a determination not to become like her father and brother, and to ensure that she has work that she finds purposeful. Hollway and Jefferson (2000) employ the concept of the "defended subject," which is "simultaneously psychic and social" (p. 24) to understand the dynamic and narratives produced in interviews. It is "a product of a unique biography of anxiety-provoking life-events" and of how "they have been unconsciously defended against" (Hollway and Jefferson 2000, 24). Thinking about Julia as a "defended subject" brings another perspective to her busyness and struggles to succeed, and leads us also to notice her hard work to overcome difficulties, please her father, and defend herself against failure and unhappiness.

We argued in chapter 4 that we saw value in reading psychologically and sociologically based accounts against each other; neither offered a "full picture" of the subject, but each generated significant and distinctive insights. In the case of Julia, we can see that she is both an embodiment of the "New Times," reflexive, enterprising subject, and of the "hard work" ethos of Regional High. But her subjectivity is also formed in family narratives and events, and in the particular biographical histories that motivate people in complex and often ambivalent ways. Changes in the form of gendered subjectivity are manifested in and need to be interpreted at both levels.

Both Julia and Keren attended school in a large regional city and in their first year after leaving school had remained there, but had big plans for how to construct their futures and create an independent life, doing things that they found exciting and important, looking outward away from their local community, even as they remained linked into it. We want to briefly place these experiences against two of the boys in our study who also lived in Cubbin, Alan from Regional Tech and Andrew from Regional High. The point is not to make a blunt gender contrast but to draw out some of the different and emergent emphases in how futures, independence and autonomy, and sense of community are being worked out.

Alan lives in a small country town outside Cubbin and his father works in the capital city, about one and one-half hours away by public transport, where he commutes daily. The family, Alan says, choose to live in the country town for "lifestyle reasons": they are not locals, they are not dependent on work in the area. He enjoys country activities, but his imagination and outlook are strongly fueled by an orientation to the "outside" world—to the metropolitan area and to "overseas.". Alan's mother migrated as an adult to Australia from North America, and she remains in regular contact with her family there.

When we first meet Alan at age 12, he talks with evident excitement and pride of his family's recent overseas trip to see his relatives, and also, as a bonus, to visit Disneyland. His sense of self is keenly and positively constructed in terms of a certain ambivalence to his local community and a sense of status because of his international connections. His having two passports, his potential ability to work both in Australia and in North America, his confident knowledge of a world beyond the small town in which his family has chosen to live—these are repeated themes in his representation of himself to us. We too represent a metropolitan world, we come from the city, we drive in to the country town, do our work, and then leave. Alan speaks to us as one who also knows about city life and a social world not confined to a country town.

During Year 11 and early Year 12 Alan says he will probably move away from the area and go to university in a capital city. He makes interstate trips to University Information Days and inquires about courses at various universities, but throughout the year he appears desultory and cannot seem to focus on work. A long-term relationship with his girlfriend breaks up, he loses interest in many of the hobbies he once had, he considers that he might fail a subject and then withdraws from it in order to concentrate more attention on the subjects he has a chance of passing. He starts to wonder whether he will in fact go to university.

In Year 12, Alan places himself under considerably less pressure than many of his contemporaries at the other schools we are studying. He has, by his own reckoning, never had to work really hard at school, but, as external examinations are approaching, he wonders whether he will be able to succeed. He starts to make critical comments about the school, about not being pushed, whereas earlier this had not been an issue for him. In fact, he seemed to like the latitude the school afforded him and the relative freedom and cultural authority he had. His final examination results are not as good as he had hoped and restrict his choice of university. Whereas when younger, he had looked to life outside the country town as intrinsically more interesting, he now retells stories, generic "urban myths" of the difficulties of city life, and as one of the factors making transition hard for some of his peers. He speaks of his friends having housing difficulties, of drugs, crime, and people losing their way: "He says he failed because of that [sharing a house with a drug user] but I think he's just got lazy and decided to go out every weekend" (first postschool interview, 2000). In the end, Alan decides to enrol at the local university, partly because his results limit his options (the local university has lower entry score requirements than most of the metropolitan universities), and partly because it is cheaper to study locally than move to the city. He chooses a combined degree in Business and Asian Studies, reflecting his interest in a world beyond the local and an interest in living and studying overseas (there is a placement in Japan for part of the course). He enjoys the course, and favorably compares his experiences with those of his friends who moved to the city. He speaks warmly of the small class sizes, of knowing the lecturers and other students, of it being a friendly place. He acknowledges that he will need to leave the local town once he finishes studying. "The type of degree I'm doing is not going to have much of a place in Cubbin so I'll be looking around at Melbourne or Sydney or wherever for a job" (second postschool interview, 2000).

For Alan there is ongoing mediation of a sense of place and belonging and a desire to be elsewhere. On the one hand, he is drawn to the sense of possibility afforded by "overseas" and city life, but, on the other, he enjoys and chooses a sense of belonging and feeling embedded in his local community. He is active in a local community group that conducts historical reenactments of war battles. Such local activities outside school were particularly important for many of the young people in Cubbin, and, as we discuss further, were frequently spoken about by the boys.

Andrew, from Regional High, is actively involved in local sporting clubs in Cubbin, and misses these connections when he moves to university in the city. He is the first one in his family to attend university and, while he is proud of his achievements, he is ambivalent about the university and city life. At school, Andrew has a "nice-guy," witty, and playful persona; as one of his friends said to us, "he wants to be Mr. Perfect and have a good time," and Andrew does not appear unhappy with this description. In interviews he is genial and confident, talks frequently about his sports, and, like other students at Regional High, emphasizes the value of hard work and having goals to aim for. He takes on a kind of avuncular attitude toward his peers, and even to us.

Andrew has always wanted to go to university and throughout school speaks confidently of his aspiration. He was interested in medicine, but he gradually shifts his expectations in line with his anticipated Year 12 results. He enrolls in a degree in medical science at a new, relatively low-status university, and maintains a longer-term view that he could always transfer to medicine. To us at least, Andrew does not talk of any disappointment and continues to be proud of his achievements and happy with his decisions. He is awarded a small scholarship by the university, and this further adds to his sense of feeling successful and on the road to a successful future. Nevertheless, he does find being at university and living in residential accommodation at university difficult and misses his hometown, where his status and the class and cultural relativities are familiar. He is well known in Cubbin for his sporting achievements and his humorous, easygoing manner. Andrew is one of the most outspoken students we interview regarding Regional High's being "as good as a private school." He is conscious of the status being at the school brings to young people in Cubbin. But he seems unaware that such status does not translate into other social contexts outside the town.

Andrew recognizes that he may have to stay in a large metropolitan city for his work, but would prefer to undertake a career that allowed him to move back to a country town: "Um, just it's sort of good just sort of being able to walk down the street of Cubbin and knowing a few people rather than just sort of walk around here and just [be] another face in the crowd so, I guess yeah I've just really been brought up in Cubbin and so that's where I'm most comfortable" (postschool interview, 2000). Andrew remains proud of his achievements and has elements of the enterprising hard work that characterizes the Regional High ethos, but at university he appears to become less sure of himself, less confident of his place in this new environment and the experience of encountering a different view of himself. He appears unfamiliar with the signifier of the university's location. It is a low-status, new university intended to service the western suburbs (in parts economically disadvantaged and ethnically mixed), and he finds it difficult to articulate why he finds this so unsettling

> *Andrew:* Ah, it's very different [at university] from what I've encountered in the past, there's a fairly strong, ah, ethnic flavor to the students there, which is sort of, coming from Cubbin it's not really something that you're used to, um, but apart from that it's, um, yeah it's similar, like everyone there's studying, and, focused on that usually, um, but yeah, probably just the ethnic side of it.
>
> (Andrew, postschool interview, 2000)

Andrew travels home most weekends as his part-time job and sporting clubs are located in Cubbin. The city remains an "other" place, one of difference and disconnection.

As with Julia, Keren, and Alan, Andrew's story is not simply one reducible to gender differences. It is interwoven with stories about class, ethnicity, location, schooling, and family dynamics. There are elements of a scaling back of ambition, of finding out what is realistic and possible, but also elements of uncertainty. His mediation of community and future is deeply connected to being in a place where he is well known, where familiarity does not include ethnic or cultural diversity, and where there is some continuity in his sense of self in relation to others. While Alan has some ambivalence about his local community and considers a future elsewhere, Andrew looks to his own future as a re-creation or repetition of his past. For both, themes of community and connection are prominent. For Keren and Julia, and for many of the other girls we interviewed, there was a marked energy and optimism about the future and a clear sense of working to find themselves. They did not deny or avoid the "pull of connection and community" but negotiated that in conjunction with a strong sense of their own ambitions and possibilities, their own striving for independence and autonomy, with a determination and strategizing that exceeded the developmental narrative of individuation. For boys, achievement and autonomy arguably continue to be more socially emphasized as a project than they are for girls. But, as our case study discussions have suggested, themes of community and connection are pronounced themes for the young men as they make their way in a new world. They do seem less secure and confident about their futures as young adults than they did in early secondary school, and in comparison to many of the young women we interviewed. This is not to suggest that there has been a reversal or inversion of the gender binaries, but rather to point to some emergent themes in the changing forms of masculinity and femininity as we see these young men encounter dilemmas that have been typically aligned with femininity, and these young women work toward an autonomous future.

Autonomy, Connection, Individualization, and Gender Difference

The patterns and themes we have drawn out in these case studies echo some of the arguments made by Arnot (2002) in her analysis of the recontextualization of gender codes. On the one hand, she argues, women appear to be responding to "new forms of modernity by transforming traditional class-based femininities and sexual relations and replacing these with more personalized and more reflexive processes of decision-making" (259). Young men, on the other hand, "may well find themselves attempting to cling on to traditional male roles, traditional family structures and local (territorial and community) identities" (261).

Within psychological discourses, how individuals negotiate the desire for both individual autonomy and relationships with others is typically characterized as a gendered problem, with young women represented as particularly vulnerable, and the pull of connection and community regarded as less of a pressing issue for young men. Here the work of Carol Gilligan and colleagues (1982; Gilligan, Lyons, and Hanmer 1990; Taylor, Gilligan, and Sullivan 1997), while regarded as controversial and disputed by many feminists, has nevertheless been very influential (Barrett 1999; Davis 1994). In short, Gilligan argued that as girls grow up they experience a conflict between desires for autonomy and desires for connection. At adolescence girls are "tempted to solve these problems by excluding themselves or excluding others" (Gilligan, Lyons, and Hanmer 1990, 9).[3]

Gilligan's work has been widely criticized for its universalizing pronouncements about girlhood based primarily on the experiences of middle-class North American girls, as well as its essentializing of femininity and insensitivity to social context, relations of difference, and changing historical times (e.g, *Feminism and Psychology* 1994). Many critics have emphasized the lack of attention to context and difference but have also tended to understate the new insights that flowed from this work. Here we want to draw attention to some specificity in the ways these matters of community and autonomy are being taken up in these particular times. Further, as our case studies suggested, there has been some exaggeration of the absence of such concerns about connection and community among boys. More specifically, we suggest that the claim that girls face a tension between autonomy and connection pays little attention, on the one hand, to the manner in which that dilemma is also negotiated by young men today or to the changes that feminism and other cultural trends have made to the gendered associations of this dilemma. Girls are not, we have suggested, so constrained or burdened by autonomy and success (or choosing between autonomy or connection), nor boys as indifferent to desires for connection and community.

The concepts of "autonomy" and "connection" are one useful focus when we consider the themes emerging in our interviews, and they are concepts that have been widely influential in discussions and interventions in relation to gender. But we also need to consider another important perspective on these matters, one that focuses on broad patterns of social change rather than gendered difference within that. This is the double-edged character of "autonomy" in contemporary times and (Rose 1999) new forms of selfhood and autonomous subjectivity.

The pursuit of autonomy might also be seen as one way of describing what Beck and Beck-Gernsheim (2002) represent as a feature of contemporary processes of individualization. The processes of self-making involved in this pursuit of autonomy also recall Nikolas Rose's (1999) analysis of the rise and effects of a "culture of the self." Autonomy is also historically aligned with masculinity, with femininity represented as "not autonomy," as feminist theorists from Simone de Beauvoir onward have critically shown. Young women's embrace of autonomy is as much a consequence of cultural imperatives to individualization, to calls to "be your own person" as it is an artifact of feminism. Seeing young women's desire for autonomy as evidence of the freedom of women from passivity and emotional dependence invokes the success of feminism, but tends to neglect the ways in which the practices of autonomy are linked to the emergence and regulation of particular kinds of individuals. But women's quest for individuality is differentiated from that of men because of women's historical association as incapable of and excluded from such a subjectivity and because of the association of women with care and connection, which are typically counterposed as in conflict with autonomy.

Nikolas Rose argues that, in current times, psychological knowledges and techniques structure the way in which we understand and know ourselves and mediate our social and personal experiences.[4] This represents a new form of subjectification (in the Foucauldian sense of regulation of the self) rather than simple emancipatory possibilities toward greater self-knowledge. Autonomous individuals know and conduct themselves through these psychotherapeutic lenses and discourses—they constitute the contemporary form of government of the self and of others. There is an emphasized process of scrutinizing relationships—those of and with other people, as well as the project of relating to oneself—leading to a "new culture of the self" (Rose 1999, 91).

> The individual is to adopt a new relation to his or her self in the everyday world, in which the self itself is to be an object of knowledge and autonomy is to be achieved through a continual enterprise of self-improvement through the application of a rational knowledge and technique. . . . Hence the norm of autonomy produces an intense and continuous self-scrutiny, self-dissatisfaction and self-evaluation in terms of the vocabularies and explanations of [psychotherapeutic] expertise. (Rose 1999, 93)

In such "big picture" arguments, however, there is limited attention given to the particular ways in which these new forms of the self are either gendered or enacted by situated, embodied individuals. In cultures saturated with knowledge of gender difference, particularly the feminization of affect and relationships and the masculine connotations of the norm of autonomy, such therapeutic techniques of the self are going to resonate differently for girls and boys.

In the following section, we turn to a close study of two young men with different class backgrounds who attend two different schools—Brett at Regional Tech and Marcus at Suburban High—and explore how they negotiate the dilemmas of connection and relationships and becoming their own person.

Masculinity, Community and Self/Other Relationships

At the end of elementary school, Brett described himself as "helpful" and a good friend. As he grows up, he continues to understand himself in this way: standing by his mates is important for him, a matter of honor and pride. He hopes his friends know that "I'd do anything for them if they needed to and that. If it was in limits. I'd stick by them." (Year 9, age 15). He enjoys recreational shooting, has a thought-out opposition to restrictive gun laws, and disdains authority (particularly teachers and the police), but in his experience in the workplace respects his bosses. He holds strong populist-conservative political views (believes some of Pauline Hanson's views are okay: "she's standing for the Australians") (Year 12, age 18) and expresses chivalrous/patriarchal attitudes to women and girls: "I wouldn't hit a girl, unless if she was trying to kill me or something . . . if . . .a girl hit me or something, I'd just keep walking. I wouldn't hit a girl. It's wrong" (Year 9, age 15). But throughout school, girls occupy a marginal place for Brett compared to the world of his mates. Work and social life are important, and the things that matter most are "getting a job, friends, family, school at the start" (Year 11, age 17, 1998). He spends most of his time out of school and on the weekends with his mates, shooting and "mucking around with cars." Friends are important to Brett, and are a strong part of his life and his identity. But, for him (in contrast, for example, to someone like Nicky—see chapter 5), this is just something that is. It is not an issue that needs to be reflexively mined or consciously brought into a project about who he is or who he might be.

Brett imagines a conventional future—the nuclear family and a male breadwinner in regular work. In his final year of school, he sees himself in a few years' time as having: "Oh, steady job. My own house. Oh, and [in] quite a few years, settle down, have a family, I suppose" (Year 12, age 18). But it is not a scenario he appears to have actively determined. It is expressed more as the unfolding of a perceived inevitable future. In many respects, Brett continues to embody a relatively traditional form of country-town white working-class masculinity. His identity is tied up in sport, cars, his mates, and manual or trade work; he describes himself as "easygoing" and the future, from his point of view, is unproblematic: he will, as his peer at the school Keren also says, "take things as they come" (Year 12, age 18).

In his senior years of school, Brett began an internship in engineering and welding, taking some subjects at school, others at a local college of Technical and Further Education (TAFE) and spending two days a week working as a welder in a truck-building factory. In our last interview with him, he was struggling to complete the formal requirements of the course and had effectively left school. A large part of the attraction of the internship was that it placed him among workmates who treated him as an adult. Throughout his schooling, he is impatient to move beyond that infantilizing domain, which stands in the way of his entering manhood.

> You go to work they treat you like an adult; at [TAFE] they treat you like an adult, but here they just treat you like a kid really, a little child.
>
> Yeah, I feel a lot older, in the workplace. They all know I'm a lot younger but they all treat me like one of the adults. Except like telling me what to do. If we are doing a job and something goes wrong, like I put in my input about it too, like what I think should happen, instead of sitting back and not allowed to say anything.
>
> (Brett, Regional Tech, Year 12, age 18)

In the world outside, however, things have changed. The decline of the manufacturing sector, the growth in rural and youth unemployment, a restructured labor market (Kenway and Kelly 2000), and its attendant ideas of the "flexible workforce," combine to produce for young men such as Brett a likely future of insecure, limited, or no paid work. When we do our final postschool interviews, Brett is in fact unemployed. In such an economic context, "mates" and interpersonal relationships become increasingly important and in a sense occupy the space once filled by the sociality and purposefulness of paid work. Brett finds these associations in a sporting club as well as in friendships and regular parties (and misdoings). Brett's work experiences are also depicted in terms of his positive and affirming interactions with workmates.

For another young man, at the same school and similarly on the margins of the labor market, the local athletics club provided a forum for connection and regular commitment. This person, Dirk, had a less troubled pathway through school—he was not such an overt troublemaker, but his story is similar. In the early years, he says that his thinking about the future is "take it as it comes"; in the later years of school, he is enthusiastic only about his trade subjects and workplace experiences and fails to complete his academic subjects; he strongly wants to enter a trade; his preference is carpentry, but he is prepared to enter any other if that is not available. These are the traditional masculine working-class aspirations, but, like Brett, when we revisit him at 18, Dirk is without work because the carpenter to whom he been apprenticed had experienced tough times, and no other opportunities were available.

For Brett, as for the other students in our project, identity is bound up in the choices he makes, and in Brett's case particularly his resistance to his school, no matter how much it tries to encourage and find appropriate courses for him. His identity as someone who does not get on at school, who resists schooling, is an identity and identification that would be at home in Paul Willis's (1977) account of working-class boys at school three decades ago.

With us, both Brett and Dirk appear uncomfortable reflecting on their emotional life and what each thinks about himself. They do not seem to be immersed in the modes of self-scrutiny discussed by Rose (1999), nor do they understand themselves within the discourse of "choice biography"; they, traditionally, "take things as they come." These young men presume a traditional masculine experience and role—the expectation of work, of being a breadwinner, and of settling down with family—despite the changed economic and social circumstance they inhabit. On the one hand, these boys appear to embody a relatively traditional, even an emphasized and intransigent form of white, provincial, working-class masculinity. Being with mates is linked with a repertoire of masculine activities and values that appear relatively unchanged by feminism or related social changes such as Giddens describes as the "transformation of intimacy" (1992). On the other hand, their marginal connection to the labor market and the pleasure they derive from relations with friends and workmates point to a retraditionalized masculinity that is anchored not in paid work, but in relationships.

Marcus embodies a different kind of masculinity, but one that is also rearticulated along narratives of the self and relationships. Marcus attends Suburban High, an "arty," government school in a middle-class suburb of a large city, which we discussed in chapter 7.

The school has a reputation for being tolerant and socially inclusive and has a number of programs for "at risk" students, such as a breakfast club for homeless students and an extensive pupil welfare and support program. Students tell us that it accepts "difficult" students who have been expelled from other schools. Positive social and interpersonal relations among students and between students and teachers are actively promoted and recognized by students as an attractive aspect of their school. Students talk positively about the care they receive at the school, and of the personal approach of the teachers: at the end of their secondary schooling, all students regarded this as an important part of their schooling experience. Marcus thinks "it's a good school in a lot of ways like the attitudes of the teachers, like they don't push you a whole lot, but they, most of the teachers you know, care about your education and don't really treat you like some sort of number really" (Year 9, age 15). Reflecting back on the school, Marcus says,

> It wasn't a disciplinarian sort of school . . . developing sort of the alternative side as opposed to your disciplinarian go ahead and succeed in life sort of thing . . . [how he saw private schools] . . . as far as looking outside the square seeing how other people live, um, you know, seeing a wider variety of people I think you get to know at state school, I think yeah I learnt a lot from my time at [. . .], probably brought me down to earth made me I don't know, maybe less arrogant or something.
>
> (Marcus, in year after leaving school, Suburban High, age 18)

The school promised a "second chance" for all, another chance to remake oneself, to not mindlessly conform but to work out one's own goals and values. It encouraged a therapeutic approach to students' problems; talking through issues, visiting the counselor, self-understanding. The school also encouraged political awareness of difference: "That's one of the good things about it. Sort of accepting you and stuff. Um, yeah, generally sort of, yeah, you know it's not cool to be racist and stuff like sexist, so they're pretty nice sort of people." (Year 9, age 15).

Marcus embodied the habitus of Suburban High in a very striking way. Toward the end of secondary school, he is preoccupied with working out what he wants to do, but with a focus on working on his emotional well-being, on sorting himself out—self-discovery—rather than planning strategically for his immediate future. Marcus, and several other students, speak of the possibilities of self-improvement as self-knowledge: "I think you should live by your own sort of, set your own sort of standards and morals and ethics and stuff, and live by that" (Year 9, age 15).

He has a romantic view of the quest for self-knowledge, from drugs to overseas travel, and thinks he might be an artist.

> I don't want to have a meat and 3 veg sort of life, if you know what I mean . . . I don't want to be your ordinary sort of person that lives in a house with two kids and a wife and stuff. I sort of want to, I want to like experience other things, experiment with things.
>
> I've got loads of stupid ideas going through my head, but, things like moving away to, you know traveling around a lot. I don't really like the idea of being settled in one place, I like to move around a lot. And, um, I don't want to have a boring life, I want to, I want to, you know, make something of my life and not just something, you know, uninteresting.
>
> (Marcus, Suburban High Year 9, age 15)

At 18, he came back from an overseas student exchange but was not motivated to return to secondary school in Australia to complete Year 12 as he was not sure it was the right thing for him to do. He is unable to commit to a particular job, even a part-time casual one—he just has to find himself. He is immersed in understanding and making the self: for him, "choice biography" produces overwhelming indecision and inertia.

> I really haven't found any direction at all, yet really, don't know exactly what I want to do, I'd like to write, I'd like to travel, I know I want to travel in my life, that's for sure, that's a priority for me to get out and see different things, but haven't really found my direction in life, in terms of career, don't know what I'm going to do.
>
> (Marcus, in year after leaving school, age 18)

The schools' pedagogic and pastoral care strategies and Marcus's orientation to understanding the personal are psychotherapeutic in the sense discussed by Rose (1999). They constitute a culture of the self that privileges self-knowledge and relationships and requires endless self-monitoring.

In these two examples of Brett and Marcus, we see traditional forms of masculinity alongside retraditionalized and more therapeutic forms. In one sense, this assessment appears consistent with the youth research literature on "normal or traditional biographies" and "choice biographies": that is, young people who pursue a relatively traditional pattern of transition through school and work and anticipate conventional gender roles, and young people who, in Gidden's sense, pursue a detraditionalized pathway and emphasize choice and flexibility in their imagined futures (du Bois-Reymond 1998; Dwyer et al. 1998). Such categorizations can convey a sense of the broad patterns of difference in young people's identity and future making, but (insofar as they are shorthand descriptions for complex processes) they can also risk reifying biographies as categories.

Moreover, in Marcus's story, we can see that the supposed "choice biography" of contemporary times, when it is taken on, is not simply an empowering moment of opportunity, but also is a form of subjectification that, in its relentless self-scrutiny, can have its own reflexivity dangers. In the case of Brett, friendship and relationships with his mates are clearly important, and are likely to become more so. At the same time, his self-identity remains linked to getting work, being independent, and experiencing a traditional future as a breadwinner. He has a confidence in who he is that is not shared by Marcus, even though his economic prospects are bleak. For Brett, the question of "Who am I?" is not particularly compelling, meaningful, or pertinent precisely because he feels both sure of himself and uninterested in the level of (femininized?) introspection such a question requires. Marcus's sense of self is characterized by intense reflexivity and by the task of sorting himself out—in relation to others and to his true self—independently of the world of work; the question of "Who I am?" is a guiding one. Marcus's work is his biographical project—an emblematic subject of modernity.

In terms of the self as a project, in general, girls more than boys in our study more readily (or more fully) took on the kind of self-reflection and scrutiny evident in Marcus's story. But working-class girls attending the same school as Brett and Dirk shared in their refrain and proclamation of "taking it as it comes," the almost superstitious resistance to proclaiming high hopes for the future or detailed strategic planning of the steps to get there. Nevertheless, there were signs that their trajectory was not identical with the boys in our study. The girls might talk as if the future or their fate "just happens" or just unfolds, but, as our earlier example of Keren suggests, they were persisting in different contexts and with different opportunities.

Conclusion

Giddens (1992) speaks optimistically of the possibilities afforded by the transformation of intimacy and the project of making the self. He identifies feminism as the agent of change, arguing that the new possibilities it has opened up for relationships and intimacy signal the promise of democracy. Rose locates the focus on relationships and quest for the "personal" as representing new forms of governing the self (1999). For Rose, turning the self into a biographical project is understood not as a guarantee of autonomy or of ontological security, but rather as an artifact of the predominance of psychotherapeutic knowledges. They represent for Rose a particular set of strategies in the history of practices of freedom and practices of the self.

We have brought together elements of these two different lines of argument, and of some parallel and influential feminist debates, to examine some of the socially specific and local ways in which young women and men are negotiating autonomy and becoming "their own person" within a broadly characterized culture of the self and in the wake of feminism and changing gender relations.

One evident element of changing times in relation to the time and place in which we did our study was the changes in what was said and what was deemed proper to say about gender, discrimination, and equal opportunity. In terms of self-conscious discourse, at least in the context of school, the people we spoke to were quick to say that there was no discrimination in relation to sex, that gender was not an important marker in terms of futures and possibilities. At the same time, traditional ways of viewing men versus women persisted in their narratives: "males are just normal"; women are too concerned about appearance. There was little interest in discussing the politics or context that made different things matter for men or women; and resistance by boys in their early and mid-high school years to any need to think differently about who they might be (compared with their fathers) or what they needed to do. Gender difference was not an interesting topic for them, and there was a widely shared apolitical assumption that sexism was easily identified as any explicit or formal difference of treatment on the basis of gender.

The narratives we have discussed here are not necessarily helpful ones for either the girls or the boys in this study. It does matter more than ever if boys leave school before graduation, yet the very success of girls is creating some unwillingness on their part to engage with schooling in the same way. And girls, lulled by the sense that there is now formal equal opportunity, are not well prepared for the situation they find from their mid-twenties, when wage and promotion patterns are strongly differentiated by gender. Issues about how workplace and domestic demands can really come together are not the subject of scrutiny in the way they were in the wave of Australian feminism of the 1970s and 1980s that enacted new workforce legislation.[5]

In the stories of individuals we discussed in this and earlier chapters, we see some of the unevenness and complexity of change. While schools might be, as Rose suggests, drawn into the processes of constructing a new government of the self to produce new kinds of "autonomous" self-marketing individuals, the emphases of the culture of the four schools we studied took this up in markedly different ways, and the differences are echoed in the stories we hear from Marcus compared with Brett and Dirk, or Nicky compared with Keren and Julia. And for the girls who were so energized and excited when they daydreamed of the future at 18, the new "subjectification" that demands an autonomous self is not all dangerous and negative (at least not at this stage of their lives).

Our aim in this discussion has not been to develop simple gender contrasts or come up with a grand new theory or account of gender difference. Instead we have tried to illuminate some of the ways in which different young women and men are negotiating some conventionally and strongly gendered themes, such as autonomy, connection, relationships, and individualization. And we have tried to point to some of the complex ways in which gender relations today, in a postfeminist, late-modern, and neoliberal era, are subject to both change and continuity. These dual processes and gender configurations are central, not peripheral, to the form of contemporary social life and to possibilities for making modern lives.

CHAPTER 9

Schooling, Schooling Politics, and Making Modern Lives

This has been a book about subjectivity and the making of selves in the context of contemporary schooling and contemporary times. As we have been writing, a new national debate has broken out in Australia about the values young people acquire in schools, provoked by Prime Minister John Howard's charge that parents were choosing private schools for their children because these offered clearer and firmer values. Public schools, he argued, were losing the confidence of parents because they were "too politically correct" and also "values neutral"—an interesting combination, to say the least.

The debate about values and about public and private schools encapsulates a number of the themes about subjectivity and schooling that we have tried to explore in this book. There is a widespread sense of New Times and frequently expressed concerns among politicians and parents as well as theorists about how young people today are forming themselves in relation to a future world and society that seem to have changed dramatically. The interest in a changed social world and in processes of self-formation is both about work, careers, pathways, and patterns, and about relationships, community, and values about self and other. There is interest in and concern about how such changes are being felt and lived, and also in what schooling (as well as parents) should be doing today. At the same time, such debates are far from being transparent.

The Australian prime minister who instigated this recent debate with some overt criticism of the "political correctness" of public schooling is one whose government has committed larger amounts of funding to subsidizing private schools, and one who won an election in good part by playing on fears of the population about "the other" in the form of refugees. The values this government wants to encourage as a response to the "New Times" are values of enterprise and Christianity and the traditional, Western, nuclear family. The debate about values and schools is overtly about how to sustain work as well as maintain a healthy community, but it is also part of the longstanding political use of schooling as an ideological weapon in which some parts of the community are blamed for their failure to be successful or to be the mainstream, or in which schooling is blamed because jobs have changed or disappeared, or some aspects of civil life (crime, violence, driving behavior, eating behavior, and so on) are found wanting. The blaming of schools for social orientations of the citizenry is a common historical strategy that hides the unequal and different resources (not just material ones) with which different schools and families operate.

And the debate is not transparent in yet another way. It alludes to schools as if they are themselves transparent and easily reshaped institutions, as if the values they convey in their brochures are the same as those they enact in their practices, and as if young people at school can be easily manipulated in their views of the world by the technical operations of what schools teach. We have looked close-up at the complexity of different young people at four different schools, schools with different histories and location, young people from different backgrounds in the same school and similar backgrounds at different schools, and at what they said about schools, self, and politics when they first came to the school and over the next seven years. In doing so, we wanted to show how their engagement with schooling and with particular schools over the teenage years does become part of the making of self, the making of inequalities, and the making of society.

One of our themes is that schools do enter into the making of the self and the production of inequalities, work trajectories, and social relationships beyond school, but we emphasize two further elaborations of these processes. First, we try to show that the forming of subjectivity in the context of school should be seen from the perspective of processes and projects of becoming, not just from a perspective of reflecting (social discourses), or of mediating (dispositions, experiences, and cultural capital brought to the schooling arena), though these too deserve recognition. This is evident, for example, in how the young people we interviewed located themselves and expressed views related to race and immigration. Their ways of talking did carry some imprint of different school cultures, one of which, for example, emphasized the politics of distribution, and another the politics of recognition; yet another spoke with a liberal discourse of free speech and rights that is possible when one's own position is securely of the elite. And they also bore the marks of particular family experiences and emphases: Stephanie, a girl who is aware of her own parents' origins in Europe, not Australia, has a different relationship to the debates about national belonging than the other students from more long-standing Australian heritage whom we interview at the same school. But the young people's identifications and placing of themselves were also expressions of their own hopes and longings in relation to their future self and the future community and their place in that.

To make these points might seem like old news, or even common sense, but if so, it is a common sense that is not shown in the ways that many politicians, or policy-makers, or theorists approach the issues. In accounts of schooling and inequalities, a sense of complex subjectivities at work often recedes. In theories of subjectivity, schooling is often at best a stereotyped and formulaic presence. And elsewhere, and over and over, debates about schooling and research on schooling take place as if schooling is basically a technical and managerial operation, as if young people are not complex subjects, but bundles of effects whose causes can be experimentally determined. Vocational education or careers education, for example, is approached as if it is simply a matter of giving enough information about the choices, and as early as possible. From our longitudinal study, it is evident that the orientation to a job future is very differently experienced at 12 than at 17, and that questions or information about it are received very differently at those ages. Actual social experiences matter too. The fact that most of the young people we happened to follow had mothers who at some point in the course of our study undertook further study themselves, and that a number of fathers were out of work, is drawn on in their deeper sense of where they might be going and in how different young people interact with the agendas of schooling and the culture of their own schools.

Our second broad theme about these processes of subjectivity was to give a particular perspective on how patterns of social inequalities and differences are reinforced and produced and reproduced in the course of schooling. What we found in our project, and have argued in this book, is an account that emphasizes the local effects of particular schools as well as the impact of schooling generally, of schooling as a comparatively experienced institutional and discursive feature of the society. We draw attention to effects of the form of schooling—the differences in the relative demographic, community, and historical locations from which different schools necessarily operate—and also to the discursive uptake by particular schools, their particular school cultures, and how this mediates particular social and political values and particular senses for an individual of their potential or lack of potential. We showed in earlier chapters that what the four schools in this study did, as well as how this was perceived by students, parents, and the community, was heavily mediated by social distinctions of the school setting, location, history, and previous family experiences. In the first year of our study, at the most elite school, all of those we interviewed talked of some poor teaching and inadequate facilities in the computer area, but for none of them did this signal that they were getting a poor education. Community perceptions and history constructed this as a good school, and its elite networking operations framed any particular moves it made in relation to curriculum or teaching. Conversely, the poorest school in our study was doing a lot of things that most of those who deal with schools today, or with working-class children, highly recommend. It had a lot of technology, it worked to make curriculum relevant, it attempted to make provision that would keep young people engaged and give them better possibilities for work. But the weight of family history and peer culture, the community and media designation of the relative place of this school and the suburbs where these young people lived, meant that this continued to be an uphill battle. The public school in our study that wanted to be "like" a private school had to work hard and repetitively at this.

However, within this broad context, schools do still make choices about how they operate and the values they transmit (but not, of course, choices from a level playing field, untrammeled by history, place, and resources). In our study, this is shown most interestingly by the different values, trajectories, and interviews at 18 of the young people attending Regional High compared with those attending Suburban High. At Regional High, there was little of the "politically correct" valuing of each person of which the Australian prime minister complained. What was conveyed was strong instrumental values, a sense that this was a hard competitive world: that the task during school was to show one's school to be "as good as" the private schools.

The orientations to making one's way in the world were to work hard, to plan, to have goals, to know different ways of achieving them. If young people from this school did not get the score they hoped for in their final examinations (and the broad relativities of schooling discussed in the previous paragraph are one reason why this was not uncommon), they embarked on another way of getting there. At 18, Stephanie had begun a technical college diploma course rather than a university course, but one that had the potential to allow her to transfer to the degree course in the same area; Andrew was doing medical sciences rather than a medical degree, but had visions of a future move to eventually become a doctor as he had hoped; Jackie was busy working in a part-time job and getting herself fit so she would pass the rigorous physical entrance examination for the police force; Julia was studying the course she had chosen (nursing), but not in the university of her first choice, and was making viable plans that would extend her directions, financial support, and opportunities in the near future. And John had left school at the minimum age and dropped out of sight: this was not a school that gave a lot of attention to nurturing those with difficulties.

At Suburban High, by contrast, the school had a long-standing culture of valuing the "inclusiveness" that the conservative prime minister implicitly derides. Here both teachers and students repeatedly see the distinctive features of this school as its valuing of (ethnic) diversity and its attempts to look after each individual, to give them second chances if they needed it. Although the overall pattern of final-year results relative to intake was not so different at this school from that of Regional High, the orientations to self and future developed in each school context were markedly different. Over the years of the interviews, at Regional High, the young people talked a lot about their goals and activities (they led busy lives with part-time work, very active sports involvements, dance classes). At Suburban High what was emphasized was not goals, but rather the scrutiny of the self. What most (not all) of those we talked to here were prepared to dwell on at some length was "Who am I?," "What is my personality?," "What kind of person do I want to be?" At 18, when the young people from Regional High were firmly at the beginning of their postschool career or job trajectory (both in our own outside judgment of this and in their own self-perceptions), the young people from Suburban High were still quite heavily preoccupied with these other introspective questions. At this school, Madeleine has started an arts course at university but dropped out within the first two months; Amelie began a university nursing course, but is also considering dropping out; Nassar and Jenna are still at school because they had not taken a full course in the previous year; Marcus has not been able to face returning to school and completing high school after his period of study abroad; and Helen has finally found a university course that seems to suit her (introspective) interests: Women's Studies.

In terms of young people and pathways, one reading of the summarized outcomes of where the people from each school end up (or of outcomes relative to SES or outcomes relative to gender) seems unsurprising: looking close-up does not alter the patterns of factual outcomes we can read from databases. What our close-up and longitudinal account gives more sense of is the ambivalence and emotional tensions through which individual subjects are making their way to these first postschool steps; some changing meanings of what outcomes mean in relation to particular lives (and possible futures); and some concrete sense of how lives are affected by particular schools and different orientations and trajectories set up for the medium and longer term than those postschool pathways indicate.

From a substantial history of sociological studies of schooling and inequalities, we are already accustomed to seeing young people's class, gender, race-differentiated engagement with school as mediated by forms of culture clash between those modes of comportment, speech, dispositions, orientations that school values and those brought to it by particular groups. But our close-up study offers some other perspectives on how lives are made in particular school contexts. In a number of chapters, we discuss Keren, who, like most of her peers at her school (Regional Tech), comes from a working-class background, has parents without successful school experiences themselves, and in some areas of the academic curriculum struggles with the work. But in this school, Keren's discourse of "taking it as it comes," of not tempting fate by being too lavish in her ambitions, does not preclude her staying on and ending up in a course to become a registered nurse and to begin an independent life about which she is very happy. The school's limited (or "realistic") expectations about where students would end up meant that it gave support to some of Keren's academic needs (extra tutoring in mathematics, for example) without exerting an atmosphere of competitive striving or pressure on her to succeed or to have particular goals that she might have experienced at the other school in our study, which might have been too much for her. We suggest too that her story is something of a gendered story. Her own mother is returning to study while our study proceeds. Her gendered class identity does not require the rejection of school as part of "being a man" that we see in Brett's story at the same school. And the same school culture has different effects for Alan, a boy from a more cosmopolitan background, than for Keren. Here the lack of pressure, the lack of competition, means that he settles for work and outcomes that are respectable (a computer course at the local university), but are less than he might have obtained at the other school in this town, and are diminished from his earlier ambitions to move out of the town and study at some more prestigious and metropolitan institutions.

At the most elite school too, we showed similar ways in which trajectories for individual lives are not simply about the match or lack of match between habitus or dispositions and the mainstream curriculum. The school culture and values enter individual lives, though the trajectories they embark on are differentiated and can involve conscious rejection of the school. Diana's running away from this school is driven in part by her dislike of its values, but in part by her unhappiness that she is not valued in its setting. Three years later, she is studying law at university in a different state, with ambitions and ways of thinking about what she has achieved and where she is going that are not highly differentiated from her peers who remained at the school. Gillian came to this school with a strong self-narrative about being a good person who cares for others and appreciates what opportunities the school can give her. Her sense of herself as an outsider diminishes over the years of schooling and her career aims move from a more ordinary one (teaching) to one that is highly selective in its intake (arts therapy). The interviews with students at this school indicate that they see its own values as concerned with social success and distinctiveness across a broad array of activities. The school develops a strong emphasis on a school community that will be a continued feature of the social lives of those who go there, with hierarchies of insiders and outsiders both in peer relations inside the school and in university life beyond school. Gillian negotiates these themes in ways that are continuous with her earlier sense of self and biographical agendas. Her incorporation of some of the school codes does modify some of her outlook, but also provides her with a sense of other possibilities and a new but complementary sense of who she is.

In their various ways, Alannah, Nicky, and Peter are also carrying their experiences as part of their school community into their post-school lives. These three young people are now in universities and courses other than the one large elite university to which students from this school proceed en masse. They are highly conscious of now having few of their school friends around them at university, and dwell on how this feels, though such experiences are the norm for students from the other schools in our study. The two young women in particular continue a life in which the social relationships and networks maintain a high continuity with those they set up in their school years. Nicky, whose story we discussed in chapter 5, wants to remain part of the elite school community, to embody its practices of distinctions, and also hopes to be a mother when young, a desire—or the articulation of a desire—that is unusual among many of her peers at City Academy. Nicky does not imagine her future life as one of full-time work, but one of having a "good life" and this, in the realm of her experience, seems both desirable and materially possible, even though it does place her somewhat outside the "aiming for success" in working lives and multiple pathways that other girls from City Academy articulate. The pathways data on the courses and outcomes of such young people are only a small part of the story of who they now are and the trajectories they are embarking upon.

We started our study with an interest in what has changed in contemporary times—how young people form identities, educational choices, pathways, and values in a period when gender "equal opportunity" policies are old news; jobs have changed dramatically; the demographics of family and community life are experienced as being disrupted, and are under scrutiny by politicians and theorists. Our account and our argument in this book are that for young people going through school this is a period of continuity and change in a context of continuity and change.

In some respects, the rhetoric about "New Times" is easily exaggerated. The schools, the trajectories, the gendered outcomes show some remarkable continuities with patterns and theories that are well established. In some respects, the story of Brett and Dirk and Talik and how they experience school and the search for jobs could be inserted in sociological school ethnographies of 30 or 40 years ago with little sense of anachronism. Talk of "New Times" should not be an excuse for exaggerating "individualized" self-making and ignoring the patterns of class-based differences that remain a central feature of how schooling as an overall system operates and produces effects. Nevertheless, as we discuss in our chapter on "class," what we are trying to get a sense of here (or multiple perspectives on) are these ongoing processes of "reproduction" within a changing world and within some changing meanings of what is powerful and less powerful, given a changing economy and culture. That is, we are trying to understand both what is the same and what is different about schools and the social world now, emphases represented in the broader picture by the theories, respectively, of Bourdieu compared with those of Giddens or Beck.

In terms of what is changing or what is different about current times in relation to the lives of young people at school, this study has drawn attention to a number of recurring issues.

First, on the mooted issues of changing gender relations and their impact, the young people in our study have been touched by what they see in their parents' lives, and by those discursive changes to how gender difference is now represented in school policy and in the public sphere. In the high school years at least, the girls have a different sense of their future life than research tended to show at the beginning of the attention to girls in the 1970s. Their narratives about the future do not depict a relatively brief postschool phase of work and study followed by a long period of domestic responsibilities. Indeed, in most cases, the latter concerns seem not to be a strong part of their own thinking about the future. What the girls in our study talk of to us (with only a couple of exceptions) is about their ambitions for independence and excitement (jobs and travel in particular) and not their hopes for a future family. Instead, for many, there is a sense of excitement and yearnings for independence. They handle relationship with their boyfriends, but this does not appear to dominate their choices and thinking about their postschool futures.

Or is it that this is the story they feel able to tell us? Although "equal opportunities" rhetoric has opened up certain ambitions and orientations to the future for them, it brings with it a sense that gender difference must be denied, that it is not appropriate to examine or dwell on different gendered behaviors and why they might arise. In the early stages of our study (when they were aged about 12 to 15), the middle-class girls tended to talk about their rebellion against their mothers and desire to be free of that restriction; the working-class girls were empathetic to their mothers and spoke of their mothers' good wishes for them. But a lot of girls from both backgrounds also told us that their own mothers at some point returned to study and changed jobs themselves in the course of our research, and spoke positively of that, while a mother whose daughter calls her "a real mum mum" is treated as a negative role model from her daughter's point of view.

With the boys in our study, there is some awareness of actual changes in family patterns, but uncertainty about what, concretely, their future family life will be like. At the same time, there is a relatively unshaken continuing belief that "males are just normal" or, put another way, that male experiences are the norm. The social and subjectivity changes associated with feminism seem to have a much stronger impact on young women than young men, and it is the young women—across all four different schools—who appear to be managing new work and social changes with more confidence.

A major discussion in recent times has been about what is happening to community and social relationships, evident in a range of theoretical discussions about, for example, increased individualization (Beck and Beck-Gernsheim 2002), or declining social capital (Putnam 2000). The close-up interviews with both boys and girls in our study showed a considerable concern with and orientation to issues of community. The boys in the Regional Tech looked to strong associations outside school, in sporting and gun clubs and other community associations (and David at Regional High through car workshop and racing involvements). These boys from Cubbin found a post-school move to another city a difficult one to make, and often preferred to return home at weekends to continue their existing patterns of social relations.

Another live issue in relation to contemporary times is a focus on "new literacies" and the "new worker" and the modes by which people of the next generation will be expected to enter and negotiate their working life. At two of the schools in our study, City Academy and Regional High, students were actively acquiring a sense of themselves as a "portfolio" person: one who was self-conscious about representing a range of achievements and activities beyond examination results as part of what they had to offer in negotiating the world beyond school. And the middle-class girls in this study have very high levels of reflexivity in terms of how they position themselves interpersonally with us. Some of the reshaping of the curriculum, and the new literacies agenda, is about acquiring much more self-consciousness about how things are produced and read by different people in different settings. These modes of the middle-class girls are potentially highly advantageous attributes in negotiating working life, though they also bring with them a high degree of critical self-scrutiny that may turn in on the self and undermine one's self-confidence. Nevertheless, the vocational education literature today is full of hopes about workers learning to become "flexible lifelong learners." The contrast between the interviews, as well as pathways, of the girls at City Academy and the boys at Regional Tech points to the irony that a powerful discourse in relation to those in nonuniversity-based jobs calls up as desired attributes what might be seen as gender-class dispositions rather than teachable orientations. At Regional Tech, the school tried to provide entry-points to work for its students, usually through personal networks, but what these students acquired little of was a perspective on the bigger scene and on how they could do more than try to emulate their parents' lives "taking it as it comes."

Our book has also touched on the specificities of lives in contemporary times, in particular the issue of young lives in Australia that share and are involved in broader global movements, but are also grounded in a particular history and construction of schooling. In the state in which we carried out our study, the history of a strong well-established group of private schools from which a large number of those in powerful positions are drawn is a feature of the system. The private schooling sector is attracting growing numbers in a context where parents' anxieties about the future for their children are increased by uncertainties about how the world is changing. Commentators have often remarked on some differences they observe between Australian and U.S. cultural styles. In Australia, people are less comfortable talking about themselves; there is not the evangelical public confessional religious tradition or the contemporary secular replicas of these in television talk shows; ambition is treated with some suspicion (unless in sports); there is a "tall poppy" syndrome in which people who achieve success are readily criticized. For our study this means that even our attempts to ask directly about "self" often bring limited responses: much of the story we tell here has to operate by reading what is implied across a range of talk about many topics.

A study that is interview-based and with relatively small numbers is, of course, a limited means of offering any grand or generalized insights about what is changing for individual lives in these times, but, as we have argued, we did not carry out our study as if we were blank slates—we worked on our seven years of interviews, along with three further years of reviewing our 400 odd transcripts and tapes in dialogue with other research, other theories, and other discussions about social change and subjectivity. What we have tried to do in this book is offer some ways of seeing young people's engagement with schooling in their lives, and to deliberately adopt different types of perspective on this. In chapter 4, we discussed some of the different theoretical concerns that animated our study, and argued for the value of an approach that aimed to keep different (sometimes competing, sometimes complementary) perspectives in focus and to work with and across them in a reflexive and critical manner. Different theoretical approaches open up different ways of seeing, providing contrasting lenses for viewing the complex interplay between subjectivity, schooling, and inequality. As we have argued, individual lives are not reducible to a single theoretical framework—no matter how neat and coherent that might ostensibly seem—biographical formation exceeds the theories that seek to account for it. Our opening epigraph from Seyla Benhabib was chosen because we see it as making a related point: "there is a never a single set of constitutive criteria to appeal to in characterizing complex social practices." The transposition for us is that there is never a single set of *conceptual* criteria to appeal to in characterizing complex *social and biographical* processes.

We work in faculties of education and in part our interests are framed by what is being projected as policies for schools. A further framing of this study is an attempt to raise issues about processes of inequality and about the *relevance of meanings and subjectivity* for policy-making about school—policy-making should not only be concerned with factors and facts. We also have children ourselves, and parents' questions and concerns are, rightly, not identical with those of policy-makers. We believe that inequalities and difference and what schools do in relation to this need more and better attention than they get; but, at the same time, we do not want to write a story of individual lives in which the middle-class young people at school are only the demeaned "other" of the impassioned story on behalf of the working class, or where boys are the cardboard "other" of girls (and vice versa). Our chapter on national identity and issues of politics and race is about trying to see the complexities at work in this context—to observe the patterns of disadvantaging but also to explore values and meanings being built in ways that are very different from binary categories and typologies in which one is racist and another not. In deciding to undertake a study that would work qualitatively with young people over an extended time, we are almost inevitably framing a humanist story as well as an analytic one.

Schooling is the social institution that we subject all young lives to, and all those lives matter. But the humanist attention to people and not just types is not about a withdrawal from concerns about the politics or the analytics of schooling. We wanted to show what young people draw on, as well as the resources they are working with in developing values and personal and social agendas over these years; we wanted to depict them living and making lives in particular times and particular places. All these lives matter, theoretically as well as in daily life, but, in daily life as well as theoretically, the social patterns being built by individual lives and the unfairness in these processes also matter.

Appendix 1

Participant Snapshots

Suburban High

At this school we had rather more students in our study than we had originally intended—at least in part because a couple of those originally interviewed as friends proactively organized themselves into the study. Those we followed were:

Helen

Helen gave the impression of someone with strong opinions, but one who would not easily talk. Her self-descriptions often refer to her as "shy." Throughout the six years of the study, she consistently talks of not knowing what she wants to do, or where she wants to go, though, at 18, she is at university and enjoying courses in Women's Studies. She is close to her mother, an ex-teacher and union organizer, who has a senior executive position with a large nonprofit youth organization. Her father is a school principal, and she has stepsiblings from his earlier marriage (two older brothers and an older sister). Her mother went to a private school and her father attended various state schools. During her senior years of high school, Helen has a close boyfriend who lives in another city, and whom she visits every weekend.

Amelie

Amelie is an extrovert who we discover, retrospectively, was struggling with schoolwork at primary school and in the early secondary years, but who at 18 has passed her final year certificate and is taking a degree in nursing. She has close family ties to New Zealand (her father's birthplace), and in the course of the study is also affected by the suicide of someone with whom she was close. Her father is a self-employed gardener, after being laid off from his previous job as a fitter, but he used that opportunity to retrain as a gardener and now takes on apprentices. Her mother was initially a full-time homemaker, but did a part-time degree in accounting in the period when Amelie was at school, and now keeps the books for the gardening business. She has a brother who is just slightly older.

Madeleine

Madeleine's father has a senior job in the media, and often raises with her the issue of whether she should be at private school. She resisted this when choosing secondary schools, but at the end of the study is aware that this decision had some costs. For most of the study, Madeleine lives with her mother, but moved to live with her father for the final year of high school when her mother relocated to a seaside town. Madeleine's mother had gone to private school but did not graduate, and has had a range of different semiskilled jobs. Her father has a degree in journalism and recently has returned to work on a Master's degree. Madeleine also has an older brother. Madeleine speaks quietly and seems disengaged, not just from the interviews or from school, but from life. She begins a university degree, but has already dropped out when we interview students just three months into the new academic year.

Jenna

Jenna finds being at school a drag. In the early years she enjoys art and drama and possibly woodwork, but never likes mathematics and English, and is critical of teachers. During year 11, she makes a decision to drop some subjects and take an extra year to complete school. In the early years of high school, she nominated being a vet or a flight attendant as possible futures; in later years, she talks about being a photographer. Jenna's parents separated in the course of our study. At 18, Jenna is continuing with her disrupted final schooling subject.

Talik

Talik's parents are Turkish and migrated to Australia before he was born. They speak Turkish at home, and he attends Turkish language school on Saturday mornings, and has social networks in the Turkish community. He also is very keen on basketball, and plays in teams in and out of school. His father is a taxi driver, though there was a period when he worked with Talik's mother, making clothes to sell at markets. His mother now works as a nursing assistant in facilities for old and disabled people, working through an agency. Prior to that, she took a course in English. Talik has a younger brother at the same school. In terms of future ambitions, Talik mentioned only basketball in the first three years of our study, but later became interested in IT. He hoped to do a university qualification in this area, but his scores did not allow immediate entry, and at 18 he is doing a computer qualification at TAFE.

Daniel

Daniel is a personable and articulate student who talked his own way into our cohort. His father is a psychologist, his mother runs a small business, and he has an older sister. He plays lacrosse, and at the beginning of our study dreams of being in an Olympic team and eventually managing a farm. Daniel has some learning difficulties and the school organizes a special timetable for him; he leaves school at 16 to begin an apprenticeship in greens-keeping (i.e., gardening for specific sporting purposes). He does the first two years of the apprenticeship, but, when we last talk to him, has withdrawn and is just working as a casual employee in gardening.

Marcus

Marcus is an articulate and reflective individual, a very good cricketer, but also someone who throughout our whole study spends a lot of time thinking about who he is, his choices, where he wants to go. His father is a youth worker who began but did not finish university, and in the later years of the study was managing a boardinghouse for Aboriginal students in a remote community (Marcus joined him for some months). Marcus's mother did not complete year 12, but now owns and runs two dress shops. Both parents are of Anglo-Australian background. He has one older brother, now at university. In year 11, Marcus took an exchange to another country that he loved, but difficulties arose, partly of his own making, and he was forced to return home early. He planned to return to school for year 12, but could not face doing that and instead did some casual work, spent time with his father, and made plans about a future return to overseas travel. His earlier aspirations had been to "not lead a boring life."

Nassar

Nassar's family came from South Asia in the middle of his primary school years. He found the different style of Australian school a challenge, but when we began the study is obsessed with science and being a scientist, although his mother would like him to be a doctor. Nassar likes to talk, but does not seem to have many friends at school. In the early years, he is very close to and concerned about his mother. In later years, he becomes obsessed with computer chat rooms. Both academically and psychologically he is under considerable strain in the later years, and has periods away from school. In the final year of our study, he has returned to try to complete year 12, but is now aiming for a TAFE diploma in computers rather than the ambitions he had mentioned earlier whose entry requirements were well above his academic achievements. At the beginning of our study, Nassar's father was working in a factory, and by the end he was employed as a "human resource person." Nassar's mother was working as a part-time cook as well as studying for an Arts degree, and in the final year of our study was doing honors in that. Nassar's parents separated in the course of our study. He is an only child.

Regional High

Julia

Julia is serious and self-contained, and talks often about planning her own life. She is of Anglo-Australian background; her father completed high school (year 12), previously worked in a bank, and now manages a petrol station; her mother left school after year 10 and is a hairdresser, and Julia has one older brother. Throughout high school, Julia has a very full array of out-of-school activities: she studies dance, referees basketball, works part-time, and has an older boyfriend whom she sees most nights. In the early years of high school, Julia talked about wanting to work with animals or be a physiotherapist or psychologist; in the senior years, she aims to do social work or psychology or nursing; at 18 she is undertaking a degree in nursing at the university in her hometown, but planning to apply to join the airforce and complete her nursing qualification elsewhere.

Jackie

Jackie is cheerful and maintains a consistent sense of what she wants to do (become a police officer) from the middle years of high school. She seems not to get caught up in stresses about school results, university ambitions, and so on, brushing off suggestions from teachers or others about other careers she might consider. She is, however, concerned about, and at times disturbed by, friendship issues. Jackie is of Anglo-Australian background; both parents were teachers during her early school years. They later bought and managed a motel during much of the period of this study. Toward the end of our study, they sold the motel, and, at the end, Jackie's mother had returned to work as a teacher, and her father was not working. Jackie has an older sister. In year 9, Jackie says she is considering either interior decorating or police work, and in the following years settles consistently and strongly on becoming a police officer as her ambition, though she does work with a florist who offers her the opportunity to continue with them. Jackie passes her final school certificate and secures a university place, but decides to work for a year first and acquire experiences that will improve her chances of acceptance in the police force (to which she will apply at 19).

Stephanie

It was several years into the project before we realized Stephanie's parents were of Cypriot-Turkish background. She is blonde, with an unmarked Australian accent, and initially did not mention her family background in interviews. Stephanie's father owned a fish and chip shop and later worked in a secondhand store, but did not like working for a boss and went on unemployment benefits; at the end of the study, her father was still looking for work. He left school in about year 9. Her mother is now PA to a firm of accountants. She had initially worked in the fish and chip shop, then completed a writing course, and had had temporary jobs in secretarial and clerical work. Her parents had migrated from Cyprus to Germany then England then Australia; her mother had completed year 11 in England. Stephanie has one older and one younger brother. In the middle of high school, Stephanie's parents separated, and her mother moved to a new house just outside the city; by the end of the study both parents were living there. Stephanie talked every year of wanting to travel and have a good job. She mentioned modeling and being a lawyer, but for the final three years of high school was clear that she wanted to do hotel management. Stephanie's results were not as good as she had hoped so she was not able to directly undertake a university degree following year 12; instead she embarked on a diploma in hospitality, one that would give her entry to hotel work, and enable her to work toward a degree later.

Andrew

Andrew has the manner of an avuncular older person. Even in grade 6, he liked to crack jokes and flirt with the interviewer. His ambition was to do medicine, and he reminded us of some of the traditional family doctors one sees in television programs or films set in the 1940s and 1950s. Andrew's father started as a mechanic and has worked as a service manager and then technician in a larger auto dealer. His father left school at 15 or 16 and did an apprenticeship and took courses at trade school. His mother is a registered nurse. According to Andrew, his mother had been under pressure from her family to do well at school and attend university, but the pressure had been too much and she left midway through year 12. She worked as a sales representative, and has retrained as a nurse in the time since Andrew started high school. He has a younger brother, and they live in a desirable suburb near the school. Andrew initially wanted to be a lawyer or a doctor. His final school HSC score was not high enough for admission to the extremely competitive medical degrees in this state (students normally need scores in the top 1 percent to take these courses that are entered directly as undergraduates). However, Andrew has instead enrolled toward a Medical Sciences degree and is considering applying later for graduate entry toward a medical degree.

David

David had some trouble with bullying in the early years of high school, but was determined to succeed; at 18, he was studying mechanical engineering at a metropolitan university. His consuming passion was working on cars with his uncle, and his dream was to be part of a racing team. David and his family had moved from a farm to the city midway through his primary years because of a family dispute that permeated a lot of the interviews. They live in a high status area near the school, and David talks often about his family being the object of considerable envy. He also attributes his being bullied to this envy and to his being different from and more focused on his studies than his peers. He tells us his father had gone to private school until year 10, then been forced to help on the farm. After leaving the farm, he had started at the bottom at a truck yard, and worked his way up to become manager. He had completed school at night. David's mother had finished her schooling at a technical institution, but she too had not been able to go on to the career she wanted because of family responsibilities. Later she qualified and worked in real estate, and more recently in a shop. David has a younger brother and a younger sister. David consistently had talked about wanting to do an Engineering degree with an aim of later joining a Formula One racing team.

John

John dropped out of school as soon as he was legally able (aged 15) and when last we were able to talk to him (the following year) had a part-time job in a supermarket. John lived with his father, who was on a pension, and missed very much his mother, who had remarried and lived in a distant town. John resided with them for a couple of years, but it had not worked out, and he was living with his father again by the beginning of our study when he was in grade 6. His sister, a single parent with a baby, also lived with them. In the early years of school, when we asked about future jobs, John always mentioned the police or the airforce. But the teachers had predicted John would leave school early, following the paths of his brothers, and were not surprised when he did not return our attempts to contact him later, saying that the family was suspicious of authorities and how information might be used.

Regional Tech

We initially approached some more people at this school, and began our study with six students, but one of them decided not to continue after the first interview.

Keren

Keren was engaging and talkative when we started, had some difficult periods in early high school, and was more self-reflective and self-conscious at the age of 18. When we first interviewed her, Keren was living in a trailer park in a country town, which her mother managed, and doing a solid amount of domestic work herself. A stepfather whom she didn't like, was on the scene. Two years later, he had departed (to Keren's relief). In the period of our study, Keren's mother took a series of qualifications: in nursing and social welfare, and then in psychology, and was working as a rehabilitation nurse. In terms of her own ambition, Keren was one of the most vocal expressors of "take it as it comes," but, over the course of the study, she did name a number of postschool occupational ideas. In the early years of high school, she talked of becoming a cook (when she was doing a lot of cooking in the trailer park), then followed some ideas about childcare or primary teaching, and then nursing. At 18, she was taking a one-year registered nursing qualification, and was moving into her own apartment, and was very happy about that.

Kylie

Kylie lived in the small town that was one of the feeder areas for the technical school in our study, and was self-contained and strong-willed. She left school in year 11, after a fight with a friend. In the early interviews, she consistently mentioned wanting to be a chef, and when she left school she initially began a qualification in this area in TAFE. However, she did not continue with this, and by age 18 had moved to work full-time at McDonald's, where she had previously worked part-time. But she was enthusiastic about both the friendship and career paths available there, was in related sporting teams and taking training courses offered through her employer, and was adamant that school had not been a good place to be for her.

Alan

One of Alan's parents was Canadian, and he had a more cosmopolitan experience than most of the students at his school: he had traveled to Canada, and in the course of the study took part in a camp for potential leaders from across the whole state. In the early years of the study, Alan was absorbed in sports, especially swimming; in the middle years of the study, Alan had a close girlfriend and was intensively involved in an association that recreated and reenacted historical events on horseback. Alan's course at 18—a degree program in computer studies—was in the area he had named as his future interest in the first year of high school. But, in the middle school, he was not oriented to the future; in the course of the project his ambitions changed from wanting to go to a university in a major city to a decision to attend the local university. His father commuted to work in the city. He had completed year 10, then done an apprenticeship, and now worked in an office and participated in the navy reserves. His mother completed school, and started as a nurse, but became a kindergarten assistant after her children were born. She has done some studies in sociology in the period of our own study. Alan has two younger brothers.

Dirk

Dirk's parents were Dutch, and, when he was in primary school, they returned to Holland for a short period and had considered staying. Neither parent had continued much beyond the period of compulsory schooling (in Holland) and they had migrated to Australia as adults, before they had children. In Australia, his father, now retired, worked on the railways; his mother worked in a factory when they were in Holland, but in Australia has been a housewife, but has also done further studies at TAFE (in nursing and in history). Dirk has three older sisters, one older brother, a twin sister, and a younger brother. Dirk is not much interested in schoolwork (other than the vocational subjects), and is mainly interested in sports—he remains an active member of a local athletic club throughout the study. The outcomes and occupations of his siblings were unusually diverse: one sister was a secondary teacher, a brother works in McDonald's, another sister works in an office, another is a swimming instructor, and his twin sister at 18 was going to university, while Dirk himself was unemployed (because his employer was unable to maintain his apprenticeship) and looking for another apprenticeship or other work.

Brett

In the early years of high school, Brett's main enjoyment came from his out-of-school involvement in a gun club, with his father and other friends. He initially had wanted to join the army, but in the course of school (and our project) becomes progressively disenchanted and in trouble with the school. He does some dual accreditation subjects in a factory, which he likes, but at 18 is unemployed and looking for factory work. His parents are Anglo-Australian and when we interview Brett his father has been on sickness leave from his factory job.

City Academy

The six students in our study who began in this school are:

Peter

Peter has a twin brother, he is good at sports and music, and in his later years wins a scholarship at the school, but also has a number of experiences of not quite winning: his rowing crew consistently loses, and his final results are not as good as his twin brother's. He is in an academically selected group in the school who do a different final school certificate, yet he feels his results are not as strong as his high-achieving peers. But he enjoys and is actively involved in both sporting teams and musical groups associated with the school. Peter's father has a degree in accounting and now owns a small business. His mother qualified and worked as a nurse, traveled and worked in various jobs, and now works in the family business, but has also recently completed further qualifications in management. They are a close family who engage in sports and musical activities together. In the later school years, Peter mentions wanting to be an engineer, then, later, a physiotherapist. At 18 he is enrolled in Engineering at university.

Lee

Lee's father is a lawyer, and his mother is a teacher, and both identified with Labor rather than conservative politics. Throughout the interviews, Lee was insistent on his individuality and his interests in music (and later his involvement in drugs), and was unhappy at City College, which he saw as a conservative and conformist institution. He has one sister who is at a different private school. Lee's parents responded to his unhappiness at the school by finding a more congenial community-based and countercultural private school that he attended after year 9. Around that time, he showed more interest in both his Chinese heritage (mother's side) and opportunities for travel, but later in our study was not available for interview because his involvement with drugs had led to a period of hospitalization.

Sophie

Sophie is a very bubbly and enthusiastic person. She loves dance, and has passed high-level qualifications, and has a close family whom she enjoys. Her father is a senior member of the judiciary, and her mother works in social welfare. Both went to private schools (her father went to the same school that she now attends). Her mother has recently been doing a professional writing course. She lives in a wealthy suburb. She has an older brother, and, at 18, she is undertaking the same degree course that he did—in Commerce at the highest-status university in the city. She had earlier considered taking time out after school to be involved full-time in dance.

Nicky

Nicky is an effervescent individual who at the beginning of our study is bursting to tell all the different things she might like to do (including having children young); she is also full of enthusiasm about the school. At 18, after thinking about naturopathy as her career direction, Nicky is taking a course in fashion design and missing the close and extensive friendship networks of City College (most of whom go on to a different university, the one attended at 18 by Sophie and Gillian). Her father is a lawyer who went to this school; her mother did a music degree but is not in paid work ("she's a real mum mum"), but is heavily involved in school fund-raising committees. Nicky has two older brothers and one younger one. She lives in an established solidly wealthy suburb.

Alannah

Alannah's passion is horses, and her interviews are full of horsey metaphors, but she also helps out in her father's business. Her father completed a degree in economics, and her mother had finished year 12, then gone to a finishing school. Both had attended private schools. She has a younger brother. The family live in the ring of wealthy suburbs associated with the elite private schools in this city. At 18, Alannah is enrolled in both a university commerce degree and a part-time TAFE diploma, and is continuing to work part-time.

Gillian

Gillian lives in a suburb (and attended a primary school) some distance from City Academy and considered more working class. Few young people from that suburb attend private schools. At the beginning of the study, Gillian seems awkward and is highly self-conscious that she seems different from most of her fellow students; by year 12 she is on the committee organizing the social events, and appears much happier and more relaxed. Her father is a senior teacher in a private school and her mother is a journalist, and she has two younger sisters. In the early years, Gillian talks of wanting to be a special education teacher for children with disabilities; in the later years she becomes interested in music therapy, and at 18 is enrolled in this course at a prestigious university.

Diana

In the first half of our study, Diana was one of the most evidently unhappy people. She talked often about the pressures she felt in terms of her parents' expectations, and also the pressures that the school generated; her unhappiness was intensified after a period of exchange to another country at the end of year 9 that, on her own account, was not only not a happy experience, but gave her too much time to think about what she was unhappy with in terms of the school, friends, and her life. She is articulate and comes from a comfortable suburb, but not one within the inner network of elite locations often associated with this school. Her father is a doctor, and her mother a nurse who now works in his surgery; by the end of our study, the mother has returned to school to undertake a qualification in building construction. During year 10, Diana dramatically runs away from the school and from home to another state—but to the home of a family friend. She completes her schooling at a state school there, is enthusiastic about the experience, and does well in the different environment. At 18, Diana has embarked on a law degree in that state, but is making plans to arrange a transfer back to her home state.

Appendix 2a
Summary of Pathways

(Status when interviewed in mid-year 2000, when students were 18)
By Gender (N = 26: 14 girls, 12 boys***)***

Education/Work Status at 18

Completed school by end 1999	11 girls; 5 boys
University studies in 2000	8 girls; 4 boys
TAFE studies in 2000	2 girls, 1 boy
Other training in 2000	2 girls
Unemployed or casual working 2000	2 girls; 4 boys

One girl is doing combined university degree and TAFE diploma and is counted twice.

Occupations and Courses at 18

Girls	*Boys*
Law	Mechanical engineering (2)
Commerce	Medical technology
Music therapy	Computer studies (2)
Arts	Schooling interrupted—school/work status uncertain (3)
Arts/business administration	Gardening
Nursing (3)	Unemployed—seeking factory work or trade (2)
Dress design	
Hospitality	
Work/police force	
Completing school	
Casual (part-time) work (2)	

Appendix 2b
Who Got What—School Contrasts

School	*Sex*	*Uni/TAFE/ Other at Age 18*	*Status of Institution*	*Course/Vocation*
City Academy (Private, Metropolitan)				
	M	Uni	Elite uni	Mechanical engineering
	M	Rehabilitation	—	*Changed schools at 15, schooling not completed
	F	Uni	Well-ranked tech uni	Dress design
	F	Uni	Elite uni	Commerce
	F	Uni	Elite uni	Music therapy
	F	Uni and TAFE	Middle-ranked uni	Arts degree and Dip Business Admin
	F #	Uni	Uni in another state	Ran away at 16; Now doing law
High School (Regional)				
	F	TAFE	Higher-status technical	Hospitality diploma
	F	Uni	Provincial, low-status uni	Nursing degree
	F	Working	—	Preparing to enter police force
	M	Uni	Middle-ranked uni	Mechanical engineering
	M	Uni	Lower-status university	Medical technology
	M*	Casual/unemployed	—	*Left school at 15
High School (Metropolitan)				
	M	TAFE	Lower-status	Computer diploma
	M*	Casual jobs	—	*Took exchange year and has not resumed studies

School	Sex	Uni/TAFE/ Other at Age 18	Status of Institution	Course/Vocation
	M*	Working	—	Left school at 15 and began landscape apprenticeship; did not complete
	F	Uni	middle-status university	BA in Women's Studies
	F	Uni	Provincial and lower-status university	Nursing
	F	Casual work	—	Began uni but dropped out
	F*	Completing year 12	—	*Chose to take year 12 over 2 years
	M*	Taking year 12	—	*Psychological disruptions
Secondary (Ex-tech) School (Regional)				
	F	Work-based training (with TAFE)		One year nursing diploma
	F*	Part-time work		*Left school at 16, began TAFE hospitality course but discontinued, now doing work-based training
	M	Uni	Low status	Computer studies
	M*	Unemployed		Seeking factory work
	M*	Unemployed, seeking apprenticeship		Partially completed (failed) year 12; began apprenticeship apprenticeship but employer not able to continue

* did not complete schooling

changed schools during study

TAFE: Technical and Further Education system of colleges

Appendix 2c: Future Daydreams and Plans

This table presents a summary of student responses to questions about their future—what they wanted to do when they were older. Sometimes students responded with a clear career choice, other times not. If the entry is blank it means the question was not asked or the student was not interviewed in that round.

Student	Yr 7 1st	Year 7 2nd	Year 8 1st	Year 9	Year 10	Year 11	Year 12	Postschool (actual)
Julia Regional High	Animals,	Physio-therapist	Psychologist			Social work, psychology or nursing		Nursing
Jackie Regional High	Nothing specific			Police officer or interior decorating	Police force	Work then police	Work, then police force	Working, preparing to enter police force
Stephanie Regional High	Fame, work	Travel, university zoologist	Travel, lawyer	Good job, travel	Hotel management TAFE	Hospitality, TAFE	University to study hospitality	Hospitality diploma
Andrew Regional High	Lifestyle	University	Lawyer	Chef, pastry cook		Medicine	N/a	Medical technology at university
David Regional High	Businessman, geologist, nothing definite	Mechanic, motor sports		Mechanic, maybe in the army	Engineering	Engineering and a racing team	Uni and racing	Mechanical engineering
John Regional High	Police force	Police officer		Helicopter driver or policeman	Airforce		N/a	Left school at 15
Kylie Regional Tech	Not asked	Chef	Chef	N/a		Chef	N/a	Working after discontinuing TAFE course

Dirk Regional Tech	"A good job"		No daydreaming	N/a		Apprentice-ship in woodwork	Don't know	Began apprenticeship but employer unable to continue
Brett Regional Tech	Not asked	Army, own a gun stall	Army, builder, mechanic	Something with wood or electronics	Apprentice-ship—carpenter or joiner		Job	Seeking factory work
Keren Regional Tech	Don't think about future	Chef		Chef and a "karate dude"	Childcare or catering	Maybe childcare	Primary school teaching—university	Nursing diploma
Alan Regional Tech	Computers—programmer	Chef	Doesn't daydream	Doesn't think about it		Accounting or commerce	University	Computer Studies at university
Madeleine Suburban High	Vet, animals Doesn't know	Vet		No real answer		Doesn't know	Doesn't know	Began uni, dropped out
Helen Suburban High	Nothing definite yet	No real answer		No daydreaming	Can't decide	Doesn't know	Doesn't know—maybe job or uni/TAFE	University—women's studies
Amelie Suburban High	Police force	No real answer	Vet	No future dreams	Vet, psychology	Doesn't know	Army/nursing	Nursing at university

Student	Yr 7 1st	Year 7 2nd	Year 8 1st	Year 9	Year 10	Year 11	Year 12	Postschool (actual)
Talik Suburban High	Basketball player	Basketball, comedian	Basketball	No answer	Good job, motor industry	Info tech and business management	Information systems at uni	TAFE—computing diploma
Daniel Suburban High	Family		Apprentice-ship	Sport—lacrosse	Gardening	Dreams of wealth and early retirement		Left at 15 and began land-scaping apprentice-ship (didn't complete)
Jenna Suburban High	Vet, flight attendant	Vet, flight attendant architect		Don't think much about it	Photographer	Wondering about jobs but not sure	Photography	Did year 12 over 2 years
Marcus Suburban High	Zoologist	No real answer		Commune, build a hotel in Bali	Doesn't want a boring life	Not sure—going on exchange		Took exchange year and didn't finish yr 12
Nassar Suburban High	Scientist	Fun, family		N/a		Medicine	Defense forces	Doing year 12
Diana City Academy	Journalist, model	No career answer—own house		Travel		Not thinking about it		University—law

Peter City Academy	Don't think about it			Doesn't think about it		Engineer, physio-therapist/ medicine	Physio-therapy or engineering	Mechanical engineering
Nicky City Academy	Photographer /busker, family	Fashion designer, photographer	Kindergarten teacher, lawyer	Lots of different ideas	Aromatherapy, art	Lots of ideas		Fashion design at university
Sophie City Academy	Nothing defi-nite—maybe animals	No real answer		No job ideas	Dance then uni	Dance, arts and social science at uni	Dancing, uni	Commerce degree
Alannah City Academy	Vet	Lots of ideas and nothing definite	"Marry someone rich!"	Doesn't think about it	Family but not sure of jobs	Media	Uni	Arts degree and dip busi-ness admin at university
Gillian City Academy	Environment worries—no career ideas	Teach in a special school	"to help people"	Working with disabled people		Special education	Uni then a job	Music therapy at university
Lee City Academy	Doesn't know	No serious thoughts		Writing				At 15, changed schools; schooling not yet finished

Notes

Chapter 1

1. We have not used a pseudonym for the Victorian state capital city Melbourne because there are state differences in Australia that are relevant, and the city is large enough for schools to not be easily identifiable. However, in terms of the provincial city, which we have named Cubbin, individuals and schools would be more readily identifiable if we had not used a pseudonym.

Chapter 2

1. Not everyone uses the terms this way. Gee (2000/01) provides a review of the usefulness of "identity" in educational research and draws attention to a range of different ways this term is used, several of which overlap with what we are naming here as "subjectivity."
2. In selecting excerpts for the compilation videos we chose several key questions (e.g., How would you describe yourself? Tell us what you think about the future?) from interview schedules for each year and then excerpted the relevant sections from the individual videos. We did not "customize" video compilations, in the sense of choosing certain questions for each person, in part because we did not want to embarrass or make students feel uncomfortable by looking at excerpts we alone had decided were significant for them, and in part because we wanted to be able to compare their responses and for them to have a good sense of their "growing up" over the period.

Chapter 3

1. In the Australian vernacular, this is an unambiguous insult. "Tip" refers to a garbage dump, and "tech" is an abbreviation of "technical schools"; schools more oriented to the manual trades and vocational education, and in this town especially, have a clear reputation for serving working-class and poor families. Even though technical schools no longer formally exist, many schools that were previously "techs" continue to have forms of curriculum as well as reputations that echo their technical school origins. The stories that circulated about this former Technical School, particularly from kids at the local High school, often referred to the school as dirty, violent, having lots of fights, full of trash, a school that you would not "choose" to go to if you could help it, or if your parents lived in a "better" suburb.
2. In Willis's study the working-class "lads" used this as a disparaging term for those who play the academic game.
3. The education system in the state where our study was based differs from that of many U.S. states in that it has relatively little external high-stakes testing. Indeed, there is just one point at which that becomes important: the final school examination taken at the end of year 12 (the Victorian Certificate of Education), which produces results on each subject, but also a single combined "tertiary entrance score" in which each student is ranked against all other students in the state, and is also fed into an index that publicly rates schools against each other.
4. At one level, the contrast between academic and vocational is not as clear-cut as it might seem since going to university is itself a highly vocational path. But the traditional binary designation "vocational" versus "academic" continues to operate when "vocational" refers to courses oriented to jobs that will be entered directly from school. Nevertheless, these formal divisions are in the process of changing as schools now allow dual accreditation of some subjects as credit toward a vocational certification award and as accruing points for the university admissions index score.

Chapter 4

1. Claire Colebrook (2000) argues, following the work of Delueze and Guattari, that traditional understandings of the subject have been "tied to a strategy of being and essence, rather than becoming"; see also Grosz (1999).
2. A "pen pal" was someone whom you might never have met but corresponded with via letters. They were often initiated through schools and it was a common practice when we were growing up. You would often begin such a letter with an introduction and description of yourself. Transformations in communication—email, texting, digital cameras, etc.—have undoubtedly changed this practice.
3. Further distinctions can be made in relation to contemporary uses of "reflexivity." There are at least three main ways in which reflexivity is commonly deployed: sociology of reflexivity (as we are discussing here); reflexive sociology (as, e.g., in the sociological project of Bourdieu (Bourdieu and Wacquant 1992, Kenway and McLeod 2004); and methodological reflexivity (Pillow 2003), an orientation that also characterizes our own methodological approach (McLeod 2003; McLeod and Yates 1997; Yates 2003).

4. Bourdieu's book specifically on gender, *Masculine Domination* (2001), is a clear illustration of this problem—it asserts the adequacy of the approach by largely ignoring the issues that have been raised by feminist theories about what it does not address, such as the impact of feminism on gender relations and the contradictory aspects of subjectivity and desire.
5. We thank Valerie Walkerdine for this observation, made in response to a version of this discussion presented at the conference "Everyday world life and culture of young girls" Feminist Research Centre, University of Oslo, August 20–22, 1998, and acknowledge the valuable discussion and exchanges provided by all the participants at this seminar.

Chapter 5

1. This is a common representation of the divide between cultural studies and sociology, particularly among British commentators; see also Barrett (1992) and McRobbie (1996).
2. These methodological issues of significance and interpretive "warrant" in relation to small-number research are discussed in more detail in Yates (2003).
3. This contrasts with some of the other experiences of school culture and family habitus that we have discussed earlier. Gillian's story in the previous chapter is an account of how the habitus of the school is gradually acquired, so that she moved from feeling ill at ease and out of place, to feeling at home and began to embody the practices of the self and forms of distinction that characterize successful (female) students at City Academy. In the example of Nassar in chapter 3, there is a contradiction between the habitus of the school and his family culture; and much of his experience at school is dominated by trying to work out the codes of his new school, codes that remained opaque to him, even though the school had an overt commitment to cultural inclusiveness and respect for differences.
4. However, in contrast to Proweller's study (1998), none of our participants indicated that their mothers had given them explicit advice of the need to forge a career that would offer them protection in the case of a divorce

Chapter 6

1. "The Immigration Restriction Act was the key part of a package of legislation passed by the new Federal Parliament in 1901, aimed at excluding all non-European migrants. This package included the Pacific Islander Labourers Act and Section 15 of the 1901 Post and Telegraph Act, which provided that ships carrying Australian mails, and hence subsidized by the Commonwealth, should employ only white labor. Its sentiments were in line with Australian nationalism in the late 1880s and 1890s, and moves to restrict non-European immigration to most of the Australian colonies dating back to the 1850s. The mechanism restricting immigration could not be overtly based on race as this was opposed by Britain and frowned upon by Britain's ally, Japan. Instead, the basis was literacy, assessed by a Dictation Test. Similar Dictation Tests, based on legislation used in Natal in South Africa, had been introduced in Western Australia, New South Wales and Tasmania in the

late 1890s. The Immigration Restriction Act enabled the government to exclude any person who 'when asked to do so by an officer fails to write out at dictation and sign in the presence of the officer, a passage of 50 words in length in a European language directed by the officer.' The Dictation Test could be administered to any immigrant during the first year of residence. It was initially proposed that the Test would be in English, but it was argued that this could discourage European migration and advantage Japanese people, and Americans of African descent. Instead, any 'European language' was specified. In 1905 this was changed to 'any prescribed language' to lessen offense to the Japanese. From 1932 the Test could be given during the first five years of residence, and any number of times. The Dictation Test was administered 805 times in 1902–03 with 46 people passing and 554 times in 1904–09 with only six people successful. After 1909 no person passed the Dictation Test and people who failed were refused entry or deported. The Act, frequently amended, remained in force until 1958." Council for the Centenary of Federation (2000) Commonwealth of Australia http://www.founding docs.gov.au/text_only/places/cth/cth4ii.htm

2. This has since been published as J. McLeod and L. Yates (2003) "Who is 'us'? Students negotiating discourses of racism and national identification in Australia," *Race, Ethnicity and Education,* 6 (1):29–49.

Chapter 7

1. In that study, defined as those groups not in the top or bottom percentiles of measurements provided by the Australian Bureau of Statistics [ABS].
2. One of us grew up in Cubbin. Late in the project, she was visiting her family when her mother drove her around a new housing development near Regional High and commented "That's where the snobs live." Her mother came from a working-class background and had herself been to a lower-status school than Regional High. In contrast, David, a student at Regional High, who lived in the "establishment" wealthy area of the town, dismissively described this same type of housing development as "where the nouveaus live."

Chapter 8

1. To make this argument alone would to some extent be simply to take issue with abstraction and with what theory is and does.
2. Such responses are interesting in light of current concerns—from policy-makers, teachers, and parents—about boys' performance at school and their general social and emotional outlook. These adult worries have not shaken the boys' and girls' own beliefs that the boys are fine and do not need any special programs or interference.
3. Studies by Gilligan and her colleagues have developed beyond this early work with some regard to criticisms that we note here. Our purpose here is not to review this body of work, but to focus on the themes from that initial work that are so well known, and that have been influential well beyond academic research and discussion contexts.

4. Rose explains: "Today, psychologists elaborate complex emotional, interpersonal and organization techniques by which the practices of everyday life can be organized according to the ethic of autonomous selfhood. This know-how has been disseminated by two main routes. The first route works through reshaping the practices of those who exercise authority over others—social workers, managers, teachers, nurses—such that they exercise their powers in order to nurture and direct these individual strivings in the most appropriate and productive fashions. Here one sees the elaboration, in a plethora of self-instruction manuals, training courses and consultancy exercises, of a new set of relational technologies that appear to give professional authority an almost therapeutic character. The second route operates by what one can term the psychotherapies of normality, which promulgate new ways of planning life, and approaching predicaments, and disseminate new procedures for understanding oneself and acting upon oneself to overcome dissatisfactions, realize one's potential, gain happiness and achieve autonomy" (Rose 1999, 90).
5. The legislation remains, but is largely meaningless now that work is ruled by individual bargaining rather than regulation of conditions, and in which more and more is demanded of workers (Pusey 2003).

References

ABS [Australian Bureau of Statistics]. 2004. *Australian Social Trends* 2004 http://www.abs.gov.au/.

Adkins, Lisa. 2000. Objects of innovation: Post-occupational reflexivity and re-traditionalisations of gender. In *Transformations: Thinking Through Feminism*, edited by Sara Ahmed, Jane Kilby, Celia Lury, Maureen McNeil, and Beverley Skeggs. London: Routledge.

———. 2002a. *Revisions: Gender and Sexuality in Late Modernity*. Buckingham, UK: Open University Press.

———. 2002b. Reflexivity: Freedom or Habit of Gender? Paper read at After Bourdieu: Feminists Evaluate Bourdieu, Conference, University of Manchester, http://les.mac.ac.uk/sociology/Seminar/afterbourdieu.shtm, 11 October 2002, at University of Manchester.

Ang, Ien. 2000. Identity Blues. In *Without Guarantees: In Honor of Stuart Hall*, edited by Paul Gilroy, Lawrence Grossberg, and Angela McRobbie. London: Verso.

Anyon, Jean. 1983. Intersections of gender and class: accommodation and resistance by working-class and affluent females to contradictory sex-role ideologies. In *Gender, Class & Education*, edited by S. B. Walker and L. Barton. London: Falmer Press.

Apple, Michael. 2000. *Educating the 'Right' Way: Markets, Standards, God and Inequality*. New York: Routledge.

Arnot, Madeleine. 2002. *Reproducing Gender? Essays on Educational Theory and Feminist Politics*. London: Routledge.

Arnot, Madeleine, Miriam David, and Gaby Weiner. 1999. *Closing the Gender Gap: Post-war Education and Social Change*. Cambridge: Polity Press.

Bagnall, Nigel. 2000. The balance between *vocational* secondary and general secondary schooling in France and Australia. *Comparative Education* 36 (4):459-476.

Baker, Bernadette, M., and Katharina Heyning, eds. 2004. *Dangerous Coagulations: The Uses of Foucault in the Study of Education*. New York: Peter Lang.

Ball, Stephen. 2000. Performativities and fabrications in the educational economy. *Australian Education Researcher* 27 (2):1–24.

———. 2003. *Class Strategies and the Education Market: The Middle Classes and Social Advantage.* London: RoutledgeFalmer.

Ball, Stephen, Meg Maguire, and Sheila Macrae. 2000. *Choice, Pathways and Transitions Post 16: New Youth, New Economies in the Global City.* London: RoutledgeFalmer.

Barrett, Michele. 1992. Words and things: materialism and method in contemporary feminist analysis. In *Destabilizing Theory: Contemporary Feminist Debates,* edited by M. Barrett and A. Phillips. Cambridge, UK: Polity Press.

———. 1999. *Imagination in Theory: Culture, Writing, Words and Things.* New York: New York University Press.

Bauman, Zygmunt. 2000. *Liquid Modernity.* Cambridge: Polity Press.

———. 2001. *The Individualized Society.* Cambridge: Polity Press.

Beck, Ulrich. 1992. *Risk Society: Towards a New Modernity.* Translated by M. Ritter. London: Sage.

Beck, Ulrich, and Elisabeth Beck-Gernsheim. 1995. *The Normal Chaos of Love.* Translated by M. Ritter and J. Wiebel. Cambridge, UK: Polity Press, in association with Blackwell Publishers.

———. 2002. *Individualization: Institutional Individualism and Its Social and Political Consequences.* Translated by P. Camiller. London: Sage Publications.

Beck, Ulrich, Anthony Giddens, and Scott Lash. 1994. *Reflexive Modernization: Politics, Tradition and Aesthetics in the Modern Social Order.* Stanford: Stanford University Press.

Behar, Ruth. 1996. *The Vulnerable Observer: Anthropology That Breaks Your Heart.* Boston: Beacon Press.

Bendle, Mervyn F. 2002. The crisis of "identity" in high modernity. *British Journal of Sociology* 53 (1):1–18.

Benhabib, Seyla. 1995. Feminism and Postmodernism. In S. Benhabib, J. Butler, D. Cornell, and N. Fraser, *Feminist Contentions: A Philosophical Exchange.* New York: Routledge.

Bernstein, Basil. 1977. *Class, Codes and Control.* Vol. 3. London: Routledge & Kegan Paul.

———. 1996. *Pedagogy, Symbolic Control, and Identity. Theory, Research, and Critique.* London: Taylor & Francis.

Bettie, Julie. 2003. *Women Without Class: Girls, Race and Identity.* Berkeley: University of California Press.

Bloustien, Geraldine. 2003. *Girl Making: A Cross-Cultural Ethnography on the Processes of Growing up Female.* New York: Berghahn Press.

Bourdieu, Pierre. 1976a. The school as a conservative force: scholastic and cultural inequalities. In *Schooling and Capitalism: A Reader,* edited by R. Dale, G. Esland, and M. MacDonald. London: Routledge & Kegan Paul.

———. 1976b. Systems of education and systems of thought. In *Schooling and Capitalism: A Reader,* edited by R. Dale, G. Esland, and M. MacDonald. London: Routledge & Kegan Paul.

———. 1977. *Outline of a Theory of Practice.* Cambridge, UK: Cambridge University Press.

———. 2000. *Pascalian Mediations.* Translated by R. Nice. Cambridge UK: Polity Press, in association with Blackwell Publishers. Original edition, Editions du Seuil.

———. 2001. *Masculine Domination.* Translated by R. Nice. Stanford: Stanford University Press.

Bourdieu, Pierre et al. 1999. *The Weight of the World: Social Suffering in Contemporary Society.* Translated by P. P. Ferguson, Cambridge, UK: Polity Press in association with Blackwell Publishers.

Bourdieu, Pierre, and Jean-Claude Passeron. 1977. *Reproduction in Education, Society and Culture.* Translated by R. Nice. London: Sage.

Bourdieu, Pierre, and L. J. D. Wacquant. 1992. *An Invitation to Reflexive Sociology.* Chicago: University of Chicago Press.

Braidotti, Rosi. 1994. *Nomadic Subjects: Embodiment and Sexual Difference in Contemporary Feminist Theory.* New York: Columbia University Press.

Brantlinger, Ellen. 2003. *Dividing Classes: How the Middle Class Negotiates and Rationalizes School Advantage.* New York: RoutledgeFalmer.

Britzman, Deborah. 2000. 'The Question of Belief': Writing Poststructual Ethnography. In *Working The Ruins: Feminist Poststructural Theory and Methods in Education,* edited by E. A. St. Pierre, and W. Pillow. New York: Routledge.

Butler, Judith. 1990. *Gender Trouble: Feminism and the Subversion of Identity.* New York: Routledge.

——. 1999 Performativity's social magic. In *Bourdieu: A Critical Reader,* edited by R. Shusterman. Oxford: Blackwell.

Chappell, Clive, Carl Rhodes, Nicky Solomon, Mark Tennant, and Lyn Yates. 2003. *Reconstructing the Lifelong Learner: Pedagogy and Identity in Individual, Organisational and Social Change.* London: Routledge.

Cohen, Phil. 1997. *Rethinking the Youth Question: Education, Labour and Cultural Studies.* London: Macmillan.

Cohen, Phil, and Ainley, Pat. 2000. In the country of the blind? Youth Studies and Cultural Studies in Britain. *Journal of Youth Studies* 3 (1):79–95.

Colebrook, Claire. 2000. A grammar of becoming: Strategy, subjectivism, and style. In *Delueze and Feminist Theory,* edited by I. Buchanan, and C. Colebrook. Edinburgh: Edinburgh University Press.

Collins, Cherry, Jane Kenway, and Julie McLeod. 2000. *Factors Influencing the Educational Performance of Males and Females in School and Their Initial Destinations after Leaving School.* Canberra: Department of Education, Training and Youth Affairs.

Connell, R.W. 1995. *Masculinities.* St. Leonards, NSW, Aust: Allen & Unwin.

——. 2002. *Gender.* Cambridge, UK: Polity.

Connell, R.W., D. J. Ashenden, S. Kessler, and G. W. Dowsett. 1982. *Making the Difference: Schools, Families and Social Division.* Sydney: George Allen & Unwin.

Cosslett, Tess, Celia Lury, and Penny Summerfield, eds. 2000. *Feminism and Autobiography: Texts, Theories, Methods.* London: Routledge.

Davis, K. 1994. What's in a voice? Methods and metaphors. *Feminism & Psychology* 4 (4):353–361.

Dillabough, Jo-Anne, and Arnot, Madeleine. 2001. Feminist sociology of education: Dynamics, debates and directions. In *Sociology of Education Today,* edited by J. Demaine. London: Palgrave.

Dolby, Nadine. 2000. The shifting ground of race: The role of taste in youth's production of identities. *Race Ethnicity and Education* 3 (1):7–23.

Dolby, Nadine, and Dimitriadis, Greg, eds. 2004. *Learning to Labor in New Times.* New York: RoutledgeFalmer.

Donald, James. 1991. On the threshold: Psychoanlysis and cultural studies. In *Psychoanalysis and Cultural Theory: Thresholds,* edited by J. Donald. London: Macmillan.

Driscoll, Catherine. 2002. *Girls: Feminine Adolescence in Popular Culture and Cultural Theory*. New York: Columbia University Press.

Du Bois-Reymond, Manuela. 1998. 'I don't want to commit myself yet': Young people's life concepts. *Journal of Youth Studies* 1 (1): 63–79.

Du Gay, Paul. 1996. *Consumption and Identity at Work*. London: Sage.

Dwyer, Peter J., A. Harwood, and D. Tyler. 1998. *Life Patterns, Choices, Careers: 1991–1998*. Research Report, Youth Research Centre, Faculty of Education: University of Melbourne.

Dwyer, Peter, Debra Tyler, and Johanna Wyn. 2001. Journeying through the Nineties: The Life Patterns Project 1991–2000. Melbourne: Youth Research Centre, University of Melbourne.

Dwyer, Peter J., and Johanna Wyn. 2001. *Youth, Education and Risk: Facing the Future*. London: RoutledgeFalmer.

Erikson, Erik. 1968. *Identity: Youth and Crisis*. New York: Norton.

Evans, Karen. 2002. Taking control of their lives: Agency in young adult transitions in England and the New Germany. *Journal of Youth Studies* 5 (3):245–269.

Feminism and Psychology. 1994. Special issue on The Harvard Project on Women's Psychology and Girls' Development. 4 (4).

Fine, Michelle. 1994. Dis-stance and other stances: Negotations of power inside feminist research. In *Power and Method: Political Activism and Educational Research*, edited by A. Gitlin. New York: Routledge.

——. 1997. Witnessing Whiteness. In *Off White: Readings on Race, Power and Society*, edited by M. Fine, L. Weis, L. Powell, and L. M. Wong. New York: Routledge.

Fine, Michelle, and Lois Weis. 1998. *The Unknown City: The Lives of Poor and Working-Class Young Adults*. Boston: Beacon Press.

Foucault, Michel. 1982. The subject and power. In *Michel Foucault: Beyond Structuralism and Hermeneutics*, edited by H. L. Dreyfus, and P. Rabinow. Chicago: University of Chicago Press.

——. 1988. Technologies of the Self. In *Technologies of the Self: A Seminar with Michel Foucault*, edited by L. H. Martin, H. Gutman, and P. Hutton, London: Tavistock Publications.

Francis, Becky, and Christine Skelton, eds. 2001. *Investigating Gender: Contemporary Perspectives in Education*. Buckingham, UK: Open University Press.

Fraser, Nancy. 1997. *Justice Interruptus: Critical Reflections on the 'Postsocialist' Condition*. New York: Routledge.

Freebody, Peter. 2003. *Qualitative Research in Education: Interaction and Practice*. London: Sage.

Furlong, Andy. 2003. Reconceptualising youth transitions; Research on transitions in the UK. Paper presented at Deakin University, Geelong, Aust, Sept 5, 2003.

Furlong, Andy, and Fred Cartmel. 1997. *Young People and Social Change: Individualization and Risk in Late Modernity*. Edited by A. Warde, *Sociology and Social Change*. Buckingham, UK: Open University Press.

Gatens, Moira. 1991. *Feminism and Philosophy: Perspectives on Difference and Equality*. Bloomington: Indiana University Press.

Gee, James P. 1999. New people in new worlds: Networks, the new capitalism and schools. In *Multiliteracies: Literacy Learning and the Design of Social Futures*, edited by B. Cope and M. Kalantizis. London: Routledge.

———. 2000-2001. Identity as an analytic lens for research in education. In *Review of Research in Education*, edited by W. G. Secada. Washington, DC: American Educational Research Association.

Gee, James P., Glynda Hull, and Colin Lankshear. 1996. *The New Work Order: Behind the Language of the New Capitalism, Studies in Education.* St. Leonards, NSW: Allen & Unwin.

Gewirtz, Sharon. 1998. Conceptualising social justice in education: Mapping the territory. *Journal of Education Policy* 13 (4): 469-484.

Gewirtz, Sharon, Stephen Ball, and Richard Bowe. 1995. *Markets, Choice, and Equity in Education.* Buckingham, UK: Open University Press.

Giddens, Anthony. 1991. *Modernity and Self-Identity: Self and Society in the Late Modern Age.* Cambridge, UK: Polity Press.

———. 1992. *The Transformation of Intimacy: Sexuality, Love and Eroticism in Modern Societies.* Stanford: Stanford University Press.

Gilbert, Pam, and Rob Gilbert. 2001. Masculinity, inequality and post-school opportunities: Disrupting oppositional politics about boys' education. *International Journal of Inclusive Education* 5 (1):1-13.

Gilligan, Carol. 1982. *In a Different Voice: Psychological Theory and Women's Development.* Cambridge: Harvard University Press.

Gilligan, Carol, Nona P. Lyons, and Trudy J. Hanmer, eds. 1990. *Making Connections: The Relational Worlds of Adolescent Girls at Emma Willard School.* Cambridge: Harvard University Press.

Gilroy, Paul, Lawrence Grossberg, and Angela McRobbie, eds. 2000. *Without Guarantees: In Honour of Stuart Hall.* London: Verso.

Giroux, Henry. 1997. Rewriting the discourse of racial identity: Towards a pedagogy and politics of whiteness. *Harvard Education Review* 67 (2):285-320.

Gitlin, Andrew, ed. 1994. *Power and Method: Political Activism and Educational Research.* New York: Routledge.

Gordon, Tuula, Janet Holland, and Elina Lahelma. 2000. *Making Spaces: Citizenship and Difference in Schools.* London: Macmillan.

Gordon, Tuula, and Elina Lahelma. 2003. From ethnography to life history: Tracing transitions of school students. *International Journal of Social Research Methods* 6 (3).

Grenfell, Michael, David James, with Philip Hodkinson, Diane Reay, and Derek Robbins. 1998. *Bourdieu and Education: Acts of Practical Theory.* London: Falmer Press.

Griffin, Christine. 1993. *Representations of Youth: The Study of Youth and Adolescence in Britain and America.* Cambridge, UK: Polity Press.

Grosz, Elizabeth, ed. 1999. *Becomings: Explorations in Time, Memory, and Futures.* Ithaca: Cornell University Press.

Hage, Ghassan. 1998. *White Nation: Fantasies of White Supremacy in a Multicultural Society.* Sydney: Pluto Press.

Hall, Stuart. 1996. Who needs 'identity'? In *Questions of Cultural Identity*, edited by S. Hall and P. du Gay. London: Sage.

Hall, Stuart, and Paul Du Gay, eds. 1996. *Questions of Cultural Identity.* London: Sage Publications.

Harris, Anita. 2004. *Future Girl: Young Women in the Twenty-First Century.* New York: Routledge.

Hatch, J., and R. Wisniewski. 1995. *Life History and Narrative.* London: Falmer Press.

Haug, Frigga. 1987. *Female Sexualization: A Collective Work of Memory.* Translated by E. Carter. London: Verso.

Hey, Valerie. 1997. *The Company She Keeps: An Ethnography of Girls' Friendships.* Buckingham, UK: Open University Press.

Hollway, Wendy. 1994. Beyond sex differences: A project for feminist psychology. *Feminism & Psychology* 4 (4):538–546.

Hollway, Wendy, and Tony Jefferson. 2000. *Doing Qualitative Research Differently: Free Association, Narrative and the Interview Method.* London: Sage.

Johnson, Lesley. 1993. *The Modern Girl: Girlhood and Growing Up.* Sydney: Allen and Unwin.

Kamler, Barbara. 2001. *Relocating the Personal: A Critical Writing Pedagogy.* Albany: State University of New York Press.

Kamler, Barbara, Jo-Anne Reid, Rod MacLean, and Alyson Simpson. 1994. Shaping Up Nicely: The Formation of Schoolgirls and Schoolboys in the First Month of School: A Report to the Gender Equity and Curriculum Reform Project. Canberra: Department of Employment, Education and Training.

Kehily, Mary Jane. 2002. *Sexuality, Gender and Schooling: Shifting Agendas in Social Learning.* London: RoutledgeFalmer.

Kenway, Jane, and P. Kelly. 2000. Local/global labor markets and the restructuring of gender, schooling and work. In *Globalisation and Education,* edited by N. Stromquist, and K. Monkman. Lanham, MD: Rowman and Littlefield.

Kenway, Jane, and Kraack, Anna. 2004. Reordering work and destabilizing masculinity. In *Learning to Labor in New Times,* edited by N. Dolby and G. Dimitradis. New York: Routledge.

Kenway, Jane, and Julie McLeod. 2004. Bourdieu's reflexive sociology and "spaces of points of view": Whose reflexivity, which perspective? *British Journal of Sociology of Education* 25 (4):525–544.

Kingston, Margot. 1999. *Off the Rails: The Pauline Hanson Trip.* Sydney: Allen & Unwin.

Kvale, Steinar. 1996. *InterViews: An Introduction to Qualitative Research Interviewing.* Thousand Oaks, CA: Sage.

Lahelma, Elina. 2002. School is for making friends: Secondary school as lived and remembered. *British Journal of Sociology of Education* 23 (2):368–381.

Lamont, Michele. 2000. The rhetorics of racism and anti-racism in France and the United States. In *Rethinking Comparative Cultural Sociology: Repertoires of Evaluation in France and the United States,* edited by M. Lamont and L. Thevenot. New York and Cambridge: Cambridge University Press.

Lareau, Annette. 2003. *Unequal Childhoods: Class, Race and Family Life.* Berkeley: University of California Press.

Lather, Patti. 1991. *Getting Smart: Feminist Research and Pedagogy with/in the Postmodern.* New York: Routledge.

———. 1994. Fertile obsession: Validity after poststructuralism. In *Power and Method: Political Activism and Educational Research,* edited by A. Gitlin. New York: Routledge.

Lawler, Steph. 2000. *Mothering the Self: Mothers, Daughters, Subjects.* London: Routledge.

Lesko, Nancy, 1996. Past, present, and future conceptions of adolescence. *Educational Theory,* Fall, 46 (4):453–472.

———. ed. 2000. *Masculinities in Schools.* Thousand Oaks, CA: Sage.

———. 2001. *Act your age! A Cultural Construction of Adolescence.* New York: RoutledgeFalmer.

Lingard, Bob, and Peter Douglas. 1999. *Men Engaging Feminisms: Pro-Feminism, Backlashes and Schooling.* Buckingham, UK: Open University Press.

Lovell, Terry. 2000. Thinking feminism with and against Bourdieu. *Feminist Theory* 1 (1): 11–32.

Lucey, Helen, and Diane Reay. 2000. Social class and the psyche. *Soundings* 15: 139–154.

Luke, C., and V. Carrington. 2000. Race Matters. *Journal of Intercultural Studies* 21 (1):5–24.

MacDonald, Kevin. 1999. *Struggles for Subjectivity: Identity, Action and Youth Experience.* Cambridge, UK: Cambridge University Press.

MacIntyre, Stuart, and Anna Clark. 2003. *The History Wars.* Carlton, Vic, Aust: Melbourne University Press.

MacLure, Maggie. 2003. *Discourse in Educational and Social Research.* Buckingham, UK: Open University Press.

Mansfield, Nick. 2000. *Subjectivity: Theories of the Self from Freud to Haraway.* Sydney: Allen & Unwin.

Marks, Gary, N., and Julie McMillan. 2003. Declining inequality? The changing impact of socio-economic background and ability on education in Australia. *British Journal of Sociology* 54 (4):453–471.

MCEETYA [Ministerial Advisory Committee on Employment, Education, Training and Youth Affairs]. 2000. New Framework for Vocational Education in Schools: A comprehensive guide about pathways for young Australians in transition. Melbourne: Curriculum Corporation.

McLeod, Julie. 1993. Impossible fictions: Utopian visions and feminist educational research. *Melbourne Studies in Education,* Special Issue, "Feminism and Education":107–118.

——. 2000a. Metaphors of the self; Searching for young people's identity through interviews. In *Researching Youth,* edited by J. McLeod and K. Malone. Hobart, Aust: Australian Clearinghouse on Youth Studies.

——. 2000b. Subjectivity and schooling in a longitudinal study of secondary students. *British Journal of Sociology of Education* 21 (4):501–521.

——. 2001. When poststructuralism meets gender. In *Governing the Child in the New Millennium,* edited by K. Hultqvist and G. Dahlberg. New York: Routledge.

——. 2002. Working out intimacy: Young people in an age of reflexivity. *Discourse: studies in the cultural politics of education* 23 (2):211–226.

——. 2003. Why we interview now: Perspective and reflexivity in longitudinal study. *International Journal of Social Research Methodology* 6 (3):201–211.

——. 2005. Feminists re-reading Bourdieu: Old debates and new questions about gender habitus and gender change. *Theory and Research in Education* 3(1):11–30.

McLeod, Julie, and Lyn Yates. 1997. Can we find out about girls and boys today, or must we just settle for talking about ourselves. Dilemmas of a feminist, qualitative longitudinal research project. *Australian Education Researcher* 24 (3):23–42.

——. (1998) How young people think about self, work and futures, *Family Matters,* 49: 28–33.

——. 2003. Who is "us"? Students negotiating discourses of racism and national identification in Australia. *Race Ethnicity and Education* 6 (1):29–49.

McNay, Lois. 1992. *Foucault and Feminism: Power and Gender and Self.* Cambridge, UK: Polity Press.

——. 1999. Gender, habitus and the field: Pierre Bourdieu and the limits of reflexivity. *Theory, Culture and Society* 16 (1):95–117.

——. 2000. *Gender and Agency: Reconfiguring the Subject in Feminist and Social Theory.* Cambridge, UK: Polity Press.

McRobbie, Angela. 1996. Different, youthful subjectivities. In *The Post-Colonial Question: Common Skies, Divided Horizons,* edited by I. Chambers, and L. Curtis. New York: Routledge.

Modjeska, Drusilla. 2000. A writ served. *The Australian Review of Books* 5 (6):6–7.

Moore, Henrietta (2001) A "masterclass" in subjectivity. In *Feminist (Re)Visions: Landscapes, Ethnoscapes, and Theoryscapes,* edited by G. Currie and C. Rothenberg, Lanham: Lexington Books.

Morley, David, and Kuan-Hsing Chen, eds. 1996. *Stuart Hall: Critical Dialogues in Cultural Studies.* London: Routledge.

Nayak, Anoop. 1999. "White English Ethnicities"; Racism, anti-racism and student perspectives. *Race, Ethnicity and Education* 2 (2):177–202.

Nielsen, Harriet Bjerrum, and Monica Rudberg. 1995. Gender recipes among young girls. *Young: Journal of Nordic Youth Studies* 3 (2):71–88.

Nielsen, Harriet Bjerrum. 1996. The magic writing pad—on gender and identity. *Young: Journal of Nordic Youth Studies* 4 (3):2–18.

Nielsen, Harriet Bjerrum, and Monica Rudberg. 1994. *Psychological Gender and Modernity.* Oslo: Scandinavian University Press.

OECD. 2004. Knowledge and Skills for Life—First Results from PISA 2000. Report of the Program for International School Assessment.

Olneck, Michael. 2000. "Can multicultural education change what counts as cultural capital?" *American Educational Research Journal* 37 (2):317–348.

Peel, Mark, and Janet McCalman. 1992. Who went where in *Who's Who 1988*: The Schooling of the Australian Elite. Parkville: History Department, University of Melbourne.

Perera, Suvendrini. 1999. Whiteness and its Discontents: Notes on politics, gender, sex and food in the year of Pauline Hanson. *Journal of Intercultural Studies* 20 (2):183–198.

Phoenix, Ann, and Barbara Tizard. 1996. Thinking through class: The place of social class in the lives of young Londoners. *Feminism and Psychology* 6 (3):427–442.

Pillow, Wanda. 2003. Confession, catharsis or cure? Rethinking the uses of reflexivity as methodological power in qualitative research. *Qualitative Studies in Education* 16 (2):175–196.

Plumridge, Libby, and Rachel Thomson. 2003. Longitudinal qualitative studies and the reflexive self. *International Journal of Social Research Methods* 6 (3):213–222.

Popkewitz, Thomas S, and Marie Brennan, eds. 1998. *Foucault's Challenge.* New York: Teachers College Press.

Power, Sally, Tony Edwards, Geoff Whitty, and Valerie Wigfall. 2003. *Education and the Middle Class.* Buckingham, UK: Open University Press.

Probyn, Elspeth. 1993. *Sexing the Self: Gendered Positions in Cultural Studies.* New York: Routledge.

Proweller, Amira. 1998. *Constructing Female Identities: Meaning Making in an Upper Middle Class Youth Culture.* Albany: State University of New York Press.

Pusey, Michael. 2003. *The Experience of Middle Australia: The Dark Side of Economic Reform.* Cambridge: Cambridge University Press.

Putnam, Robert D. 2000. *Bowling Alone: The Collapse and Revival of American Community.* New York: Simon & Schuster.

Reay, Diane. 1995a. Using habitus to look at "race" and class in primary school classrooms. In *Antiracism, Culture and Social Justice in Education,* edited by M. Griffiths and B. Troyna. Stoke-on-Trent: Trentham Books.

———. 1995b. "They employ cleaners to do that": Habitus in the primary school. *British Journal of Sociology of Education* 16 (3):331–371.

———. 1997. Feminist theory, habitus, and social class: Disrupting notions of classlessness. *Women's Studies International Forum* 20 (2):225–233.

———. 2001. The paradox of contemporary femininities in education: Combining fluidity with fixity. In *Investigating Gender: Contemporary Perspectives in Education,* edited by B. Francis and C. Skelton. Buckingham, UK: Open University Press.

Rizvi, F. 1993. Children and the grammar of popular racism. In *Race, Identity and Representation in Education,* edited by C. McCarthy and W. Crichlow. New York: Routledge.

Roman, Leslie G., and Linda Eyre, eds. 1997. *Dangerous Territories: Struggles for Difference and Equality in Education.* New York: Routledge.

Roman, Leslie G., and T. Stanley. 1997. Empire, emigres and aliens: Young people's negotiation of official and popular racism in Canada. In *Dangerous Territories: Struggles for difference and equality in education,* edited by L. G. Roman and L. Eyre. New York: Routledge.

Roman, Leslie. G. 1996. Spectacle in the dark: Youth as transgression, display, and repression. *Education Theory* Fall, 46:1–22.

Rose, Nikolas. 1989. *Governing the Soul: The Shaping of the Private Self.* London: Routledge.

———. 1996. *Inventing Ourselves: Psychology, Power and Personhood.* Cambridge, UK: Cambridge University Press.

———. 1999. *Powers of Freedom: Reframing Political Thought.* Cambridge, UK.: Cambridge University Press.

Scheurich, J. J. 1995. A postmodernist critique of research interviewing. *Qualitative Studies in Education* 8 (3):239–352.

Schirato, Tony, and Jen Webb. 2003. Bourdieu's concept of reflexivity as metaliteracy. *Cultural Studies* 17 (3):539–552.

Shusterman, Richard. 1999. *Bourdieu: A Critical Reader.* Oxford: Blackwell.

Skeggs, Beverely. 1997. *Formations of Class and Gender: Becoming Respectable.* London: Sage.

St. Pierre, Elizabeth. A., and Wanda Pillow, eds. 2000. *Working the Ruins: Feminist Poststructural Theory and Methods in Education.* New York: Routledge.

Steedman, Carolyn. 2000. Enforced narratives: Stories of another self. In *Feminism and Autobiography: Texts, Theories, Methods,* edited by T. Cosslett, C. Lury, and P. Summerfield. London: Routledge.

Stronach, Ian, and Maggie MacLure. 1997. *Educational Research Undone: The Postmodern Embrace.* Buckingham, UK: Open University Press.

Summers, Anne. 2003. *The End of Equality: Work, Babies and Women's Choices in 21st Century Australia.* Sydney: Random House.

Tamboukou, Maria. 2003. *Women, Education, and the Self.* New York: Palgrave.

Taylor, Jill McLean, Carol Gilligan, and Amy M. Sullivan. 1996. Missing voices, changing meanings: Developing a voice-centered, relational method and creating an interpretive community. In *Feminist Social Psychologies: Internation Perspectives,* edited by S. Wilkinson. Buckingham, UK: Open University Press.

———. 1997. *Between Voice and Silence: Women and Girls, Race and Relationship.* Cambridge: Harvard University Press.

Teese, Richard. 2000. *Academic Success and Social Power: Examinations and Inequality.* Carlton South: Melbourne University Press.

Teese, Richard, and John Polesel. 2003. *Undemocratic Schooling: Equity and Quality in Mass Secondary Education in Australia.* Melbourne: Melbourne University Press.

Thomson, Pat. 2002. *Schooling the Rustbelt Kids: Making the Difference in Changing Times.* Sydney: Allen & Unwin.

Thomson, Rachel, Robert Bell, Janet Holland, Sheila Henderson, Sheena McGrellis, and Sue Sharpe. 2002. Critical moments: Choice, chance and opportunity in young people's narratives of transition to adulthood. *Sociology* 6 (2):335–354.

Thomson, Rachel, and Janet Holland. 2003a. Making the most of what you've got: Resources, values and inequalities in young people's transitions to adulthood. *Educational Review* 55 (1):33–46.

———. 2003b. Hindsight, foresight and insight: The challenges of longitudinal qualitative research. *International Journal of Social Research Methodology* 6 (3):233–244.

Tripp, David. 1993. *Critical Incidents in Teaching: Developing Professional Judgement.* London: Routledge.

Tsolidis, Georgina. 2001. *Schooling, Diaspora and Gender: Being Feminist and Being Different.* Buckingham, UK: Open University Press.

Walker, J. 1988. *Louts and Legends: Male Youth Culture in an Inner-City School.* Sydney: Allen & Unwin.

Walkerdine, Valerie. 1988. *The Mastery of Reason: Cognitive Development and the Production of Rationality.* London: Routledge.

Walkerdine, Valerie, and Helen Lucey. 1989. *Democracy in the Kitchen: Regulating Mothers and Socialising Daughters.* London: Virago.

Walkerdine, Valerie, Helen Lucey, and June Melody. 2001. *Growing Up Girl: Psychosocial Explorations of Gender and Class.* London: Palgrave.

Webb, Jen, Tony Schirato, and Geoff Danaher. 2002. *Understanding Bourdieu.* Sydney: Allen & Unwin.

Weis, Lois. 1993. White male working-class youth: An exploration of relative privilege and loss. In *Beyond Silenced Voices: Class, Race and Gender in United States Schools,* edited by L. F. Weis and M. Fine. Albany: State University of New York Press.

———. 2004. Revisiting a 1980s "moment of critique": Class, gender and the new economy. In *Learning to Labor in New Times,* edited by N. Dolby and G. Dimitriades with P. Willis. New York: RoutledgeFalmer.

Weis, Lois, and Michelle Fine, eds. 2000. *Construction Sites: Excavating Race, Class, and Gender Among Urban Youth.* New York: Teachers College Press.

Wexler, Philip. 1992. *Becoming Somebody: Toward a Social Psychology of School.* London: Falmer Press.

Willis, Paul. 1977. *Learning to Labour.* Aldershot: Saxon House.

Wyn, Johanna. 2000. The postmodern girl: Education, "success" and the construction of girls' identities. In *Researching Youth,* edited by J. McLeod and K. Malone. Hobart, Tas, Aust: Australian Clearinghouse for Youth Studies.

Yates, Lyn. 1997. Gender equity and the boys' debate: What sort of challenge is it? *British Journal of Sociology of Education* 18 (3):337–347.

———. 1998. Constructing and deconstructing "girls" as a category of concern. In *Education into the 21st Century: Dangerous Terrain for Women?,* edited by A. Mackinnon, I. Elgqvist-Saltzman, and A. Prentice. London: Falmer Press.

———. 2000. "The facts of the case": Gender equity for boys as a public policy issue. In *Masculinities at School,* edited by N. Lesko. Thousand Oaks, CA: Sage.

———. 2000a. Representing "class" in qualitative research. In *Researching Youth,* edited by J. McLeod and K. Malone. Hobart: Australian Clearinghouse for Youth Research.

———. 2001. Selves, social factors, school sites and the tricky issue of "school effects." *Change: Transformations in Education* 4 (2):15–29.

———. 2003. Interpretive claims and methodological warrant in small number qualitative longitudinal research. *International Journal of Social Research Methods* 6 (3):223–232.

———. 2004. *What Does Good Education Research Look Like? Situating a Field and Its Practices.* Maidenhead and New York: Open University Press.

Yates, Lyn, and Leder, Gilah. 1996. *The Student Pathways Project: A Review and Overview of National Data Bases*: Canberra: Department of Education and Training.

Yates, Lyn, and McLeod, Julie. 2000. Social Justice and the Middle. *Australian Education Researcher* 27 (3):59–77.

Index